ROUTLEDGE LIBRARY EDITIONS:
ADVERTISING

ADVERTISING AT THE CROSSROADS

ADVERTISING AT THE CROSSROADS

Federal Regulation vs. Voluntary Controls

MAX A. GELLER

Volume 2

Routledge
Taylor & Francis Group
LONDON AND NEW YORK

First published in 1952

This edition first published in 2013
by Routledge
4 Park Square, Milton Park, Abingdon, Oxon OX14 4RN
605 Third Avenue, New York, NY 10017

Routledge is an imprint of the Taylor & Francis Group, an informa business

British Library Cataloguing in Publication Data
A catalogue record for this book is available from the British Library

ISBN: 978-0-415-63749-7 (Set)
eISBN: 978-0-203-07915-7 (Set)
ISBN: 978-0-415-81774-5 (Volume 2)(hbk)
eISBN: 978-0-203-58355-5 (Volume 2)

Publisher's Note
The publisher has gone to great lengths to ensure the quality of this reprint but points out that some imperfections in the original copies may be apparent.

Disclaimer
The publisher has made every effort to trace copyright holders and would welcome correspondence from those they have been unable to trace.

ADVERTISING AT THE CROSSROADS

Federal Regulation vs. Voluntary Controls

By

MAX A. GELLER, Ph.D.

THE RONALD PRESS COMPANY · NEW YORK

Library of Congress Catalog Card Number: 52-9274

PRINTED IN THE UNITED STATES OF AMERICA

TO MY WIFE WHOSE

FORBEARANCE, UNDERSTANDING, AND ENCOURAGEMENT

HAVE MADE THIS WORK POSSIBLE

PREFACE

Advertising today is not only under sterner scrutiny by the various federal regulatory and judicial bodies but is also facing an ominous storm of public criticism because of certain abuses. This two-fronted attack seriously worries me, both as an advertising agent of long experience and as a business executive with advertising problems of my own. One of the big questions troubling advertisers, agencies, and media is whether advertising will be subject to increasingly stringent governmental controls or whether it will forestall such action by mature self-regulation. In this book I have attempted to face the issue squarely and realistically, and to point out several constructive measures that advertising must initiate in its self-interest. Otherwise public indignation will inevitably result in restrictive federal regulations.

In analyzing the problems that confront advertising, I have had to go beyond a mere account of its development or even a discussion of the trend in federal administrative and judicial decisions concerning its regulation. The heart of the issue is the relationship of advertising to our economic and social structure. In the past fifty years the annual advertising expenditures have jumped from $95,000,000 to more than $6,500,000,000. Advertising is thus not simply a facet of "big business"; it is a big business itself.

The result is that advertising must now be appraised in the light of national policy and public interest. In a period when the national purpose is to combat inflation, these huge tax-deductible expenditures have the opposite effect. Advertisers and their agencies might well take cognizance of the recommendation by the President's Council of Economic Advisers to tax advertising and the manner in which such a threatened tax was avoided in Britain by voluntary controls. Nor can the media ignore their responsibilities, particularly periodicals, which enjoy a bounty from the public treasury in the form of second-class mailing privileges, and radio and television stations, which are licensed to use property belonging to the nation. They have a duty to curb advertising policies that are not in the public interest.

I need hardly add that I am not opposed to advertising; and I would be the last to deny the vitally important function it renders in our system of production and distribution. Yet it would be a foolish and short-sighted policy to disregard the mounting criticism as of negligible import. I believe that the interest of advertising will best be served by a candid recognition on the part of business and the profession itself of their obligation to lead the fight in upholding standards of decency, honesty, and responsibility.

Thanks are due to many who have contributed directly and indirectly to this book. I desire especially to express my deep obligation to the following: my good friend and former colleague, Professor Rinehart J. Swenson of New York University, who suggested the approach to this study and whose guidance has proved invaluable; Sidney Schulman, for his unstinted aid in legal research and critical appraisal of the material dealing with the various regulatory bodies; my good friend and associate, Max Tendrich, for his painstaking proofreading and the gathering and analyzing of the statistical material; and to Dr. Gerard Priestley for his criticisms and suggestions. I also wish to thank Barbara Tilney, Joan Plaut and my daughter Harriet Greenfield, who have provided excellent secretarial and editorial assistance. Lastly, I hope that my daughter Genevieve G. Geller will find here some justification for having "goaded" me back to school to complete my Ph.D. studies after an eighteen-year lapse and for her unwavering faith in a book that she has waited so long to see completed.

MAX A. GELLER

New York, April, 1952

ACKNOWLEDGMENTS

The preparation of this book has been greatly facilitated by the cooperation of individuals, government officials, and advertising media and associations who have responded so generously to requests for statistics and other material. Needless to say, no one mentioned is responsible in any way for the use to which the material has been put, for the statements made therein, or for the views expressed in the subsequent pages.

In acknowledging this assistance, I wish to express my appreciation for the help rendered by the following:

Stephan Spingarn, Commissioner, Richard Whitely, Director of the Deceptive Practices Division, and Alan B. Hobbes, Office of the General Counsel—all of the Federal Trade Commission; Earl Minderman, Assistant to the Chairman of the Federal Communications Commission; the Office of the Solicitor of the Post Office Department; the Office of the Commissioner of Internal Revenue and the Alcohol Tax Unit of the Treasury Department; Philip Maguire, of the law office of Becker, Maguire, and Reich; the legal staff of Delson, Levin and Gordon; the Readers' Service Departments of *Printers' Ink, Advertising Age, Broadcasting-Telecasting,* and *Variety*; the Radio and Television Research and Sales Departments of the American Broadcasting Company, the Columbia Broadcasting System, and the National Broadcasting Company; the staff of the American Association of Advertising Agencies; the staff of the Magazine Advertising Bureau; the Research Departments of the individual magazines who compiled statistics on circulation and advertising; and the staff of the Direct Mail Advertising Association Inc. for the material on direct mail.

M. A. G.

CONTENTS

APPENDIX

TABLES

ADVERTISING AT THE CROSSROADS

Chapter 1

THE ADVERTISER AND THE CONSUMER

THE IMPACT OF ADVERTISING ON THE CONSUMER AND THE HOME

All the efforts of advertising are directed against one group —the consumer. Of the basic economic groups in our modern society, the ultimate consumer is the largest and his interest the most akin to the general interest; yet he is the least organized, the least articulate, and the least recognized of all the groups in the dynamics of policy formation. The consumer's position is inherently weak, since his interest is diffused too widely to lend itself to effective organization.

In the theoretical system of classical economics, the consumer played a leading role. Adam Smith's well-known comment on this point is worth citing:

> Consumption is the sole end and purpose of all production; and the interest of the producer ought to be attended to only so far as it may be necessary for promoting that of the consumer. The maxim is so perfectly self-evident, that it would be absurd to attempt to prove it.[1]

The actual position of the consumer in our modern economic life, however, is far from being sovereign. Technological development, which has produced a multiplicity of similar products, has made the consumer's choice or selection more difficult. The vast volume of advertising of branded products,

[1] Adam Smith, *An Inquiry Into the Nature and Causes of the Wealth of Nations* (New York: Modern Library, Inc., 1937), p. 159.

each screaming for acceptance for one reason or another, has widened further the gap between the classical theory of economics and actuality.

Because of the impact of technology and advertising, consumer legislation was developed and administrative agencies were formed to protect and represent the consumer. Government intervention followed the usual pattern: unregulated private enterprise, spurred by the profit motive, developed abuses which the government alone had the power to correct. The government is the "policeman" to whom the people turn for protection when self-help proves inadequate. In order to understand better the regulatory policies of the government, in so far as they affect advertising, it is helpful to examine briefly their *raison d'être*.

It has been charged that advertising is, at times, crude, vulgar, and offensive. Even consumers who have a considerable tolerance for "puffery" and exaggeration in advertising criticize many advertisements as being in "bad taste," "indecent," "suggestive," or based on the fear motive to an undue degree, and using questionable testimonials and pseudo-scientific claims. It is said that murder mysteries on the radio and the low neckline on television have deleterious effects on our youngsters and the family as a whole. "Soap operas" are regarded as particularly obnoxious by some psychologists and sociologists. There is much to these charges, but as with most generalizations, they are perhaps too superficial.

Some people object to any advertising in behalf of products which they consider harmful, such as cigarettes, liquor, or drug preparations. Many contend that advertising is uneconomical and that the same products in a different package vying for the consumers' dollars constitute a great economic waste. Again, there is a measure of truth in this assertion, but the generalization is, as usual, too sweeping.

On the other hand, equally extreme claims are made in defense of advertising methods. Irritated by the charge that advertising executives are "Babbitts," fattening upon the credulity of the uninformed, *Printers' Ink* once made the following retort:

> The literati seem to look with amused tolerance upon the man who produces and sells meat, automobiles, butter, oil, shoes, and cheese. . . . The packers have contributed more to the health and general welfare of the country than all the writers combined.
>
> The conviction persists that these gentlemen, so handy with English, are lampooning men who are vastly more useful and important than themselves.
>
> The manufacturer of a good piece of merchandise is usually much more of a benefactor to humanity than the writer of magazine articles or books which ridicule him.[2]

There is as little balance in this attitude as in the boast of Frank Presbrey that "advertising probably is our greatest agency for spreading an understanding and love of beauty in all things."

The honest advertiser, when queried, will admit without any hesitation that advertising is not intended to be objective or impartial, but, on the contrary, is meant to be strongly biased according to his commercial interests. He will say that the great majority of advertisers are as honest as most other men, admitting that among advertisers, as in every field of human endeavor, there are charlatans and cheats. Advertising has only one job to do—to sell goods or services. The consumer must be piled up with as many goods and services as he can possibly be made to take, because only thus, says the advertiser, can mass production be kept going at full blast. This is important, according to the advertiser, because only then can we have full employment. We enable "our consumer" to pay for the goods and services which the advertiser wishes to

---

[2] Quoted from Frank Presbrey, *The History and Development of Advertising* (New York: Doubleday, Doran Co., Inc., 1929), pp. 608–9.

sell him. Advertising is, therefore, the motive force which keeps the economic merry-go-round in perpetual motion.

Thus, the fact is stressed that without adequate production we cannot satisfy even normal consumption; likewise, that without consumer demand the wheels of production must come to a stop, with unemployment and depressions as the result. An interesting exposition of this viewpoint in a judicial decision is to be found in the case of *Ford Motor Company v. Federal Trade Commission* [3] where the Circuit Court said:

> Advertising goes hand in hand with volume of production and retail distribution. It operates to increase the demand for and availability of goods and to develop quickly consumers' acceptance of the manufactured products. Expressed another way, it breaks down consumers' resistance, creates consumers' acceptance, and develops consumers' demand. . . .
>
> The use of advertising as an aid to the production and distribution of goods has been recognized so long as to require only passing notice. The economy of mass production is just as well known, and the effects of advertising may be described as mass selling without which distribution would be lessened and a fortiori production correspondingly decreased.

No one who views advertising objectively can deny that it has made important contributions to our standard of living. F. P. Bishop's comments on this point are appropriate:

> Whatever the motive and whatever the means, it is probably true that commercial advertisers have done more than all the doctors, the scientists, the schools, and the social workers to make cleanliness "popular," and to impose the sanctions of social disapproval on those who are careless in this respect.
>
> Commercial advertisers have helped to persuade new generations of the public not only to wash, but also to clean their teeth, brush their hair, and to look after themselves in a dozen different ways calculated to improve their health and appearance and to make the world a pleasanter and brighter place to

---

[3] 120 F. (2d) 175 (1941), cert. denied 314 U.S. 668, 62 S. Ct. 130 (1941), 86 L. Ed. 534 (1941).

> live in. . . . and in so far as the efforts of the advertisers have helped to educate the public in dental hygiene it may be claimed that the habit moulding power of advertising has served society well.
>
> The same is true of hygiene in the home. The National Institute's list of heavily advertised commodities includes disinfectants and insecticides, household soap, cleaners and polishers, toilet tissue, vacuum cleaners, mangles and wringers. In the use of all these and many other articles the commercial advertiser can claim to have been the most effective educator of the average housewife. He has encouraged her to take a pride in her home; he has helped to bring labour-saving equipment within her reach; he has given her new ideas about furniture, carpets, curtains, and the like. His support has made possible the many "home" journals and magazines which supply her with many household hints and point the way to improvements. The voice of the housewife is not often, if ever, heard in support of the academic critics who condemn modern advertising.[4]

All this shows that advertising can make a luxury of yesterday into a necessity of today and that our standard of living has been raised by the mass production of automobiles, radios, television sets, and other modern conveniences. The advertiser, nevertheless, will concede that his motive is not to render a social service or to aid our economic welfare. The only thing he is concerned about is selling his product. He "sets his sights" for the consumer. If he shoots too high or too low in his presentation, he will miss his target and, therefore, lose sales volume.

The copy appeal, selected by the advertiser, represents his studied and deliberate appraisal of the consumer. If advertising campaigns featuring such obnoxious themes as "B. O.," "Halitosis," "A Bridesmaid Often, But Never a Bride," or "His Boss Turned Him Down Because He Didn't Use X Shoe

---

[4] F. P. Bishop, *The Ethics of Advertising* (London: Robert Hale, Ltd., 1949), pp. 139–40.

Polish"—to mention just a few—have succeeded, then, perhaps, the intellectual level of the consumer is more acutely evaluated by the advertising agency than by the sociologist or psychologist.

An excellent illustration of the stimuli to which the average consumer will respond is to be found in an article written by a well-known copywriter.[5] He lists ten chief motives or desires which prompt the average consumer to "buy":

1. *Money and Better Job.* There must be some kind of shortcut to getting ahead faster.
2. *Security in Old Age.* When I get along in years I want to be able to take it easy.
3. *Popularity.* It's fun to be asked out all the time, to be wanted by everyone.
4. *Praise from Others.* Praise from others is a nice thing to get and I like to get it when I deserve it—and I often do.
5. *More Comfort.* A lot of people, who are not as industrious or capable as I am, seem to have more comforts. . . . So why shouldn't I spread myself once in a while?
6. *Social Advancement.* Where would a person be if he never tried to better himself and to meet and associate with better people?
7. *Improved Appearance.* It's awfully nice to have people tell you how attractive and well dressed you are. . . . If I had the time and the money that some people spend on themselves—would I show them!
8. *Personal Prestige.* I am going to see to it that my children can prove that they have parents they never need to be ashamed of.
9. *Better Health.* I don't feel any older than I did years ago. It's just that I don't seem to have the drive and the energy I used to have.
10. *Increased Enjoyment.* I work hard. I do the best I can about things . . . so why shouldn't I get as much enjoyment as I can?

---

[5] Victor Schwab, "Ten Copy Appeals," *Printers' Ink,* December 13, 1943, pp. 17–19.

It is to the many, therefore, and not the select few that most commercial advertising is addressed. Our courts, in interpreting the federal regulations of advertising, have fully recognized this fact. In the case of *P. Lorillard Company v. Federal Trade Commission,*[6] Judge Parker, speaking for the Circuit Court, said:

> As was well said by Judge Coxe in *Florence Manufacturing Co. v. J. C. Dowd & Co.* 2 Cir. 178 F. 73, 75, with reference to the law relating to trademarks: "The law is not made for the protection of experts, but for the public—that vast multitude which includes the ignorant, the unthinking and the credulous, who, in making purchases, do not stop to analyze, but are governed by appearances and general impression." See also *F.T.C. v. Standard Education Soc.* 302 U.S. 112; *Stanley Laboratories v. F.T.C.* 9 Cir. 138 F. 2d 388; *Aronberg v. F.T.C.* Cir. 132 F. 2d 165.

In the *Ford* case previously mentioned, the Court had this to say about the "average" consumer:

> The average individual does not make, and often is incapable of making, minute calculations to determine the cost of property purchased on the deferred payment plan. Mechanization, industrialization, and urbanization have transformed the structure of our society and raised to the proportions of a major social problem, the protection of the installment purchaser against his own ignorance and the pressure of his need.

Advertisers and their agencies, then, are not moralists or sociologists who try to present in their advertising an impartial, unemotional, and rational story. The advertiser can point out to the rigid moralist that when "fans" at a baseball game "boo" the umpire's decisions, they are not dishonest—they are just partisan; that the "keynoter" at a party convention who goes into raptures about his own candidates and platform and

---

[6] 186 F. (2d) 52 (1950).

then delivers a tirade against the opposing party, which he pictures as the embodiment of all evil, is not necessarily dishonest but only partisan.[7] That, says the advertiser, is precisely his case. He is concerned with selling his merchandise and he uses all the aids of pictorial presentation, and emotional and glamorizing copy, to accomplish his purpose. As long as the advertiser does not transgress the rules and regulations set up by the government, which supposedly reflect the social conscience of the community and the standard of its morals, he is just being partial or partisan in his selling efforts.

All of this, of course, points directly to the fact that rules and regulations were very much needed in this tug-of-war between the advertiser and the consumer, not to satisfy the rigid moralist, but rather to harness and control the impact of this gigantic force by which the advertiser seeks not merely to direct our existing demands but to create continuously new wants. The ethical, social, and economic problems which arise from an uncontrolled influence of such vast proportions are giving serious concern to many thinking people. Today, more than ever, it is a problem of the first magnitude.

The Advertiser

During the year 1951, the sum of $6.5 billion was spent on advertising for the purpose of persuading the consumer to purchase commodities and services. The sources of this money

---

[7] ". . . When advertisements are judged as biased or persuasive messages, they accord with what men have come to expect in persuasive messages in all walks of life. The same charges of bias, and hence of dishonesty, may be applied to the statesman in his pronouncements designed to influence the viewpoints of other statesmen, to the politician seeking votes, to the lawyer in his plea to the jury, or even to the pulpit orator seeking to save the sinner." N. H. Borden, *The Economic Effects of Advertising* (Chicago: Richard D. Irwin, Inc., 1942), p. 829.

are the persons, firms, or corporations known as advertisers. Thus the foundation of advertising is the advertiser; and just as medical science seeks the root of the disease to be cured, so also must the regulation of advertising seek to control the advertiser.

The advertiser's purpose is to create desires on the part of the consumer and to persuade him to purchase the particular product or service. Therefore, the advertiser must bring continued pressure to break down the sales resistance of the consumer and to overcome the activities of competitors.

The essential problem of the federal regulation of advertising is whether or not the advertiser is sufficiently aware of changing standards of good taste with respect to advertising. What was accepted fifty years ago may be taboo today. The Chase & Sanborn advertisement of the latter part of the last century, which claimed that coffee would cure malaria, would be suppressed today. The period during which that advertisement appeared was one in which such claims were recognized as part of the businessman's prerogative.

The advertiser's principal concern is the selling of his product. Both the consumer's sales resistance and the competition of rivals may often tempt him to distort the true quality of his product in the desire for profit. Whether such distortion is due to the enthusiasm of partisanship or willful exaggeration is not our concern. The fact remains that whatever is the advertiser's motive the results of advertising are the same; and it is because of the consequences of the advertiser's practices that federal and other regulations have been developed. In order to understand the nature of the regulations of advertising, it is important to understand the background, development, and motives of the advertiser.

The proprietor of the New Amsterdam Coffee House who hung out a sign in 1642 and the person who sought a customer for his Long Island plantation in a 1704 issue of the *Boston*

Newes Letter were both advertisers. But with an increased opportunity for profit there appeared the first organized, nation-wide advertisers, namely, the patent medicine manufacturers. It was in the early 1800's that the methods and techniques of large-scale persuasion of the public began, for the makers of patent medicines poured money into newspapers and magazines to advertise their product.[8] It was unfortunate that the American people received their introduction to advertising from charlatans who had few scruples and believed that where truth and sales conflicted, truth must be discarded. Early examples of flagrant deception designed to capture the consumer's dollar were such advertisements as Warner's Safe Kidney and Liver Cure, which was alleged to be able to cure Bright's Disease; Ayer's Cherry Pectoral, sold as a cure for tuberculosis; St. Jacob's Oil, said to cure rheumatism; Altenbeim's Magic Compound, which promised to grow hair overnight.

Although advertisements of this nature have become less frequent today,[9] the art of the patent medicine advertisement

---

[8] ". . . A study of old files of magazines and newspapers shows that advertising during the nineteenth century was devoted in large part to lotteries, transportation, books, auctions, and patent medicines. . . . The patent medicine advertising which made up a very substantial percentage of the advertising revenue of publications, was a sore spot and undoubtedly accounted in considerable part for the stigma attached to advertising at the time. In the best publications appeared many advertisements of proprietary remedies and of charms to make the user well, strong, or beautiful, which would be found only in the lowest grade magazines of the present time . . ." Borden, *op. cit.*, p. 827.

[9] At the turn of the century, the inherent danger and deception in patent medicine advertising was recognized by many publishers as detrimental to the continued reputation of their publications. As a result, many magazines excluded patent medicine advertisements entirely or attempted to eliminate the more outrageous statements. Other editors published a series of articles exposing the dishonesty of many of the manufacturers of patent medicines, e.g., those of Samuel Hopkins Adams in *Collier's* in 1904. Such articles did much to crystallize public sentiment in favor of federal regulation, which came with the enactment of the federal Food and Drug Act in 1906.

is not yet lost. The phenomenal success of the Hadacol Company a few years ago is an excellent illustration of the potency of patent medicine advertising.

Advertisers, other than patent medicine manufacturers, recognized that the problem was to use advertising for the purpose of creating good will as a means of obtaining long-run profits. In order to induce continued patronage, advertisers of the closing decades of the nineteenth century relied upon persuasive copy appeal rather than on blatant deception. Since the 1890's, Procter and Gamble, the manufacturers of Ivory Soap, have built a business empire through advertisements designed to create wants and good will. During the fifteen-year period 1936–50 this company has spent a sum in excess of $295 million to promote Crisco, Duz, Tide, and other products in addition to Ivory Soap.

A problem which always confronts the advertiser is deciding whether to continue or stop spending for advertising. That continued advertising is essential in the war against the sales resistance of the consumer is evident from the fact that when a manufacturer discontinues advertising, the public no longer purchases his product. But advertisers who have kept their brands persistently before the public have been richly rewarded. For example, smokers do not ask for "cigarettes," but for "Camels" or "Luckies"; the American housewife buys "Tide," "Duz," or "Rinso" instead of "soap"; and the family will select a "Ford," "Chrysler," or "Buick" car. Customers buy brands. Public consciousness of brand names has been developed so thoroughly that the manufacturer is protected against rebelling wholesalers, jobbers, or retailers. The latter group, in order to stay in business, is forced to stock the products which the consumer demands. This is the sort of continuing patronage, profit, and, above all, protection that moneys spent by the advertiser insure. A mere listing of the twenty-five leading advertisers for the past fifteen years is a "Who's

Who" of big business in America. Of the many thousands of corporations these twenty-five firms have spent a total of $2.8 billion for advertising during the fifteen-year period 1936–50. Table 1 lists these corporations and their individual expenditures.

TABLE 1

THE 25 LEADING ADVERTISERS: 1936–50

Advertiser	Total Advertising Expenditures
Procter & Gamble	$297,000,000
General Motors	266,000,000
General Foods	181,000,000
Lever Brothers	178,000,000
Colgate-Palmolive-Peet	145,000,000
Sterling Drug, Inc.	142,000,000
R. J. Reynolds Tobacco Co.	139,000,000
Liggett & Myers Tobacco Co.	122,000,000
General Mills Inc.	111,000,000
Ford Motor Co.	102,000,000
Chrysler Corp.	101,000,000
American Tobacco Co.	99,000,000
Seagram Distillers Corp.	98,000,000
General Electric	96,000,000
American Home Products	85,000,000
Campbell Soup Co.	79,000,000
Schenley Industries, Inc.	77,000,000
Bristol-Myers Co.	72,000,000
Standard Brands	68,000,000
Swift & Co.	66,000,000
Philip Morris & Co.	65,000,000
Miles Laboratories, Inc.	63,000,000
Coca-Cola Co.	60,000,000
National Dairy Products Corp.	57,000,000
National Distillers Products Corp.	56,000,000

Source: Barbour, Walker, Lyndon, Inc. study in *Printers' Ink*, December 1, 1950, p. 29.

Between 1940 and 1951, all advertisers spent at least $44.5 billion. Table 2 breaks this figure down into annual expenditures:

TABLE 2

ADVERTISING EXPENDITURES: 1940–51

Year		Amount
1940		$2,087,600,000
1941		2,235,700,000
1942		2,156,100,000
1943		2,496,400,000
1944		2,723,600,000
1945		2,875,500,000
1946		3,364,200,000
1947		4,259,700,000
1948		4,863,600,000
1949		5,202,200,000
1950		5,691,300,000
1951		6,548,200,000
	Total	$44,504,100,000

Source: For 1940–49, *Printers' Ink,* June 16, 1950, p. 28; for 1950–51, *Printers' Ink,* January 11, 1952, p. 36. These figures do not accurately depict advertising expenditures, because they do not include talent and production costs in radio and television, or point-of-sale display advertising which may run into the billions; if accurate total advertising expenditures were available, the grand figure for 1951 would perhaps approach $10 billion.

The 1951 total of $6.5 billion means that every second of every minute of every hour during the year, $206.11 was spent to induce the public to purchase some commodity or service. Perhaps advertising science has solved the riddle of perpetual motion.

The contest between the advertiser and the consumer is a one-sided affair. Industry and business hire the "best brains" to plan the strategy of and to conduct the sales campaign. On the other side is the poorly informed, unorganized public, often apathetic about the abuses heaped upon it. It is to protect this huge, ill-informed consumer army that federal regulations have been developed, and in succeeding chapters the adequacies of such protection will be discussed.

The Impact of Advertising on Our Economy

Although the economic effects of advertising are being assiduously studied, the role of advertising in maintaining a healthy, dynamic economy has not been adequately considered in order to formulate an over-all policy for advertising in our economy. The size and importance of advertising expenditures and the need for federal protection of the consumer's interest would indicate that the development of such a policy is the concern of the federal government.

The American economy is the richest production mechanism the world has ever known. It comprises 4 million business enterprises; it operates with a working force of 61 million, of whom 17.5 million are women; its 240,000 factories pay out $40 billion a year in wages and salaries; and its 6 million farms cover more than a billion acres. The very magnitude of this economy has made it so interdependent that the slightest interruption of its delicately balanced function threatens its very existence.

The complex, interdependent structure of the American economy and the function of advertising in maintaining full production point to the propriety of regulating advertising so as to help in controlling inflation and combating the dangers of inflation. In his economic report submitted to Congress on January 12, 1951, President Truman called the attention of Congress and the American people to the serious danger of inflation. After discussing the problem of sudden conversion to a defense economy, the President stated:

> Although we can increase production, we cannot do it quickly enough to expand the defense program, and at the same time still have as much left over for other purposes. We must put heavy restraints upon nonessential business activity. During the past few years, nearly 70% of our growing national output has gone into consumption. This has led to higher standards of living, which is the ultimate purpose of a peacetime economy. But the total supply of consumer goods cannot

be increased this year, and many types of goods must be sharply curtailed. Yet, the population will continue to grow; new families will continue to be formed; and more incomes for practically all groups will be generated by more production, more employment, and longer hours. The excess of consumer demand over available goods will rise by many billions of dollars.

This will cause intense and mounting inflationary pressures, which must be counteracted. . . .

If the inflation continues to gain cumulative force, it will multiply the cost of the defense program. It will undermine production, destroy confidence, generate friction and economic strife, impair the value of the dollar, dissipate the value of savings, and impose an intolerable burden upon fixed income groups. This must not happen.

To fight inflation, demand must be kept down until supplies can catch up. This is why we must have a stringent stabilization program. It will mean sacrifices by everybody. But under the conditions now facing us, restraints will serve the interest of all.[10]

Pursuant to the President's recommendation, Congress instituted wage and price controls, tightened credit curbs and installment buying, and increased margin requirements for stocks and commodities. The wisdom of this action was questioned by few, although the adequacy and effectiveness of such regulations troubled many.

The Committee for Economic Development, in discussing the problem of how to stop inflation in view of the prospect of a great excess of civilian consumer demands over available supplies, expressed itself as follows:

The second approach would check inflation by eliminating the excess of demand over supply rather than by trying to dam up the excess of demand behind a wall of price and rationing regulations. This approach is two-sided—to restrain

---

[10] *The Economic Report of the President,* transmitted to Congress January 12, 1951, pp. 6–7. Italics supplied.

> demand and increase supply. On the one hand, it calls for the use of taxation to reduce the incomes individuals and business have available to spend, credit controls to restrict expenditure financed by borrowed money, a program to promote savings, and maximum economy in government expenditure.[11]

In view of all the alarms sounded by the government, economic councils, and business leaders on the dangers which threaten this country because inflation is likely to become hyperinflation unless checked rapidly, it seems remarkable indeed that an advertising expenditure in excess of $6.5 billion should be permitted—with the implicit blessings of Congress —to continue its ceaseless cacophony of "buy, buy, and buy more!"

The statement that it is being done with Congressional or governmental approval is based on the fact that these expenditures are considered normal and reasonable business expenses and are, therefore, tax-deductible. The policy arrived at in 1942 by the Treasury Department in conference with advertising representatives is still the official policy of the government from a tax standpoint. Section 23(a) of the Internal Revenue Code provides that advertising expenses are deductible if they are directly connected with or pertain to the trade or business. Former Secretary of the Treasury, Henry Morgenthau, Jr., in his testimony before the Joint Committee of Internal Revenue Taxation in 1942, laid down the test of the "rule of reason" which prevails today:

> The test of whether expenditures for advertising are deductible is whether they are ordinary and necessary and bear a reasonable relation to the business activities in which the enterprise is engaged. This is not intended to exclude institu-

---

[11] Committee for Economic Development, Research and Policy Committee, *Paying for Defense*, November 16, 1950.

tional advertising in reasonable amounts or goodwill advertising calculated to influence the buying habits of the public.[12]

All this points to the fact that the billions spent on advertising in 1951 were normal and reasonable tax-deductible operating expenses. It would seem reasonable, also, to assume that in the absence of Congressional action, these expenses will continue to be deductible in the future. It is natural, perhaps, to inquire here whether the "left hand knoweth what the right hand doeth." If we are fighting inflation, and one of the important features of the battle is to curb consumer demand for civilian products which will not be available, then how can we encourage and permit the unrestrained and unregulated "all-out effort" of advertisers to sell, and sell, and sell still more?

> We did not build our standard of living on the normal demands of human beings—no one here has ever operated in a *normal* market—we have had a *stimulated* demand economy throughout our lifetime—advertising has been the great stimulator.[13]

Just as the nation must face the problem of regulating advertising and advertising expenditures in an inflationary era, so must it consider the reverse situation when it is confronted by a depression or business recession. It is interesting to note that as far back as 1927, James J. Davis, then Secretary of Labor, suggested that advertising could be used to combat business depressions. Reviewing the problem faced by a typical manufacturer when confronted with a serious slackening of demand for his product, Davis stressed the fact that the old method of coping with this problem was either to reduce wages or to discharge employees and shut down the factory.

---

[12] United States Department of Commerce, *Advertising and Its Role in War and Peace* (Washington, D. C.: U. S. Govt. Printing Office, 1942), p. 4.

[13] *Ibid.*, p. 73. Italics supplied.

The dire effect of such a step was pointed out by Secretary Davis in these words:

> Within a few hours after he [the typical manufacturer] gave notice to his workers, the word began to circulate that his plant was to be shut down. Soon, workers throughout his section of the country began to hear of it, and their hearts were chilled. Their own plant might be next.
>
> Retrenchment began immediately on the part of hundreds and then thousands of workers. Intended purchases of automobiles, household appliances, radios, books, and many luxuries were deferred. The food expense of many homes was promptly cut to a minimum. The buying power of the entire section in which the manufacturer is located was materially reduced, and the first unfavorable reaction of a vicious circle had taken place.[14]

To avoid such results, Secretary Davis urged business to employ a different technique. He contended that:

> . . . modern advertising and merchandising can be utilized to keep labor employed and thereby preserve the demand for merchandise of all kinds. . . .
>
> At the first sign of a temporary falling off in demand, he [the up-to-date manufacturer] would have called into consultation the best advertising and merchandising specialists he could find. He would have advertised in a manner that would not only support his present demand, but which would assure future demand. He would have devised new and effective sales plans. In other words, he would have done everything possible to bolster up the demand for his products before he had laid off a single workman.
>
> I am speaking advisedly regarding these measures, for I have known manufacturers who have employed them, and according to their experience, expedients of this kind bring a return that is valuable far beyond their cost. . . .
>
> Obviously, our greatest need is to preserve our established demand for manufactured products, and enough manufac-

---

[14] James J. Davis, "How Modern Selling and Advertising Can Check Unemployment," *Printers' Ink*, March 24, 1927, pp. 3 ff.

> turers have used advertising for this purpose to demonstrate that in keeping workmen employed, advertising furnishes perhaps its greatest economic value.

If, as Mr. Davis suggests, advertising can be employed to help avert or overcome business recessions, then should not the federal government encourage advertising during a deflationary period and discourage huge advertising expenditures in an inflationary one?

No answer to this question has been given as yet, principally because the federal government has not given sufficient consideration to the role of advertising and its importance in our economy. Perhaps the reason why this tremendous influence on our well-being has not received the consideration it merits and has not been properly integrated into our governmental efforts to bolster our economy is that it has come up so suddenly. Advertising, at the turn of the century, was an insignificant factor in our economy. The sum total expenditure of advertisers in all newspapers, magazines, and other periodicals totaled only $96 million in 1900; this figure mounted to $203 million in 1909; $677 million in 1921, and $3.1 billion in 1951.

It is not to be wondered, then, that not only Congress, but also our economists and even our business leaders have not as yet fully grasped the significance of a force as great as advertising. The point is that apart from remedial regulations of the excesses of advertising, the federal government has made no attempt to regulate, control, direct, curb, or harness this giant economic force.

England has recently recognized the effect of advertising upon its national economy. Faced with the problem of too much money chasing too few goods and so with a threatened collapse of the economy, British advertisers, as an alternative to a tax on advertising, voluntarily agreed to reduce advertising budgets in order to lessen the demand for luxury items, thereby easing the pressure on already deficient production.

How can the federal government cope with the problems arising from the impact of advertising on our economy? Are these problems within the scope of federal regulation? Before a discussion of any proposed answers, it is important to consider first the essential elements of advertising: the media, such as newspapers, magazines, radio, and television; the advertiser, who provides the money; and the advertising agency, which fashions and creates the advertisements and spends the money for the advertiser. Then the constitutional sources of power upon which federal regulations of advertising are predicated will be considered before coming to grips with the federal regulation of advertising and the adequacy of the instrumentalities which exist for that task.

Chapter 2

ADVERTISING MEDIA

Newspapers

Newspapers are the primary medium for advertising. When one considers their tremendous circulation—a daily circulation of more than one paper for every family in the country—and the staggering sum of money annually spent for advertising in newspaper columns, the primacy of newspapers as an advertising medium is incontestable. A large part of the advertising appearing in newspapers is of local interest. Yet the national market for so many of the products of our economy and the very nature of advertising make it inevitable that a certain measure of state and federal control impinges upon this medium.

The income from advertising, and not subscriptions or the pennies from newsstand sales, makes possible the size and the coverage of the modern newspaper. Advertising largely supports the newspaper of today, that vital stronghold for accurate reporting and free discussion. Thus the social and ethical implications of advertising extend far beyond the mere economic aspects of its function in present-day society.

In order to understand the interconnection of advertising and newspapers and the reasons for federal regulation, it is necessary to trace very briefly the evolution of the American newspaper and the role of advertising in that growth.

If one disregards the four-day existence in 1690 of *Publick Occurrences*, the first American publication to fulfill the necessary requirements for a newspaper of regular and continuing issuance was the *Boston Newes Letter.* It was published in 1704 when the population of Boston was about 8,000, and in 1719 the second newspaper in this country, the *Boston Gazette,* appeared. Newspapers soon followed in Philadelphia and New York; by the outbreak of the Revolution there were about 35 newspapers with a circulation of approximately 21,000 copies a week in a population of 2 million or so. The bulk of their advertising consisted of notices and announcements of slave sales, property sales, the availability of shipping and passenger space, and the like, as well as some advertisements for various cures and specifics.

The Revolutionary War both quickened and delayed American newspaper development. The colonists craved news of the progress of the war, but there was also a severe shortage of newsprint. And as the reading public increased, advertising had assumed new value in the eyes of the merchants. Therefore, in order to meet the demand for more news and to carry as much advertising as possible, the newspapers eliminated all display advertisements in large, bold letters and imposed a rule that all advertisements were to be entirely agate, i.e., no larger in size than the print commonly used in the ordinary news column. The increase in news material as well as the pressure for more advertising forced the newspapers to change from weekly publication to semi- or tri-weekly, and even daily publication. By 1785 there were already two daily papers in the United States.

The early years of the republic witnessed the increase in both daily and weekly papers and the extension of newspapers into regions west of the Alleghanies. Average circulation figures for all papers were extremely low, no higher than 700. Papers consisted of four pages at the most, and the price usually ranged from 6 to 11 cents, a considerable sum in an era when an average salary might not exceed $5 a week. Newspapers were largely organs of personal opinion for editors and political leaders and parties, as well as being vehicles for advertising matter.

The development of the Fourdrinier papermaking machine, among other technical improvements, contributed greatly to reducing newspaper costs; and in 1833 the first one-cent newspaper, the *New York Sun*, appeared. The *Sun* was also the first paper to cater to the general reading tastes, and by adapting a tabloid size and using newsboy distribution to sell sensationalism it reached a daily circulation of 32,000 in six years. In many ways it approximated our modern newspaper by running a want-ad page, theater and sport sections, and marriage and obituary notices; and it claimed to be the foremost advertising medium of its day. The *New York Herald*, another one-cent paper, appeared in 1835 and is important as the first really independent paper politically.

The popularity of the penny press, technological improvements in printing, better transportation facilities providing quicker distribution, and the growing literacy rate aided in the rapid growth and development of newspapers, so that by 1850 there were more than 200 daily and 2,300 weekly newspapers in America. The circulation of the dailies was up to about 1 million copies. But even though the number of newspapers and their circulation continued to grow, advertising techniques remained crude and backward. Illustrations in advertisements were lacking, and most of the penny papers continued to adhere to the "agate" rule, requiring uniformity in advertising. Most of the advertisements were short and often overlooked by the reader because it was so difficult to distinguish an advertisement from the news columns or from other advertisements.

There were several ingenious attempts made to avoid the "agate" rule, but the first consistent and substantial inroads into the power of the rule are largely attributed to one Robert Bonner. Bonner purchased a business paper in 1851 and gradually changed it into a tremendously successful magazine, *The New York Ledger*. Although the *Ledger* carried no advertising itself, Bonner advertised his publication in newspapers, the first time such a thing had been done. He broke down the "agate" rule by demonstrating to publishers that there was more revenue if greater latitude in advertising were permitted.[1] Bonner spent as much as $27,000 a week for advertising; and his display methods, based on the repetition of a single phrase, led to the development of the advertising slogan.

The Civil War had a tremendous influence on newspapers, which were used extensively by the government to sell war bonds. Hitherto, newspaper advertising had been more or less restricted to local rather than national usage. But the war bond advertising pointed the way for postwar private advertising through the newspapers on a national scale. Newspaper circulation increased tremendously, not only because of the demand for war news but also because women, replacing men in the factory, had more leisure and spending money. Newspapers were soon catering to women's interests with household features and fashion articles; now women for the first time, became an important factor in the circulation picture.

The year 1865 found America with large industrial organizations that had developed to manufacture the vast quantities of war goods needed in the preceding years. Converting quickly to peacetime consumer production, keen competition dictated the employment of advertising, particularly in the newspapers, as the best possible selling force. The desire to reach the largest possible consumer audience resulted in the

---

[1] Bonner's advertisements were so arranged that an acrostic was formed across the page by the first letter of each sentence. Another interesting sidelight of Bonner's advertising genius was his payment of tremendous sums to famous authors for serialized items and a subsequent capitalization by Bonner on the publicity accorded these large sums. Frank Presbrey, *History and Development of Advertising* (New York: Doubleday, Doran Co., Inc., 1929), pp. 236–44.

evolution of the patent-inside.[2] As a result, the advertisement in the newspapers could reach every segment of the American public.

During the remainder of the nineteenth century, newspapers and advertising grew apace with the development of big business. Political opinion and the personal element in journalism gave way to the presentation of news; centralization and standardization took over in the control of newspapers; the format and size of papers improved when increased revenues from advertising permitted the adoption of new, expensive technological developments such as the linotype; and the federal government aided these processes through low postal rates on newspapers and rural free delivery. With Pulitzer and Hearst, yellow journalism came to dominate the field; they vied for circulation supremacy among the masses in exploiting and purveying sensationalism. On the other hand, the *New York Times* was reorganized in 1896, and its editorial policy and its full and accurate reporting were aimed at a cultured and intelligent reading public, as contrasted with the more earthy and sensational approaches of the yellow sheets. Similarly, there was a class breakdown in newspaper advertising; quality goods, concerts, drama, etc. found a better advertising response from *Times* readers.

The newspapers, around the turn of the century, were filled with display advertisements and had progressed to the point where they had full-time personnel in their advertising and art departments. Education, finance, home, sport, comic, and book sections appeared, so that every cross-section of the public, no matter how diversified their interests, found some-

---

[2] The patent-inside, now known as the Sunday Supplement, consisted of a few printed pages which appeared simultaneously in many newspapers. Advertising and news copy would be sent to various central printing plants, printed, and then distributed to many rural newspapers. Frank Luther Mott, *American Journalism* (New York: The Macmillan Co., 1950), p. 585.

thing in the paper to arouse their attention. Formerly, it had been the custom for the man of the household to read the newspaper and then discard it. Now, the youngsters wanted the comics, the men the sport pages, the women the household pages. It was evident that every conceivable person who read could find something in the paper to stimulate him.

Having traced the development of the newspaper in the United States and having indicated that the newspaper possesses something of interest for every member of the family, we can now examine in somewhat greater detail the statistics on newspaper growth and circulation during the period 1940–51.

TABLE 3

CIRCULATION OF DAILY NEWSPAPERS: 1940–51

Year	Number of Weekday Papers	Weekday Circulation
1940	1,878	41,131,611
1941	1,857	42,080,391
1942	1,787	43,374,850
1943	1,754	44,392,829
1944	1,755	45,954,838
1945	1,749	48,384,188
1946	1,763	50,927,505
1947	1,769	51,673,276
1948	1,781	52,285,297
1949	1,780	52,845,551
1950	1,772	53,829,072
1951	1,773	54,017,938

Source: *Editor and Publisher Yearbook,* Bureau of Advertising, compiled at author's request. Sunday editions and newspapers published less frequently than daily have been omitted for want of accurate figures. Were those papers included, circulation figures would be substantially increased.

The 1951 daily newspaper circulation figure of 54 million, as compared with a total of 45 million families in the United States in that year, reveals that there is more than one newspaper being circulated each day for every family in the country.[3]

[3] Standard Rate and Data Service, *Consumer Markets,* 1951–52, p. 113.

Noting the extent of newspaper circulation per family, it is both interesting and important to know the volume of money that is being spent by advertisers in the newspapers in order to create wants and needs as a means of selling products. During the period 1940–51, the staggering sum of $15.7 billion was spent on newspaper advertising, broken down annually as follows:

TABLE 4

NEWSPAPER ADVERTISING EXPENDITURES: 1940–51

Year	Total
1940	$ 815,400,000
1941	844,400,000
1942	797,500,000
1943	899,900,000
1944	888,000,000
1945	921,400,000
1946	1,158,300,000
1947	1,475,000,000
1948	1,749,600,000
1949	1,905,000,000
1950	2,063,000,000
1951	2,226,000,000

Source: These statistics were compiled by Dr. Hans Zeisel, Associate Director of Research, McCann-Erickson, Inc. The figures for 1940–49 were published in *Printers' Ink* (June 16, 1950), p. 28; for 1950–51, *Printers' Ink,* January 11, 1952, p. 36.

It is unnecessary to elaborate the statement that the newspaper medium in which a total of over $2 billion was expended by advertisers during the year 1951 is a major factor in our economy. Indeed, the impact of the advertising volume in the newspapers goes far beyond the economic aspects. Linked with it are social and ethical values and problems. With more than one newspaper a day going to every family in the Uinted States and with every member of the family being reached by some phase of the editorial, as well as the advertising content, it was inevitable that some measure of regulation be invoked by the states and the federal government to curb and to restrain this great force. Subsequent chapters will consider in detail the adequacy of federal regulations and the possibility of strengthening them.

Magazines

Nearly 7,000 magazines are published in the United States and their variety is astounding: they range from the publications of learned societies, trade and professional journals, hobby magazines, to "pulps" and comics. From an advertising standpoint the most important, however, are the national magazines, a generic name for general periodicals with a national circulation. In the category of national magazines there is also great variety. Each is published to appeal to certain large classes of readers, with particular interests and desires, in places large and small throughout the country. This is the essence of "the national magazine idea," the success of which is extremely important to the national advertiser.

Nowadays, in the course of a year, well over 3.5 billion copies of magazines—more than 10 million copies a day—are sold either through subscriptions or over the newsstands. Naturally, such an enormous distribution means that the national magazine must circulate through virtually every city and town and village across the land. Thus, magazine circulations are sensitive reflectors of population shifts and buying-power changes which continually take place in America. People and their social and economic attributes are the measures of places—and so the distribution of magazine circulations, following people, is a ready measure of the value of markets.

Over the years the national magazine has grown to be the major method used by national advertisers to get a product or an idea to market. The business respect that advertisers have had for magazines has been recorded in a very tangible way; for the amount of money advertisers decide to invest each year in the ability of magazines to turn markets into customers shows a constantly climbing line when charted. In the early decades of the century national advertisers were spending considerably more in newspapers than they were in magazines: in 1915, about twice as much; in 1925, about one and a half times as much; but in 1935, only a third again as much in newspapers as in magazines. The gap was closing. Then, in 1939, magazines with $143 million of national advertising passed newspapers in national advertising for the first time. Since then magazines have never been headed. (When local advertising expenditures are included, however, newspapers still outrank by far the magazines.)

One might call the *Pennsylvania Gazette*, a weekly whose publication Benjamin Franklin took over in 1729, the first successful magazine in the United States. Like many of the eighteenth-century periodicals, it was a combination newspaper and magazine. Most of the earlier magazines were short-lived. They were generally directed to the well-to-do classes and were concerned either with literary matters or with spreading an awareness of good taste, better manners, and a mild degree of "culture." Religious magazines, which often were family periodicals as well, were common, as were temperance tracts and the abolition magazines of the era leading to the Civil War. The first successful women's magazine, *Godey's Lady's Book*, appeared in 1827, and it claimed a circulation of 100,000 in 1860. In the 1850's, better magazines, such as *Harper's* and the *Atlantic Monthly*, began to appear.

Just as in the case of newspapers, the Civil War stimulated magazine publishing; nevertheless, magazine development still lagged behind newspapers because of the following factors:

1) The American public, still not a reading public, restricted its small literary efforts and its smaller literary budget to the newspaper, which was a better buy.
2) Even so, the magazine did not cater effectively to that segment of the public which did have the reading habit.

Such short-sightedness resulted in restricting the audience to the few intelligentsia and the religious and political followers of the day.

3) For some inexplicable reason, both the publishers and the public believed that the fewer the number of advertisements, the greater the magazine's prestige. Many magazines excluded advertising entirely or imposed strict limitations on the quantity of advertising columns. This, of course, resulted in higher costs and less circulation.

Magazines are vehicles for the communication of news, of ideas and opinions, entertainment and escape, practical information and inspiration. Advertisers, no less than editors, began to recognize the function of magazines in meeting these needs of the masses. At the same time, growing circulation represented a larger national market. Thus, in the tremendous expansion and consolidation of the American economy which took place after the Civil War, the magazine increasingly assumed its role in helping to overcome the sectionalism and insularity of the American people and to fuse them into a greater homogeneity. Magazines were including more popular fiction and articles of general interest in their editorial content. Advertising was being energetically solicited, and each succeeding issue contained more and more advertisements. Increasingly, advertising was making possible the modern magazine with its improved appearance, expanded contents, larger circulation, and lower price. By 1879 there were 47 magazines of national importance with a combined circulation of 1,500,000 copies pere issue or approximately 3.1 copies for every 100 people.[4]

The postal laws of 1879, providing liberal mailing privileges through second-class postal rates, aided the magazine in achieving inexpensive and widely spread distribution; and in the

---

[4] Magazine Advertising Bureau, *The National Magazine and American Life* (New York, 1950), p. 5.

years immediately following, the magazine developed rapidly. As much as any factor, second-class postal rates made possible the national distribution of magazines.

Cosmopolitan began publication in 1889 and had a circulation of 300,000 by 1893. The leader in advertising and circulation was the *Youth's Companion.* It was on the back cover of this latter magazine in 1893 that an advertisement of the Mellin Food Company appeared at a cost of $14,000, the most expensive advertisement that had appeared up to that date.

The turn of the century was marked by expanded magazine activities,[5] and the publishing genius of Cyrus H. K. Curtis was largely responsible for such expansion. Curtis originally entered the publishing field with a weekly four-page farm paper, the *Tribune and Farmer*, and in it appeared a column written by Curtis himself, entitled, "Women at Home." This column was the subject of repeated criticism by his wife, and at Curtis's suggestion she assumed charge of the preparation of the column. Her efforts were so successful and her columns so popular that Curtis decided in 1883 to issue a women's supplement, the *Ladies' Home Journal*, which quickly became one of the leading magazines in the woman's field. The magazine's subscription price was fifty cents a year and its growth was rapid both in advertising revenue and in circulation. With its articles and features of real service to the woman, the *Ladies' Home Journal* paved the way for the tremendous influence wielded today by the woman's magazine.

Perhaps Curtis' greatest achievement was the purchase of the *Saturday Evening Post* in 1897 for the unbelievably low

[5] J. Walter Thompson was one of the dominant personalities in the magazine field at that time. Thompson had originally been a general space contractor, and having had foresight with respect to the future of magazines, he devoted his entire energy to the field. It was largely through his efforts that systematic and planned magazine advertising became standard. He soon became the foremost magazine advertising man in the country, and upon the foundation he laid rests the J. Walter Thompson Company, one of the largest advertising agencies in the world.

price of $1,000. The *Post* had originally been Franklin's *Pennsylvania Gazette,* and after many changes in form and ownership it emerged from the same printing shop in 1821 as the *Saturday Evening Post.* Although the *Post,* in the first twenty-five years of the nineteenth century printed the contributions of such writers as Edgar Allan Poe, James Fenimore Cooper, and Harriet Beecher Stowe, its circulation by 1897 was down to 2,000. Two years later the following advertisement appeared in *Printers' Ink*:

> The *Saturday Evening Post* gives you a circulation of 200,000 copies every week for one dollar per line.[6] You can buy space now for one dollar that later will cost you two dollars. The *Saturday Evening Post* is to be pushed into a circulation exceeding that of any weekly in the United States—what you have seen in the periodicals and daily papers for the past few months is but a drop in the bucket—a starter. The *Post,* as it is intended to be, hasn't started. Editorially, the best brains of America, and some of the best of England, are at work for us; mechanically, we are getting ready to print anything we may be called upon to issue, and to enlarge to 32 pages if necessary.
>
> We offer you a good investment in its advertising space at the present prices.
>
> The Curtis Publishing Co.
> Philadelphia

Curtis's success in securing large-scale advertising and promoting national circulation for the *Saturday Evening Post* and the *Ladies' Home Journal* indicates that his influence in the magazine field cannot be overestimated. These magazines not only developed, but also symbolize many of the twentieth-century concepts in the publication, financing, and distribution of the national magazine.[7]

---

[6] It is perhaps interesting to note that in 1952, the *Saturday Evening Post's* space rates are $23.30 per line.

[7] The beginning of the nineteenth century and the twenty or thirty years that followed witnessed the growth of other magazine empires. Some of these

A few selected statistics will show the relationship between advertising and the growth of the modern national magazine over the past 50 years. In 1906, *McCall's* had a circulation of 706,000 and a total of 832 columns of advertising, and by 1950, circulation had increased to 3,836,000 with a corresponding increase in the number of advertising columns to 3,301. The *Saturday Evening Post* in 1897 carried 69 columns of advertising and had a circulation of 2,231, while in 1949 its advertising was up to 16,484 columns and its circulation was 4,022,000. Comparative figures for the *Ladies' Home Journal* and *Woman's Home Companion* reveal that the *Journal's* 1900 advertising was 682 columns and its circulation, 859,000; in 1949 its advertising total was 5,849 columns with a circulation of 4,451,000. The *Companion's* 1908 total of advertising columns was 1,269 and its 1908 circulation, 503,000; but by 1950 it had a column total of 3,803 and a circulation of 4,067,000.

In order to understand better the impact of the magazine on the American home, people, and economy, it is necessary to examine magazine circulation statistics in greater detail. The penetration of the magazine into the American family is, indeed, made evident by the fact that the total average circulation per issue of sixteen of the leading magazines provides more than one magazine for every family, per issue. These sixteen magazines, their frequency of publication, and average circulation per issue are listed in Table 5.

Observing the extensive coverage of the sixteen leading magazines of all types, it is obvious that total magazine penetration must be tremendous. Table 6 effectively indicates the influence of the magazine for the period 1940–51, even

---

were: the Hearst group: *Cosmopolitan, Good Housekeeping, Town and Country;* Crowell group: *Woman's Home Companion, Collier's,* the *American Magazine;* Condé-Nast group: *Vogue, House and Garden, Vanity Fair;* and the Luce group: *Time, Life, Fortune.*

TABLE 5

SIXTEEN LEADING MAGAZINES: 1951

Magazine	Frequency of Publication	Average Circulation per Issue
Life	Weekly	5,301,331
Ladies' Home Journal	Monthly	4,458,219
McCall's Magazine	Monthly	4,011,643
Saturday Evening Post	Weekly	3,994,969
Woman's Home Companion	Monthly	3,992,005
Better Homes & Gardens	Monthly	3,563,856
Look	Weekly	3,260,927
Collier's Weekly	Weekly	3,150,444
Good Housekeeping	Monthly	3,081,960
American Home	Monthly	2,813,704
American Magazine	Monthly	2,551,008
True Story	Monthly	2,093,979
Cosmopolitan	Monthly	2,000,246
Redbook	Monthly	1,993,013
Time	Weekly	1,651,372
Newsweek	Weekly	851,036

Note: The total number of copies per issue of the sixteen magazines is 48,769,712 while the number of families in the United States is 44,646,134. Standard Rate and Data Service, *Consumer Magazine,* January, 1952, pp. 16–19; *Consumer Markets,* 1951–52, p. 113.

though the statistics represent only some 203 to 251 magazines.

Since the majority of the magazines included in Table 6 are published monthly, the figure 98.5 magazines for each 100 persons in the United States means that there are more than 11 magazines per person per year. Referring back to Table 5, it is to be observed that the circulation of *Life* is 5,301,331 copies per issue. This figure suggests that 5,301,331 persons read *Life* each week. However, it is well known that the magazine, though purchased by one member of the family, is brought into the home and read by the other members of the household. In fact, any single issue of *Life* is read by an estimated 23,950,000 persons, or 20.3 per cent of the entire United

TABLE 6

MAGAZINE CIRCULATION: 1940–51

Year	Number of Magazines	Average Circulation per Issue	U. S. Population	Circulation per 100 Persons
1940	224	94,817,238	131,954,000	71.9
1941	213	100,934,784	133,060,000	75.9
1942	203	105,704,994	133,771,000	79.0
1943	209	111,344,026	133,966,000	83.1
1944	217	115,966,726	132,552,000	87.5
1945	219	121,240,485	132,019,000	91.8
1946	239	130,897,607	139,893,000	93.6
1947	243	135,587,000	143,414,000	94.5
1948	239	140,998,562	146,116,000	96.5
1949	246	144,712,572	148,720,000	96.9
1950	249	146,679,475	151,400,000	96.9
1951	251	150,638,004	152,900,000	98.5

Source: These figures, prepared for the author by the *Magazine Advertising Bureau,* are based on magazines, other than comics, that are subscribers to the Audit Bureau of Circulation. According to N. W. Ayer & Son's *Directory of Newspapers and Periodicals,* 1951, there are 6,977 magazines in the United States.

States population 10 years or older. Since the family-wide distribution of *Life* is common to most other magazines, the same sort of projection can be made. Indicative of the importance of *Life* magazine to advertisers is that in 1951 advertisers invested $91.5 million in its pages. This was more than in any single national advertising medium. This magazine with its large circulation and readership commands a price today of $28,900, for one full color-page advertisement.

Considering the circulation figure per issue and the family projection, the magazine reaches every segment of the buying public. Because the magazine does provide such a tremendous audience and applies direct pressure on the public, the advertiser or manufacturer spends a great deal of money in magazine advertising. Table 7 lists the yearly magazine advertising expenditures for the period from 1940 to 1951, which totaled $4,574,800,000.

The magazine, unlike the newspaper, is not discarded the same day it is purchased, but often remains about the home for several days or weeks and is read and reread. The massive circulation figures in Tables 5 and 6 indicate the frequency with which the magazine carries the advertising message to the American home, and how the magazine can and does help form our habits, mores, culture, and ethics, in addition to telling us how to spend our money. Table 7 indicates the immense sums of money that advertisers are pouring into the magazines to sell their products.

TABLE 7

MAGAZINE ADVERTISING EXPENDITURES: 1940–51

Year	Advertising Expenditures in Magazines
1940	$197,700,000
1941	213,600,000
1942	198,700,000
1943	274,900,000
1944	323,600,000
1945	364,500,000
1946	426,500,000
1947	492,900,000
1948	512,700,000
1949	492,500,000
1950	514,900,000
1951	562,300,000

Source: Compiled by Dr. Hans Zeisel, Associate Director of Research, McCann-Erickson, Inc., in *Printers' Ink,* during the years listed.

It is obvious that the magazine, like the newspaper, is a giant whose efforts to sell can seriously affect our economic structure, or whose advertising content can accentuate our desires or frustrations and create needs and wants. Like any giant, the magazine has the potential to do harm and, therefore, must be regulated and controlled for the common good. Later chapters will discuss in detail the role of the federal government in controlling magazine advertising and its deficiencies and shortcomings.

Radio

One of the newest and most effective advertising media is radio. As of January 1, 1952, 42,800,000 families, or over 95 per cent of all the families in the United States, owned at least one radio set.[8] In addition to the large audience it reaches, the importance of radio as an advertising medium is that it frames the advertising message with a psychological sense of urgency that makes people buy. Unlike the newspaper or the magazine, listening to the radio does not necessitate stopping at the corner newsstand or making a special effort to sit down and absorb the contents. A flick of the switch, a turn of the dial and the siren song of salesmanship, news commentary, or propaganda finds its way into the parlor, kitchen, or bedroom.

A vital difference between radio and newspapers or magazines lies in the fact that the air waves belong to the nation. In other words, they belong to all of us; but they have been given away in the form of licenses to persons and corporations whose primary concern is profit. In Great Britain the British Broadcasting Corporation is a public corporation which accepts no advertising; but in the United States, commercial advertising alone makes it possible for the broadcasting companies to exist.

In order to understand the full impact of radio as an advertising medium on our economy and the ethical and social implications that stem from radio advertising, it is of value to sketch the origin and development of radio and the growth of radio advertising, before considering how radio, as an advertising medium, is regulated by the federal government and the adequacy of such regulations.

Extensive radio transmission began several years after Marconi startled the world with his invention. The first extensive

[8] *Variety*, January 30, 1952, p. 23.

opportunity to test the use of radio transmission for practical purposes occurred during the First World War; military communications employed radio in 1915. Some far-sighted persons were quick to recognize the profitable commercial aspects of radio advertising. The exigencies of war acted as an impetus for scientific improvement of radio facilities. By 1919 radio had advanced to the stage where a Fourth of July address, delivered by Woodrow Wilson while at sea on board the U.S.S. George Washington, was heard, although indistinctly, on shore.

Radio's commercial potential was becoming rapidly more and more evident, and in 1919 the Radio Corporation of America was organized. However, the first radio station to commence private broadcasting was Station KDKA in Pittsburgh. By the close of 1921 there were also stations in Chicago and New York. Radio's educational possibilities were demonstrated by KDKA in November, 1920, when the Harding-Cox election returns were broadcast. The first licensed station in the New York area was WJZ, in June, 1921, and the following month the famous Dempsey-Carpentier fight was broadcast. Sports broadcasts interested a tremendous segment of the public, and now provide a choice outlet for a sponsor's advertising budget.

The year 1922 was a landmark in radio history. In August the first commercially sponsored broadcast in the United States emanated from the studios of WEAF in New York. The program, sponsored by the Queensboro Corporation, cost $100 for ten minutes; a ten-minute segment today would cost $400. The more important occurrence of the year was the first network broadcast involving two stations, WJZ in New York and WGY in Schenectady.

As reception improved and as the number of sets in the United States increased, radio's importance as an advertising medium assumed new stature. Advertisers began to employ the medium more frequently, e.g., "Mineralava" sponsored

Marion Davies, then a leading motion picture star, in two ten-minute programs a week. This was another innovation in that it marked the beginning of the radio program built around a celebrated figure as a means of selling a product. The year 1923 marked the beginnings of the means by which a radio advertiser, through the channels of several radio stations, could reach a large and fertile market. A four-station simultaneous broadcast, linked together by telephone wires, connected New York, Schenectady, Pittsburgh, and Chicago, and provided a potential audience in different geographical locations for one broadcast such as could never be reached by one newspaper. Proof of the fact that the network broadcast was an effective means of selling a product was the National Carbon Company's sponsorship of the Eveready Hour, the first sixty-minute broadcast heard in several cities simultaneously.

The National Broadcasting Company began network broadcasting in September, 1926, with a total of 24 stations, and in the same year it established the Blue Network as a subsidiary. As early as 1927, radio demonstrated its ability to penetrate homes in every geographical section of the country when N.B.C. broadcast the Rose Bowl Game on a temporary coast-to-coast hook up. The success of that broadcast and its advertising potential eventually resulted in the first permanent coast-to-coast hook up in 1933 by N.B.C. The young giant was beginning to flex his muscles, and the fact that his growth was so outstanding led to the enactment and appointment in 1927 of the Federal Radio Commission. During this same year another network giant, the Columbia Broadcasting System, was born.

By 1934, radio's ability to reach and inform the public was firmly established. But the rapid growth of radio and increasing abuses were responsible for much criticism directed against the industry and public demand for more effective control. As a result, a more stringent Federal Communications Act was legislated in 1934, now administered by the Federal Communications Commission. The abuses of radio, as well as the shortcomings and problems of the Commission, will be discussed in detail in a subsequent chapter. Whether motivated primarily by an exercise of conscience or by a desire to forestall increased federal regulations, the National Association of Broadcasters, whose membership was composed of most of the broadcasters of the country, also adopted a code of self-regulation in 1939. As of 1939, the National Broadcasting Company, the Columbia Broadcasting System, and the Mutual Broadcasting System (organized in 1934) were the leading networks in the country. In 1942 the National Broadcasting Company, which owned and operated two networks, one of which was the Blue Network, was ordered by the Federal Communications Commission to divest itself of the Blue Network. This network became the American Broadcasting Company in 1945.

Having briefly traced the origin of radio and its development in the United States, we must now turn to statistical information in order to understand the massive impact of radio upon our way of life.

During the period from 1922 to 1951, the number of radio broadcasting stations increased from 30 to 2,979 stations.

This astonishing growth in the number of radio stations has been paralleled by an equally remarkable increase of network stations. As indicated previously, the radio network is the means by which one sponsor may effectively channel his advertising message to a tremendous audience by one program. Table 9 shows how the three leading networks have grown.

Taking the Columbia Broadcasting System's figures as typical, the difference between the years 1928 and 1952 represents an increase of over 1,000 per cent. Such an increase would not have been possible unless network radio advertising were effective and profitable. However, better proof of the influence of the radio in the American home may be found in

TABLE 8

NUMBER OF RADIO BROADCASTING STATIONS: 1922–51

Date	Number of Stations AM	FM
January 1, 1922	30	–
March 1, 1923	556	–
October 1, 1924	530	–
June 30, 1925	571	–
June 30, 1926	528	–
February 23, 1927	733	–
July 1, 1928	677	–
November 9, 1929	618	–
July 1, 1930	612	–
July 1, 1931	612	–
January 1, 1932	608	–
January 1, 1933	610	–
January 1, 1934	591	–
January 1, 1935	605	–
January 1, 1936	632	–
January 1, 1937	685	–
January 1, 1938	700	–
January 1, 1939	764	–
January 1, 1940	814	–
January 1, 1941	882	–
January 1, 1942	873	46
January 1, 1943	864	46
January 1, 1944	860	46
January 1, 1945	890	46
January 1, 1946	951	46
January 1, 1947	1327	186
January 1, 1948	1550	395
January 1, 1949	1906	706
January 1, 1950	2095	725
January 1, 1951	2248	660
January 3, 1952	2330	649

Source: Federal Communications Commission, License Records. *Broadcasting*, January 7, 1952, p. 93 for 1952 statistics.

statistics which reveal the increase in the number of radio sets in use and the number of homes having radios. Commencing with the year 1922, the number of radio sets in use increased from 400,000 to 90 million, with a corresponding increase in

TABLE 9

NETWORK RADIO STATIONS: 1926–52

Year (as of January 1)	National Broadcasting Company	Columbia Broadcasting System	American Broadcasting Company
1926	19	–	–
1927	48	–	–
1928	56	17	–
1929	70	49	–
1930	73	60	–
1931	85	76	–
1932	87	84	–
1933	87	91	–
1934	88	92	–
1935	89	97	–
1936	105	98	–
1937	142	105	–
1938	166	110	–
1939	105	113	–
1940	219	112	–
1941	246	118	–
1942	282	115	–
1943	137	116	–
1944	139	133	170
1945	146	145	192
1946	152	147	191
1947	158	157	218
1948	164	162	251
1949	165	167	265
1950	167	173	276
1951	176	184	289
1952	184	194	304

Source: The above figures were compiled by the Research Departments of the three networks at the request of the author. The failure to list radio stations for the American Broadcasting Company for 1943 is due to the fact that this network, formerly the National Broadcasting Company's Blue Network, had in that year been divorced from the parent network and the resulting reorganization was such that there are no accurate figures for the year.

the number of radio homes from 60,000 to 45 million.[9] Table 10 presents the year-by-year breakdown from 1922 to 1951 of the number of radios in use and the number of radio homes.

[9] The disparity between the number of radio homes (45,850,000) and the number of radio families (42.8 million) is due to the fact that many families maintain more than one establishment with one or more radios.

TABLE 10

RADIO SET GROWTH: 1922–51

Year	Homes with Radio Sets	Total Radio Sets In Use in U. S.
1922	60,000	400,000
1923	1,000,000	1,100,000
1924	2,500,000	3,000,000
1925	3,500,000	4,000,000
1926	5,000,000	5,700,000
1927	6,500,000	7,000,000
1928	7,500,000	8,500,000
1929	9,000,000	10,500,000
1930	12,048,762	13,000,000
1931	14,000,000	15,000,000
1932	16,809,562	18,000,000
1933	20,402,469	22,000,000
1934	21,456,000	26,000,000
1935	22,869,000	30,500,000
1936	24,600,000	33,000,000
1937	26,666,500	37,600,000
1938	28,000,000	40,800,000
1939	28,700,000	45,300,000
1940	29,200,000	51,000,000
1941	29,700,000	56,000,000
1942	30,800,000	59,340,000
1943	32,500,000	57,000,000
1944	33,100,000	55,000,000
1945	34,000,000	56,000,000
1946	35,000,000	60,000,000
1947	37,000,000	66,000,000
1948	40,000,000	74,000,000
1949	42,000,000	81,000,000
1950	45,000,000	90,000,000
1951	45,850,000	103,250,000

Source: *Broadcasting Magazine 1952 Yearbook,* p. 58. It is interesting to note that the radio message reaches the consumer in his car and bus (via transit radio) as well as his living room. During the year 1951 there were 20 million automobile radios in use.

A survey conducted jointly by the four major networks revealed that as of January 1, 1952, there were 105.3 million sets in the United States, or one for every citizen of voting age. Of the total number of sets, 42.8 million represents families with at least one radio; secondary and portable receivers in all radio households total 34 million; radio-equipped cars number 23.5 million; and the remaining 5 million sets are in other places.[10]

It has been observed that there are 42.8 million families listening to the radio. Assuming, at a minimum, that the family is composed of three members, there are at least 128.4 million radio listeners. The magnitude of this audience is impressive, and a market of 128.4 million listeners in their homes and automobiles, subjected to the jingle, slogan, or spoken commercial, has provided the radio advertiser with an ideal audience for his advertising message. Before proceeding to an analysis of the over-all moneys spent to educate, sell, or persuade this audience, it will be interesting to consider the expenditure involved in bringing several of the most popular radio programs to these listeners. Let us take as an example the Jack Benny show which is heard once a week for one-half hour through the facilities of the Columbia Broadcasting System and is sponsored by the American Tobacco Company. The cost to the sponsor in late 1951 was $42,535 per week for radio time and talent to send its "Be Happy, Go Lucky" slogan into 7,291,000 homes.[11] Using the figure of 2.8 persons per home it follows that this program has an audience of 20,414,800 individuals per week. On its face, the sum of $42,535 is a tremendous expenditure. However, simple mathematics reduces this to a weekly expenditure per person of two-tenths of one cent. If the American Tobacco Company attempted to reach every one of these persons by the simplest mailing device possible, individually addressed two-cent post cards, the postage alone would be $408,296. Such expenditure could not possibly convey as effective a selling message as is done by the members of the radio program.

Another example of a leading program which reaches a

---

[10] *Variety*, January 30, 1952, p. 23.

[11] Columbia Broadcasting System, Sales Department, private source. The number of homes is from *Variety*, January 30, 1952, p. 23.

large audience at a low cost per listener is the Lux Radio Theatre, which is heard over the Columbia Broadcasting System for one hour a week at a cost to Lever Brothers of $41,470 per week. Even a simple 15-minute daytime program, broadcast 5 times weekly, Monday through Friday, when the audience is smaller, will cost the sponsor of Arthur Godfrey $25,800 per week. The effectiveness of radio is demonstrated further by the "Mark Trail" program designed to capture the imagination of the juvenile audience. This program, sponsored by Kellogg's cereals, is heard for a half-hour, three times weekly, over the American Broadcasting Company network at a cost of $16,500 per week.

The above-mentioned programs, although among the leaders, represent only a very small portion of radio advertising expeditures. Radio advertisers spent during 1940–1951 a total of $5.7 billion. Table 11 lists these expenditures by year.

TABLE 11

RADIO ADVERTISING EXPENDITURES: 1940–51

Year		Total Expenditures
1940		$ 235,000,000
1941		271,200,000
1942		290,000,000
1943		344,500,000
1944		435,800,000
1945		467,700,000
1946		495,800,000
1947		555,200,000
1948		617,100,000
1949		633,800,000
1950		667,100,000
1951		690,000,000
	Total	$5,703,200,000

Source: Compiled by Dr. Hans Zeisel in *Printers' Ink* in each of the years listed. It must be noted that not all of these sums were spent on network time. By far the greater amount went into local and spot broadcasting. A spot broadcast is a segment of radio time purchased for commercial use by an advertiser on a per station basis. Local radio refers to radio time purchased by an advertiser whose principal business activity is located in the same area as the radio station.

Even these large amounts do not accurately portray the moneys spent in radio advertising. This is because the figures in Table 11 are moneys expended for time only. In addition to time, there are the production costs involved with every radio program. These include talent, announcers, publicity, and the costs of preparing commercials. Thus, actual radio expenditures, while not available, are far in excess of the figures included in Table 11.

The preceding pages have indicated that radio reaches more than 95 per cent of all families in the United States. In 1951 radio absorbed a sum in excess of $690 million for advertising time alone. The magnitude of this medium needs no further demonstration. Radio's potency demonstrates that it can do much to educate and raise the standard of living of the American public. On the other hand, it also possesses the power to misinform, deceive, and accentuate the fears, frustrations, and unsatisfied desires of the American family. In succeeding chapters the existing regulations of radio by the federal government will be discussed and analyzed, with the purpose of understanding the nature of these regulations and whether they are sufficient to channel radio along constructive lines.

Television

The youngest, the newest, and possibly the greatest potential force of all advertising media is television. The magic of television and its influence upon the American family are effectively expressed by the following quotations:

> In the ancient *Arabian Nights Tales* there was a wizard who possessed a magic stone in which he saw images of distant persons and places. In the modern Oz fantasies, which are as American as the soil of Kansas, Princess Ozma has a magic picture which reveals any person or scene the observer wishes

to see. From the Arabian Nights to the Oz books—through all the years mankind has dreamed of seeing at a distance. From the beginning of history, folklore, legendry, and wonder tales are filled with stories of crystal balls, enchanted mirrors, marvelous pictures and woodland pools—all possessing magic powers which enabled the owner to see at a distance. Now the dream has come true. The wizards of modern electronics have clutched the age-old dream and transformed it into a reality for the entertainment and benefit of all mankind. They call it—Television.[12]

Mechanically, what is Television? A tiny dot of light travels across the viewing screen, line below line, at a rate of some 15,000 lines per second. It fills in the complete area of the screen 30 times each second . . . and produces the image of a *moving* picture. On this electronic base, television is building a new entertainment form—one that is more than stage, screen, radio or print, although it contains all four. Television's fifth dimension is *intimacy*.[13]

Thus, television brings to us in one combination the information of the printed word, the immediacy of radio, the fluidity of motion pictures, the actuality of the theater, and, most important of all, the intimacy of the living room. What has been said about radio can be stated with even greater emphasis in the case of television. Television's phenomenal growth and development is breath-taking in its scope.

While only 109 television stations are in operation as against a total of 2,979 radio stations, it is an interesting fact that the Texaco Star Theater television show has had an audience of 23,880,000 for one telecast.[14] The rapid expansion of this new and powerful medium has created problems

---

[12] *Behind Your Radio Dial* (New York: National Broadcasting Co., 1948), p. 30.

[13] *Television Today* (New York: Columbia Broadcasting System, 1950), p. 27.

[14] National Broadcasting Company, Research Department.

of control. As in radio, so in television the nation has surrendered the airwaves to a comparatively small group of private individuals or corporations engaged in the pursuit of profit. Advertising and the profits derived from advertising are responsible for the astounding growth of the television industry. The influence for good or evil inherent in this expanding medium upon the life of the nation is so great that the national interest must be protected. The extent to which television is now regulated and the adequacy of such controls will be discussed later. A brief account of the growth and development of television is necessary in order to appreciate and understand the problem of federal regulation.

Although television experimentation had been in progress for many years, it was not until 1923 that an application was made for a television patent. This patent was finally issued in 1938 to V. K. Zworykin. There were, no doubt, many laboratory demonstrations of the cathode ray tube and iconoscope, but one of the most important television demonstrations was made by the Bell Laboratories in 1927 when wire television was shown between Washington and New York. The National Broadcasting Company received its first television station construction permit as early as 1928. It is also interesting to note that a color television patent was granted the same year. However, even though Zworykin had filed for a patent in 1923, it was not until 1930 that some segment of the public, albeit small, received its introduction to television. The Radio Corporation of America in that year transmitted pictures from its Station W2XBS to a screen located in a motion picture theater in New York. Apparently this demonstration indicated that television had great commercial possibilities, for soon the National Broadcasting Company officially opened Station W2XBS. Within a year, two more television stations were opened in New York by Gimbel Brothers Department Store and the Columbia Broadcasting System.

A number of large-scale public demonstrations of television followed; e.g., television's possibilities in the field of education were demonstrated in 1939 when a surgical operation, performed at a Brooklyn hospital, was televised to a group of medical students and nurses in a nearby auditorium. This surgical telecast demonstrates but one of the many beneficial ways in which this new medium can be used for the common good.

To return to television and commercial advertising, the Federal Communications Commission approved limited commercial television early in 1940. The same year witnessed a color television demonstration by the Radio Corporation of America before the Federal Communications Commission. But perhaps the most important event in 1940 was the first television network broadcast, when pictures from New York were rebroadcast through automatic radio relay to Schenectady. Later in the year, the Columbia Broadcasting System developed its mechanical system of color television which recently has been the center of the color television controversy. Television finally received the Federal Communications Commission authorization for commercial use beginning July 1, 1941.

The Federal Communications Commission order resulted in immediate application by the National Broadcasting Company for licenses to operate commercial television stations in New York, Philadelphia, and Washington. The National Broadcasting Company's first television advertising rates were $120 per hour from 6 P.M. to 11 P.M. and $60 an hour from 8 A.M. to 6 P.M. A comparison of the rates reveals the tremendous growth of television, for in 1952 the rates are $50,275 per hour for the evening and $25,138 an hour for the daytime period.

When the Federal Communications Commission order became effective in July, 1941, there were 21 television stations operating in the entire United States, although only four programs were commercially sponsored. Television had become so large by 1944 that it was necessary to create a control organization, the Television Broadcasters' Association to formulate policy rules for the industry.

By 1945 television had captured the popular imagination, and the public awaited production of the sets which the Radio Corporation of America announced would be available early in the following year at a cost of $250 to $450. Just as radio achieved new advertising importance with the development of the network, so also did television when in 1946 the first telecast was broadcast from Washington to New York over the coaxial cable. By the beginning of 1949 the coaxial cable had been developed to such an extent that the Eastern and Mid-Western states were connected and able to receive on their television screens a telecast originating either in New York, Chicago, or Omaha. Further development of the cable has progressed to the extent that now a network program can span the entire nation.

The number of seven stations remained constant from 1942 to the end of 1946 due to a "freeze" on new station construction because of the war. In 1948 after the "freeze" had ended, the number of television stations increased to 17. By January 1, 1949, this figure was up to 50 and almost doubled by January 1, 1950, reaching a total of 97. As of January 1, 1952, the number of operating television stations was 109.[15]

---

[15] Federal Communications Commission, *License Records*. The 109 stations operating as of January 1, 1952, cover 64 markets. This includes Station XELD–TV in Matamoras, Mexico, which also covers Brownsville, Texas. Because of engineering difficulties and interference problems by the television channels, the Federal Communications Commission halted new station construction on September 30, 1948. On April 11, 1952, the FCC lifted this three-and-a-half-year-old "freeze." It provided for the opening of 2,053 new stations in 1,291 communities as part of a long-range plan to bring television to the entire country. In addition, the FCC set aside for exclusive use by noncommercial, educational interests, channel assignments in 242 communities.

Television network development has kept pace with station growth. Statistics from January 1, 1946, to January 1, 1952, indicate the great increase in network television stations during this short span. In the case of the Columbia Broadcasting System there was an increase of stations from 2 to 62; the National Broadcasting Company increased from 2 to 64; and the American Broadcasting Company from 3 to 64. The principal point to be observed in these figures is television's rapid acceptance by the public. Since no network is prepared to invest the tremendous sums of money necessary for the construction of television stations unless such investment will be adequately rewarded, it is obvious that public acceptance of television has been most favorable.

An even better indication of public acceptance of this medium is to be found in the statistics showing the increase in the number of homes with television sets. In 1946 when the end of the "freeze" permitted the construction of commercial television stations, there were 10,000 television sets in use. Consider, then, the astonishing fact that as of January 1, 1952, there were 15,777,000 sets installed in homes, offices, taverns, etc. The increase from 1946 to 1952 was in excess of 150,000 per cent. The annual increases are shown in Table 12.

Television, combining the visual features of the printed word and the audible qualities of radio, surpasses both in that the television picture portrays the product in motion and use with the spoken word geared to the picture, and therefore presents a persuasive selling medium unlike anything else in

---

The allotments for education represent 11.5 per cent of the nation's available airways. To effect its long-range program of vast expansion the commission opened for further television transmission seventy new channels in the ultra high frequency (U.H.F.) field to augment the twelve very high frequency (V.H.F.) channels now in use. Only a few stations will be licensed in 1952 and take the air because of the great demands for choice channels. Such contentions must be resolved by the commission at time-consuming hearings.

the world. It offers opportunities to the advertiser that are not available to him in the other media, and he has not been slow to take advantage of this situation. Wayne Coy, former Chairman of the Federal Communications Commission, stated in an address to the Rotary Club of Chicago in 1948 that "television is the most powerful, most effective, and most profitable medium for mass merchandising yet devised." A brief consideration of the advertising activities in television will substantiate this point.

TABLE 12

TELEVISION SETS IN USE: 1946–51

Year	Total Sets
1946	10,000
1947	16,476
1948	189,900
1949	1,000,000
1950	3,950,000
1951	10,549,500
1952	15,777,000

Source: National Broadcasting Company, Research Department.

One television program, telecast through the facilities of the National Broadcasting Company and seen and heard for one hour each week in 63 television markets, costs the sponsor an estimated $90,075 per week, $45,000 of which was for talent. In December, 1951, this program reached 7,960,000 homes, and, based on an average of three viewers per home, the commercial was viewed and heard by 23,880,000 people. The approximate sum of $90,075 seems large, but when reduced mathematically to an expenditure per viewer, the sponsor has a per-person expense of only about four-tenths of one cent. On the average, there are more viewers in a television home to a particular program than listeners to a radio program on radio. While the cost to reach a single viewer in television may be higher than a listener to a radio program, the impact of a commercial with sight added to sound has made more customers of products in television homes as against nontelevision homes. An expenditure of $48,000 for a half-hour telecasting of the "I Love Lucy" show, or a $67,000 expenditure for a weekly one-hour dramatization on "Studio One," or an expenditure of $53,200 for a half-hour segment of "Your Show of Shows" are expenditures well calculated by the respective sponsors, Philip Morris, Westinghouse, and R. J. Reynolds, to do an effective job of keeping the names of their products before the public with resulting profit from increased sales.

The over-all picture of total advertising expenditures in television for the years 1949–51 is as follows: Money spent in 1949 for television time amounted to $63 million, and in 1950 to $185 million, and in 1951 to $484.4 million. The increase in 1951 over the previous year was 161.8 per cent.[16] It must be remembered, however, that, as in the case of radio, these expenditures are for time only. The "Texaco Star Theater" program, where $45,000 of the total weekly expenditure of $90,075 is used for talent and production costs, shows that the 1951 total television expenditure of $484.4 million would be increased greatly were talent and production figures added.[17]

To summarize: television has grown rapidly in stations, sets, and expenditures; and at the present time each television set has a larger audience than the radio set. The novelty of

---

[16] *Printers' Ink*, January 11, 1952, p. 36.

[17] The over-all figures on talent and production costs are not available. However, it is estimated by the Director of Research for the National Broadcasting Company that 50 per cent of program costs go for talent. Therefore, $968,800,000 is closer to the correct figure for television expenditures in 1951.

the medium is such that television viewing has become a principal pastime in America. It is television's newness and ever-increasing growth that makes it a powerful instrument for persuasion. That it may be used for education or as a means to inform the public about the responsibilities and problems of government also makes it a beneficial medium. Likewise, it may be used to promote health, tolerance, and happiness in general. On the other hand, it may be used to mislead, misinform, and deceive. This much is certain: no matter what the purpose to which television is put, it can accomplish that purpose better than any instrument of communication today. With the interests of an entire nation at stake, it is imperative that the miracle of television be properly employed. The problem of the protection of the public is, of necessity, the responsibility of the federal government. Subsequent chapters will discuss the extent to which this protection has been accorded the public.

Outdoor Advertising

Outdoor advertising is different from other media because its space unit—the poster panel, painted bulletin, or "electric spectacular"—has a fixed location: a point on a street or highway for display of an advertiser's message to all who pass.[18] The inherent difference, however, between outdoor advertising and the major media—newspapers, magazines, radio, and television--is that by its use an advertiser can reach

---

[18] A poster panel is defined as an outdoor advertising structure upon which an advertisement reproduced on paper is pasted. A painted bulletin is any outdoor advertising structure upon which the advertisement is reproduced in paint. An electric spectacular is defined as advertising copy, usually animated, constructed from sheet metal, wired for sockets and bulbs or luminous tubing, or both, with copy action controlled by flashers, circuit breakers, or motographs, and attached on an open-faced steel structure built specifically for the purpose, e.g., the Times Square area in New York City. See Hugh Agnew, *Outdoor Advertising* (New York: McGraw-Hill Book Co., Inc., 1938.)

everyone in a given market who goes outdoors. Outdoor advertising puts the advertiser's sales message, brand name, and product illustration in large size and color close to retail outlets where sales are made.

The outdoor advertising industry is an advertising service which includes selling, erecting, placing, and maintaining outdoor advertising displays on premises owned, leased, or controlled by the producer of the service. Outdoor advertising has certain advantages over the other media. By the use of the power of a picture, color, and few words, it can carry a message to the individual at a mere glance. Because outdoor advertising is geared economically for continuity and repetition, the retention of the advertiser's message or slogan is enhanced.

However, it must be noted at this point that to the advertiser and to his advertising agency, outdoor advertising has not developed into a major medium. It is used today to supplement advertising campaigns in the important media previously discussed.

Outdoor advertising was the first medium employed in the United States. The earliest recorded American advertisement was the signboard display outside the first coffee house in New Amsterdam in 1642. But this commercial sign, which is nearly always used to identify a place of business, was not a true outdoor advertisement. A true outdoor display need not be restricted to one announcement, nor need it be at the place where the product or service is offered for sale.

Poster advertising began in the United States with notices of sale of farm stock and equipment, fairs, circuses, horse races, carnivals, and medicine shows. Phineas T. Barnum was one of the pioneers in this medium, being the first to use successfuly and repeatedly poster advertising on a large scale. Though he may not have seen the advent of the electric light bulb, he did set the pattern to which electricity was eventually put. Barnum erected a series of gas or candlelight signs outside his place of amusement, the forerunner of Broadway's "Great White Way."

By the close of the Civil War, outdoor advertising had grown to the extent that there were 275 bill-posting firms employing from two to twenty men each. It was in 1867 or 1870 that the earliest recorded leasings of boards occurred in the United States, one being on the board fence around the new post office under construction in New York City. During the 1870's, theaters used poster advertising extensively, because of the improvement made in the lithographic process for reproducing pictures. Lurid portrayals on posters by burlesque shows so offended the public that some members of the bill posters' associations refused to handle offensive paper. This was the earliest recorded censorship exercised by an advertising medium over copy.[19]

In 1891 the first national association of poster men was formed. It was called the Associated Bill Posters' Association, and began the standardizations of outdoor advertising practice. Other organizations have been formed during the years to stabilize the medium as it is known today.

From 1940 to 1951 advertisers spent more than $1 billion on outdoor advertising. In comparison with the other major media, however, outdoor advertising fills a relatively minor role. In 1950 there were approximately 640 advertisers using the outdoor medium on a national level through the services of 300 advertising agencies. While we refer to the expenditures by advertisers for outdoor advertising in today's advertising picture as relatively minor, it is interesting to note that the amount spent in 1951, about $150 million, was more than one and one-half times the total of newspaper and periodical advertising revenue in the year 1900.

---

[19] G. B. Hotchkiss, *An Outline of Advertising* (New York: The Macmillan Co., 1950), p. 445.

Direct Advertising

Direct advertising is defined as "a vehicle for transmitting an advertiser's message in permanent written, printed or processed form, by controlled distribution, direct to selected individuals." [20]

Direct advertising divides itself into three broad divisions: direct-by-mail advertising; mail order advertising; and unmailed direct advertising. Direct-by-mail would be the perfect form of advertising if an advertiser could conceive a list of prospects who would all want to buy his product or service at the exact moment he told them he had it for sale. But it does not seem probable that such a list will ever be compiled. The successful direct-by-mail advertiser mails his message to "prospects" rather than "suspects." Once the advertiser has defined his "prospects" he must then secure a mailing list. Most experts agree that the list represents at least 60 per cent of the chances for successful direct-by-mail and is definitely the largest single factor in the planning and preparation of any campaign.

The usual sources for securing or building a list are:

1) Commercial list houses who furnish lists that they have compiled to an advertiser.
2) Trade directories such as the Jewelers' Board of Trade Directory.
3) City directories containing lists of all residents and business organizations.
4) Credit rating books such as Dun & Bradstreet's.
5) Telephone directories.
6) Membership lists of fraternities and clubs.
7) Voting lists.

---

[20] Direct Mail Advertising Association Inc., *The Story of Direct Advertising* (New York, 1950), p. 3.

8) Trade and consumer magazines advertisers' lists.
9) Clipping bureaus.
10) Government lists.
11) List brokers.
12) Subscription and circulation lists of magazines.
13) Company records and personnel.
14) Enclosures in advertiser's mailings.
15) Contest, coupons, fan mail.

The main uses for direct-by-mail advertising are to arouse interest and to help customers as an aid to buying; to familiarize prospects with the name of the product, its merits, and the name of the local distributor, thus removing obstacles to sales; to support the sales activities of retailers; to encourage continued patronage by present and new customers; and finally, to predispose prospects favorably so that personal selling effort will produce maximum sales returns.

While direct-by-mail advertising helps a salesman to sell, mail order advertising takes the place of the salesman. This division of direct advertising includes all methods other than personal salesmanship and space or radio advertising for inducing people to send in orders by mail.[21] Such items as sales letters or booklets soliciting orders or the huge catalogs of mail order houses are examples of mail order advertising.

Unmailed direct advertising consists of material not sent through the mails, such as store window and counter displays (point-of-purchase material), circulars handed to pedestrians

---

[21] Mail order advertisers do use space advertising for soliciting orders, usually coupons in ads. Some advertising agencies have built reputations on ability to "pull" orders from media which they have carefully researched as to mail order prospects. However, mail order advertising is a special branch of printed advertising which is not held in high respect by the advertising profession. Recently, mail order advertising witnessed the rise of pitchmen on radio and television to such an extent that entire programs were in effect commercials to "pull" orders. The many complaints of this over-commercialization have brought voluntary controls over this advertising by stations and it has been brought to the attention of the FCC.

in the streets, etc., which are delivered directly to the recipient. This division of direct advertising is used for the same purposes as direct-by-mail and mail order advertising.

Direct mail advertising is nearly as old as newspaper advertising itself. Frequently a colonial newspaper found its way to the rural areas where the advertisement was clipped and used to order a product by mail. But direct mail advertising, of necessity, lagged behind other media in the nineteenth century. Its growth depended upon adequate mail and transportation facilities to carry the advertisement to the rural consumer, the order to the manufacturer, and the purchase back to the consumer. The government, through the introduction of the one-cent postcard in 1873 and a rural free delivery system, greatly encouraged direct mail advertising. The greatest impetus to the direct mail and mail order field was the appearance of such successful organizations as Sears, Roebuck and Company and Montgomery Ward. Sears, Roebuck and Company began catalog and circular distribution in 1872 and has now progressed to the point where more than 10 million circulars and 7.5 million catalogs are distributed annually.

Direct advertising is not meant to compete with the other forms of advertising that have been previously discussed. It is used instead as a companion to increase the effectiveness of these powerful media. For the businessman whose advertising funds are limited, direct advertising may be his sole advertising medium. In almost all promotional programs, direct advertising is used irrespective of the size of the advertising budget. The following table shows the extent to which the volume of direct mail advertising has grown. These figures do not include point-of-purchase material, such as displays, but only material that was produced for and sent through the mails. These figures represent costs of postage and physical production and handling of direct advertising material.

TABLE 13

VOLUME OF DIRECT MAIL ADVERTISING: 1940–51

Year	
1940	$ 278,000,000
1941	294,000,000
1942	274,000,000
1943	298,000,000
1944	272,000,000
1945	242,000,000
1946	279,000,000
1947	483,000,000
1948	575,000,000
1949	864,000,000
1950	918,000,000
1951	1,056,000,000

Source: Direct Mail Advertising Association, Inc., Research Department.

The fact that over a billion dollars was spent in direct advertising in 1951 indicates the important share which this medium has in the impact of the advertising dollar on our national economy.

Chapter 3

THE ADVERTISING AGENCY

Development of the Advertising Agency

The most important and yet the least known factor in advertising is the modern advertising agency. Largely by design and calculation the advertising agency has refrained from publicizing itself, even though it possesses extensive facilities for exploitation and publicity. The very nature of its activities calls for the closest entente with all the channels of news, publicity, and propaganda.

The advertising agency deals directly with the media as a principal in contracting for space or time, and as a rule it is the only contact between the advertiser and the media. The power, therefore, wielded by a few thousand agencies in the expenditure of more that $6.5 billion per annum is enormous.

Advertising in the United States has had its principal growth since the turn of the present century, as indicated in the statistical data in Table 14.

Even though advertising expenditures in the 1860's were nominal, judged by present standards, advertising exerted a considerable influence on the public. According to George Wakeman, writing in the *Galaxy Magazine* in 1867, "the names of successful advertisers have become household words where great poets, politicians, philosophers and warriors of the land are as yet unheard of; where the title of Tennyson's last work is thought to be 'In A Garden' and Longfellow understood as the nickname of a tall man." [1] However, there

---

[1] Frank Presbrey, *The History and Development of Advertising* (New York: Doubleday, Doran & Co., Inc., 1929), p. 255.

TABLE 14

ADVERTISING REVENUE IN PERIODICALS: 1865–1951

Year	Amount
1865	$ 7,584,340
1880	39,136,306
1900	95,861,127
1909	202,533,235
1919	528,299,378
1929	1,120,238,395
1935	686,121,409
1940	1,095,900,000
1945	1,501,800,000
1951	3,105,300,000

Source: Based on the following sources: For 1865, U. S. Commission of Internal Revenue, *Annual Report*; for 1880–1935, Bureau of Census, *Census of Manufacturers*; for 1940, 1945, compilations of Dr. Hans Zeisel of McCann-Erickson, Inc.; for 1951, *Printers' Ink,* January 11, 1952, p. 36.

was no advertising agency at that time which could or would handle advertising in the modern accepted manner. Free-lance literary men, some of whom were newspaper reporters, were engaged by advertisers to write their advertisements.[2]

There was no newspaper or magazine directory until about 1869, nor was there an Audit Bureau of Circulation attesting to the accuracy of the publishers' circulation estimates until 1914. Although newspapers had rate cards, these cards were meaningless because each sale of space was bargained for separately. In the early years, newspaper space, as a rule, was sold by so-called advertising agents who were "space contractors," selling the space to the advertiser. The "space con-

[2] A topical style of copy was the order of the day. A Knox hat advertisement in the 1860's demonstrates how copy was tied in with the news of the day:

"Although Queen Isabella has lost her crown, the crowns of Knox's hats never come out, as everyone who purchases them at the Corner of Broadway and Fulton Street will testify. Not a man who wore Knox's hats during the earthquake in San Francisco had them shaken off. The Grecian bend may do for ladies, but all gentlemen wear Knox's hats." *Ibid.*, p. 256.

tractors" made "inside deals" whereby they retained a commission ranging from 10 to 50 per cent on the cost of the space. One of the most interesting advertising agents of the latter part of the nineteenth century was George P. Rowell. He arranged with a group of newspapers to pay them 75 per cent of the card rate, less 3 per cent cash discount if payment was made in 30 days. The cash inducement was, as a rule, so strong that Rowell did better than the remaining 25 per cent. Rowell's agency also developed the idea of coordinating the lists of newspapers with which his agency was affiliated and selling the complete list to the advertisers. This "list" system was adopted by other advertising agents or "space contractors." The only service rendered by the so-called advertising agent to the advertiser was to assist him in buying space. Writing copy or preparing the advertisement in finished form was not part of his job. The function of the advertising agent in this era has been described as follows:

> When an advertiser who is a patron of our agency applies to us for an estimate, we carry out against the name of each paper upon his list the price which we recommend him to offer. If he is not anxious about particular papers and is willing to omit any which will not contract at a low rate, considering its circulation, position and influence, the prices will be lower than they would be if he were more desirous of using all or nearly all the papers on the list. Sometimes the advertiser wishes to reach people of a certain state and is willing to invest not to exceed a sum of money which he names. In that case we should make a complete list of all the newspapers issued in that state, and against each affix a price which will be undoubtedly a low one for the service demanded. It is not expected that all will accept. Sometimes the price is made so low that it is not believed that more than one-fourth or one-third will consent to do the work at the figures named. Frequently the result is surprising, especially if the proposals happen to be forwarded when advertising business is slack. After all have been heard from, it is customary to review the correspondence in company with the advertiser, and then rea-

sonable proposals from publishers at important points who have not accepted the original propositions can be considered and acted upon.[3]

Carlton & Smith, an agency founded in 1864, represented, exclusively, religious weeklies. Among their clients in 1868 was the dry goods house of Field, Palmer and Leiter Company, later known as Marshall Field & Company. Field wrote his own advertisements. W. J. Carlton, head of the agency, branched from religious periodicals into general magazines. A few magazines which had been refusing to sell space were induced by the advertising agent's arguments to accept advertisements and to permit their publications to be added to the agent's list. That was the beginning of magazine advertising.

When J. Walter Thompson, an employee of Carlton, took over the agency in 1878, he gave special attention to the solicitation of business for general magazines.[4] Undoubtedly, much of the credit for the vast array of magazines we have in the twentieth century is due to the advertising agent's initiative in working up revenue for them.

In 1888, Rowell founded *Printers' Ink*, the bible of the advertising fraternity, and this professional magazine marks the coming of age of the advertising agency.[5]

In order to appreciate how far advertising has progressed, we need only look back to the fact that sixty years ago there were less than one dozen advertisers who spent as much as $100,000 a year.[6] The American mass market, the advertising

---

[3] *Ibid.*, p. 270.

[4] The J. Walter Thompson Co. is the largest advertising agency in the world today. In 1951 this agency billed $138 million. *Advertising Age*, February 25, 1952, p. 62.

[5] As late as 1896, advertising was still held in such low repute that a building owner placed on his property a sign excluding peddlers, book agents, and advertising men from the premises.

[6] In 1951, the 12 leading advertisers each spent over $10 million in advertising media.

agency, the national advertiser, and the media have all developed within two generations to the point where they are vital factors in our social and economic life.

The modern advertising agency came into being because, with the rapid growth and development of business enterprises, advertisers simply did not know how to use the advertising space profitably. The publishers were neither equipped to prepare hard-selling advertisements, nor were they in a position to service competing advertisers. In an age which was turning fast to specialization advertisers quickly realized that they themselves could not prepare their own advertisements and at the same time keep up with competition.

There was a real need for an objective viewpoint, an independent appraisal of the product and an analysis of the market potential and the corresponding sales opportunity. Thus, the modern advertising agency came into being at the turn of the present century.

The Role of the Advertising Agency

The agency is an organization of specialists to whom the advertiser entrusts the preparation and execution of his advertising plans. A misconception has been created in the public mind about advertising agencies, largely because the movies, stage, and novel have presented a distorted picture of the agency. F. P. Bishop describes this distortion as follows:

> As presented by playwrights and novelists the advertising man is a bone-headed simpleton living in a constant state of hysteria and whipping himself into enthusiasm over the most ludicrous trivialities. He is also a somewhat sinister simpleton; a figure of fun who can cause a shudder too, because of his ability to infect others with his own perverted sense of values, and make the whole world mad. His office (in the novels) is usually peopled by cynical and embittered young men from the universities who ought to know better and who do in fact know better, and who are cynical and embittered because

they have been seduced into prostituting their talents in this unworthy business.[7]

On the other hand, G. B. Hotchkiss views the advertising agent and his work today in a different manner:

Those who look toward advertising as a vocation naturally look first toward the advertising agencies. These, as already indicated, represent the highest development of the science, art, and strategy of advertising. However, the method of compensation has been a factor in classifying the agency as a business rather than a profession.

Undoubtedly the agencies were responsible for developing advertising into a profitable force for both the manufacturer and the publisher. The system of allowing them a commission of 15 per cent on the space used provided a strong profit incentive. The agencies still contain a large share of the most talented and skillful advertising and marketing experts in the country. They constitute the best claims of advertising to be regarded as a profession.[8]

E. E. Calkins, an able advertising agent and a partner in the firm of Calkins and Holden, has described the advertising agent as a professional man:

The work of an advertising agency is professional work. Professional service is personal service such as that rendered by a lawyer, doctor, engineer, or architect who has nothing to sell but advice; in other words, himself. The copy which the advertising agent prepares corresponds to the plans of the architect, the briefs of the lawyer, and the prescriptions of the doctor. The space, art work, printing, and other tangible materials and things which he buys are bought as an agent of the client rather than sold by him to the client.[9]

---

[7] F. P. Bishop, *The Ethics of Advertising* (London: Robert Hale, Ltd., 1949), p. 99.

[8] G. B. Hotchkiss, *An Outline of Advertising* (New York: The Macmillan Co., 1950), p. 560.

[9] *Idem.* It is interesting to note, also, that courses in advertising are now an essential part of the curriculum of many college and university schools of business or journalism.

How does the modern advertising agency function and how does it serve the advertiser? The establishment and operation of a typical modern advertising agency will serve as a good illustration. Two individuals, partners of different agencies in Chicago and New York, were once told by the president of an important tobacco company that he would entrust them with his advertising account amounting to several million dollars, if they started an advertising agency. The first requirements of this new agency were to obtain the necessary capital to equip an office, to hire the necessary staff, and, above all, to obtain recognition from the Periodical Publishers' Association (PPA) and the American Newspaper Publishers' Association (ANPA). In this manner the agency came into existence with an advertising account.[10]

How does the agency now render the required services to the account? The first step is to get the facts. The agency will seek to ascertain the background of the client, everything about the product, and its potential market. This means that the agency will prepare questionnaires to determine the competition, the distribution of the product, the adequacy of its price structure, and the past advertising history. Research must be continued even after the campaign is under way, because changes in the market can vitally affect the product appeal, the price range, and even the copy appeal.

Some agencies have their own research departments. Some even have their own "consumer panels" to make continuing studies of the effect of sales activities at the ultimate point of distribution. However, more and more, even in the larger agencies, the tendency is to use outside research organizations because it is a more economical procedure. The agency has people trained to evaluate, plan, and direct research, but the actual work is usually farmed out to outside specialists.

[10] Both the PPA and the ANPA usually require a minimum of three accounts for an agency to receive recognition.

After studying the market and the product, the advertising agency is in a position to make plans and recommendations for acceptance by the advertiser. In planning, the agency determines the market to be reached, the adequacy of the distribution and price, the appropriate media channels to carry the message to the consumer, the correct copy appeal, and the merchandising factors.

The selection of media is a very important item in the planning. It involves the choice of the right channels of communication through which to send the advertising message. It is the agency's function to determine the proper market for the particular product and then to choose the media most appropriate to reach such a market. Expert knowledge is required to make the proper choice.

> The range of choice is tremendous. There are more than 1700 daily newspapers, 650 national magazines, 1700 commercial radio stations, 4 national networks and 25 regional networks, a rapidly growing number of television stations, some 1700 business papers, outdoor plants in every sizable city and town, thousands of weekly and small-town papers, car cards, screen advertising, direct mail, dispays, etc.[11]

The media director of an advertising agency is, therefore, a very important member of the organization; he is a specialist in analyzing markets and media of all kind. He can avail himself of the Standard Rate & Data Service, which gives rates, circulations, mechanical requirements, etc., as published by the media, the annual American Association of Advertising Agencies (A.A.A.A.), market and newspaper statistics, the A.A.A.A. newspaper reader surveys, and the Audit Bureau of Circulation. He may also call on the services of media representatives who will furnish special data on the publications or radio stations which they represent. Media selection is among

---

[11] Frederic R. Gamble in *Advertising Handbook* edited by Roger Barton (New York: Prentice Hall, Inc., 1950), p. 862.

the most skilled and intricate of the advertising agency functions. Dependent upon the agency's skill, the media selection may achieve and enhance or impair and defeat the advertising plan.

Having selected the media, the agency must now determine the copy appeals and messages that will be used in these channels in order to sell the product. This calls not only for an understanding of the consumers to be reached, but also for creative talent and a rich imagination. Victor Schwab's ten precepts of what guides the copywriter are a summary of the old familiar refrain in advertising circles: "get their attention, get their interest, create desire or conviction, produce action." [12]

Where the copy calls for illustration—which is the rule in newspaper or magazine advertising—the art director, working in cooperation with the copywriter, attempts to illustrate the copy appeal. After the rough tissue, the "visual" or "finished rough" is submitted to the client for approval. When the client lacks the necessary imagination to understand the "rough," a so-called "comprehensive" layout, which looks almost like the finished advertisement, is prepared. The finished artwork is usually produced outside the advertising agency. There are special artists whose talents render themselves best to a particular type of illustration, and it is the function of the art director to select the right artist for the particular advertisement.

When the plans for copy and illustrations are completed, the agency proceeds to the next step—mechanical production. The production manager of the agency arranges with the typographer or typesetter to have copy set in type, and with the photoengraver for engravings of illustrations. As the final step the production manager orders the necessary electrotypes

[12] Victor Schwab, "Ten Copy Appeals," *Printers' Ink*, December 13, 1943, pp. 17–19. See chap. i.

or mats in needed quantities. It is the function of the production manager to know the suppliers in the particular field and to get estimates for each process so that the client may approve the cost. The production department is also entrusted with the printing of direct-by-mail matters, promotional brochures, or folders. Here, too, a knowledge of the printers and their capabilities is essential. The copywriter, the artist, and the production manager must proofread the advertisements and check the illustrations and the engravings to avoid any error.

Where the advertising agency has decided upon radio or television for the account, the task is turned over to the radio and television department. The radio program must be built to fit the market; the commercials have to be written to suit the particular program and to fit the problem created by the particular vehicle, i.e., radio or television. The agency, as a rule, will call in outside talent to help in the scriptwriting, in the direction and rehearsal of the show, and very often in the casting of performers. Radio and television require a skilled director and assistants. This branch of advertising calls for specialized talents, because even when the entire production is a "package show" [13] the agency must be in a position to appraise, evaluate, and recommend the results. The "sword of Damocles" hanging over the radio and television performers and the advertising agency is the rating indicative of the popularity of the program.

Because an agency operates under pressure of time in meeting publishing deadlines and broadcasting dates, someone in the agency is usually assigned to what is called traffic control. In a medium-sized agency, the production manager will usually function in this capacity. It is the responsibility of

---

[13] The networks or special producers create the entire show and sell it for a fixed fee to the advertising agency for the client; in such a case the agency supervises the show, but is only directly concerned with writing the commercials.

"traffic" to see that copy and artwork are prepared on schedule, that client and legal approvals have been obtained wherever necessary, and that final material is issued to reach each medium on or before its closing date.

Possibly the key man in managing an advertising account for the agency is the account executive. He is the individual employed to maintain liaison between the agency and the advertiser. He is often the individual that brings in the account. It is from him that the agency executives learn of plans of the advertiser. Client approvals of copy, art, and schedules are routed through him. The account executive, if he is gifted and versatile, will exert a great deal of influence on the account. Whether the account remains with the agency or goes elsewhere is largely his responsibility; in fact, many agencies have been formed by an account executive who so dominated an account that when he left the agency the account followed.

Having prepared the advertisement, the agency has to enter into contracts with the various media. These establish the advertising agency (not the client) as the contracting party. After the advertisement has appeared, the publisher sends the agency a copy of the magazine or a "tear sheet" from the newspaper; the broadcaster sends an affidavit or station log to show that the program was broadcast. It is the agency's function to check its media invoices against the orders and the "tear sheets" or proof of broadcast before it pays the medium. Well-regulated advertising agencies insist that the client pay several days in advance of the time when the agency is called upon to pay the medium. It is not the function of the advertising agency to providc thc funds for the client or act as his banker. It must be remembered that the obligation of the agency to the media is a primary one, and the failure of the advertiser to pay does not obviate the obligation of the agency. The agency's failure to meet its obligations when due can result in the loss of "recognition" which is the *sine qua non* of its existence.

The principal source of the agency's income is the commission allowed it by the advertising media. The service fees which it may get by special arrangements for special services are, as a rule, not an important factor in the agency's compensation.

Another form of compensation for advertising agency services would be a straight retainer against which advertising commissions are applied. This gives the advertising agency a minimum of compensation and is oftentimes used where an account is small but is potentially a big advertiser. This retainer is usually dropped when the advertiser begins spending sufficient funds to insure a profit on the account.

One of the larger agencies, N. W. Ayer and Son, which was formed on capital acquired in soliciting advertising for a group of religious periodicals, in the 1870's used the system of billing the advertiser the net rate of the space, plus an agreed percentage as their commission.

The method of agency compensation is paradoxical. The advertising agency works for the advertiser in that he does market research for the advertiser's product and writes the advertisements and processes them to completion. Nevertheless, the agent is paid by the media from which he has purchased time or space. The economics and ethics of this method of agency compensation have been questioned by many. On the other hand, after an exhaustive study of this problem, financed by media, advertisers, and agencies in 1932 and 1933, J. W. Young concluded that the compensation method now in use is the most practicable one for maintaining the best relationship between advertisers, agencies, and media.[14] Gamble supports this method of agency compensation on the theory that through the agency commission, media owners

---

[14] J. W. Young, *Advertising Agency Compensation in Relation to the Total Cost of Advertising* (Chicago: University of Chicago Press, 1933), pp. 68–69.

have built up a force of advertising agencies for the sale and service of their space and time. According to Gamble, the media owner says, in effect, to the advertiser:

> I have space to sell. In my own interests, it is important that the space shall be used intelligently and effectively. I am not able to "service" that space for you. Frankly, most advertisers are not equipped to do it either. Therefore, I will sell you the space—and if you wish it, I will provide for you the services of a group of experts who will serve you. I will pay them out of my gross receipts for space.
>
> And please note: you are not limited in your choice of agency: you may choose any agency you want, provided it conforms to my standard of what is best for advertising and therefore for me. And in serving you, as your advertising agency, it will be working directly for your interests—and indirectly for mine.
>
> Its value to me depends on what it does for you. It continues to receive compensation from me—in the form of a commission—only as long as it satisfies you.
>
> While its services are not paid by you, it is answerable to you—it must satisfy you that it is loyal to your interests—it must satisfy you that it is rendering you at least as good and effective service as you could obtain from any other agency—it must sell goods for you.
>
> If the agency does all of those things, I shall have my reward in the continuation of and the increase in the business that you place with me.[15]

One final step remains to complete the modern advertising agency picture. How does an agency proceed to get new accounts which assure the continuity of its existence? The typical advertising agency has a new business department. Very few advertising agencies advertise their services in the newspapers or magazines, out of the desire, perhaps, to remain in the background. The advertising agency may write letters to a group of carefully selected prospects pointing out the

---

[15] Barton, *op. cit.*, p. 875.

special features of its services and accomplishments. The more usual method, however, is personal solicitation by the principals or by a "new business" executive.

The agency, in its effort to get new business, will generally avoid specialized industries beyond the realm of its normal experience and will avoid also the solicitation of competing accounts. As a rule, the agency relies upon a standard presentation in the solicitation of new business. This includes the history and background of the principals and staff, the list of its accounts and a résumé of its experience and notable successes. Most important in the solicitation, however, is the personal element of confidence which the advertiser can be made to have in the agency. Upon this great intangible factor rests the success of most agencies. Nor is it to be wondered that the factor of good will and confidence is at the root of the client-agency relationship. The advertising agent is a partner in the client's business in everything except direct profit sharing. All the creations of the agency in the way of copy or art belong—by an unwritten rule in the advertising business—to the client. Many an important slogan or trade-mark was thus created by the advertising agency and became a valuable and tangible asset of the advertiser.[16] A glance at but a few well-known slogans of yesterday and today illustrate this point:

His Master's Voice
There's a Reason
Say it with Flowers

[16] "Are there any bases, after all, for distinguishing between patents and trade-marks? . . . It would ordinarily be supposed that the degree of monopoly was greater in the case of patents. Yet the huge prestige value of such names as 'Ivory,' 'Kodak,' 'Uneeda,' 'Coco-Cola,' and 'Old Dutch Cleanser,' to cite only a few, is sufficient to make one skeptical. It would be impossible to compute satisfactorily for comparison the value of the monopoly rights granted by the United States Government in the form of patents and copyrights, and the value of those existing in the form of trade-marks, trade names, and good-will." Edward Chamberlain, *The Theory of Monopolistic Competition* (Cambridge: Harvard University Press, 1936), p. 62.

Good to the Last Drop
That Schoolgirl Complexion
Ask the Man Who Owns One
You Just Know She Wears Them
I'd Walk a Mile for a Camel
Save the Surface and You Save All!
Not a Cough in a Carload
Be Happy—Go Lucky!

With this brief view of the functions and contributions of the advertising agency, it is proper to consider to what extent the social and ethical implications of advertising concern the agency.

The Advertising Code

The modern advertising agent regards himself as a professional man, applying his skill and talent in the interests of his client, just as does a doctor or lawyer, and with the same motives. The primary motive is earning a livelihood, but professional pride and service to the community are important considerations. To support this view, the agency man will point to the general code of good conduct which advertising agencies have established for themselves.[17] The pertinent provisions of the code are worth examining:

> We hold that a responsibility of advertising agencies is to be a constructive force in business.
>
> We further hold that, to discharge this responsibility, advertising agencies must recognize an obligation, not only to their clients, but to the public, the media they employ, and to each other. . . .
>
> It is recognized that advertising is a business and as such must operate within the framework of competition. It is further recognized that keen and vigorous competition, honestly con-

[17] American Association of Advertising Agencies, *Standards of Practice* (New York, 1951).

ducted, is necessary to the growth and health of American business generally, of which advertising is a part.

However, *unfair* competitive practices in the advertising agency business lead to financial waste, dilution of service, diversion of manpower, and loss of prestige. Unfair practices tend to weaken public confidence both in advertisements and in the institution of advertising.

It is on the subject of copy appeal that the standards set up in the code loom most importantly. The applicable provisions read as follows:

Advertising Copy. It is unsound and unprofessional for the advertising agency to prepare or handle any advertising of an untruthful or indecent character, as exemplified by the following copy practices disapproved in a code jointly adopted by the American Association of Advertising Agencies and the Association of National Advertisers, and also by the Advertising Federation of America:

1. False statements or misleading exaggeration.
2. Indirect misrepresentation of a product, or service, through distortion of details, or of their true perspective, either editorially or pictorially.
3. Statements or suggestions offensive to public decency.
4. Statements which tend to undermine an industry by attributing to its products, generally, faults and weaknesses true only of a few.
5. Price claims that are misleading.
6. Pseudoscientific advertising, including claims insufficiently supported by accepted authority, or that distort the true meaning or practicable application of a statement made by professional or scientific authority.
7. Testimonials which do not reflect the real choice of a competent witness.

If advertising agencies were to adhere to this code, even substantially, much of the criticism leveled against them and against advertising itself would probably disappear. But do they?

In recent issues of the leading magazines, a former opera star tells his public how to enjoy "an enchanting evening" with *Blank* whiskey; and in another advertisement he advises them that mildness, being all important to him as a singer, requires that he smoke "the cigarette that agrees with my throat" and urges them to make "the thirty-day test." In the same issues, the cigarette featuring the A.B.C.'s of smoking also features well-known personalities who have indorsed many other products. The cigarette which advises you to "Be Happy —Go Lucky" features an attractive girl in a scanty costume and low neckline. The fourth member of the "Big 4" in the cigarette field shows only an illustration of the package and says, "we're tobacco men . . . not medicine men." The latter brand has recently been the subject of a withering criticism by the federal court for misleading and deceptive advertising.[18]

These advertisements are cited not because they are typical of the majority that appear, but rather because they are sponsored by important advertisers and are prepared by leading advertising agencies. Further examples can be cited. Borden, in his analysis of twenty advertisements which were submitted to consumers and advertising men for criticism, points to some flagrant violations of the code:

1) A well-known dental product uses as the feature of the advertisement an illustration showing a closeup of the head and shoulders of a beautiful and happy-looking woman lying in bed while her husband bends over her.
2) A well-known brand of cigarettes contains pictures of and testimonials from socially prominent persons. One illustration shows women in low-cut evening gowns. Some of the statements regarding the physiological effects of cigarettes probably would be deemed questionable by physiologists.
3) This is an advertisement of a typewriter. It is gloomy, and one would have to be charitable indeed not to con-

---

[18] *P. Lorillard Co. v. Federal Trade Commission*, United States Court of Appeals, Fourth Circuit, decided December 29, 1950.

sider its theme far-fetched. The theme is an elaboration of the dire things that will happen to children who do not have typewriters. The advertisement displays a coupon prominently and urges installment purchases. The product itself is well known and entirely reputable.

4) This is an advertisement of a cosmetic, appealing to the desire for fine skin and beauty. It plays upon fear of results from improper skin care, but emphasizes the happy solution. It has a large illustration of pseudoscientific characters, and it contains testimonials from socially prominent women.

5) This advertises a well-known toilet soap. The tone of the advertisement is cheerful. The main illustration shows a beautiful, nude girl. To support its claims as an aid to good complexion, unnamed scientists are quoted. Many of the claims undoubtedly would be deemed exaggerations by many critics.

6) This advertises a product for increasing one's weight. The headline is of cartoon type, the words coming from the mouth of a professional-looking man, probably a doctor. A well-developed young woman in a bathing suit is also featured. Emphasis in the copy is placed on fear of being unattractive because thin, but the general tone is cheerful inasmuch as the cure for this situation is at hand.[19]

Is there something wrong with the advertising code? The answer, obviously, is that there is something amiss in its observance rather than in the code itself. The majority of advertisements, fortunately, are in good taste and informative.

Very often enthusiasm, partiality, and appeals to emotional responses in advertising are indiscriminately equated with unethical practices. No one really blames a salesman for becoming over-enthusiastic about his product; advertising is not unethical because it is biased or highly colored. It is difficult

---

[19] N. H. Borden, *The Economic Effects of Advertising* (Chicago: Richard D. Irwin, Inc., 1947), pp. 742–56.

to agree with A. S. J. Baster's opinion that most advertising is deceptive. He states his position rather cleverly but seems carried away by the elegance of his own rhetoric:

> Great efforts are made by copy writers to invest the most commonplace processes and objects with an emotional content. Syrup is "bucketed in the far North Woods by snowshoed woodsmen, and hauled to camp on oxen-drawn bobsleds." One wonders whether it is any better syrup for being thus bucketed and thus hauled. The behavior of banana fritters in a certain brand of cooking fat, which "takes these puffy little balls right into its deep heart and seals them in amber crispness," begins a very moving description of what everybody formerly mistook for a rather ordinary kitchen experiment; and the well-known panegyrics on "the soup that makes the meal happier," "the soup with the racy flavour, and the sparkling, sunny smile" are in a similar vein. . . .
>
> The direct function of the words and pictures of the non-informative part of an advertisement enshrouded as it is in the kind of irrelevant emotional verbiage described above, has become that of a veiled appeal to instinct, with studied avoidance of any rational judgment. In the animal world, where instinctive behavior has developed to a very high level because of urgent biological needs, this sort of advertising would precisely fit the conditions. . . .[20]

Borden answers this attack rather well in saying:

> Viewpoints such as those held by Professors Radin and Baster, when carried to their logical conclusion lead to a doctrine which denies a proper place for influence or persuasion by sellers in economic affairs. The use of influence, even in moderate degree, is characterized as dishonest and in bad taste; and the critics evidently would like to see it greatly restricted . . . As previously noted, the ethics of selling, like all ethics, are subject to constant evolution and are governed by pragmatic principles. . . .
>
> It is essential when one is appraising the honesty of advertising to try to arrive at a realistic understanding of the

[20] A. S. J. Baster, *Advertising Reconsidered* (London: P. S. King & Son, Ltd., 1935), pp. 50 ff.

> way in which people behave. Advertising is written and presented by men of firms impelled by self-interest to induce others to buy their products. Yet certain extreme critics of advertising, even while recognizing its biased source, appear to expect from advertisers an unbiased statement about the merchandise which is being featured, a statement measured by a standard of abstract truth.
>
> Messages of any kind which are designed to persuade and to influence others generally do not measure up to the standards of abstract truth. When advertisements are judged as biased of persuasive messages, they accord with what men have come to expect in persuasive messages in all walks of life. The same charges of bias, and hence of his honesty, may be applied to the statesman in his pronouncements designed to influence the viewpoint of other statesmen, to the politician seeking votes, to the lawyer in his plea to the jury, or even to the pulpit orator seeking to save the sinner.[21]

In answer to Baster's criticism, many advertising agents will agree that to be rational, advertising must be informative, but not dull, dry, and technical. The normal housewife, they say, is no more interested in the technical specifications of a vacuum cleaner than is a man in the technical details of his radio or television set. But they are interested in the labor saving and increased leisure and pleasure they can get from the product. Moreover, the advertising man will argue that since the first objective of an advertisement is to attract attention and interest, it is more desirable to give the information in a fanciful or romantic way rather than in a dull, statistical, or factual manner.

It has been argued also that the methods of the advertising agent are not those of an impartial judge, but those of an advocate eager for a verdict in his favor. The advertising agent wants to be judged by the standards applicable to a lawyer pleading for his client, rather than those which must govern the judge. The answer given by Dr. Samuel Johnson, when

---

[21] Borden, *op. cit.*, pp. 813, 829.

Boswell asked him if he did not think that the practice of the law in some degree hurt "the nice feeling of honesty," is appropriate to our discussion:

> "Why no, sir, if you act properly. You are not to deceive your clients with false representations of your opinion; you are not to tell lies to a judge."
>
> "But what do you think of supporting a cause which you know to be bad?"
>
> "Sir, you do not know it to be good or bad till the judge determines it. I have said that you are to state facts fairly; so that your thinking, or what you call knowing, a cause to be bad must be from reasoning, must be from your supposing your arguments to be weak and inconclusive. But, sir, that is not enough. An argument which does not convince yourself may convince the judge to whom you urge it; and if it does convince him, why, then, sir, you are wrong, and he is right. It is his business to judge; and you are not to be confident in your opinion that a cause is bad, but to say all you can for your client, and then hear the judge's opinion."
>
> "But, sir, does not affecting a warmth when you have no warmth, and appearing to be clearly of one opinion when you are in reality of another opinion, does not such dissimulation impair one's honesty? Is there not some danger that a lawyer may put on the same mask in common life, in the intercourse with his friends?"
>
> "Why, no sir, everybody knows you are paid for affecting warmth for your client; and it is therefore properly no dissimulation: the moment you come from the bar you resume your usual behaviour. Sir, a man will no more carry the artifice of the bar into the common intercourse of society, than a man who is paid for tumbling upon his hands will continue to tumble upon his hands when he should walk on his feet."

A realistic approach to the problem confronting the advertising agent—because of a possible conflict between his duty to his client and his obligations to society—is to admit that his ethical standard is a utilitarian rather than an ideal one. He must conform to the rules of conduct which the community has established as proper in matters of business persuasion.

These rules are embodied in voluntary codes and in state and federal laws and regulations. We are not concerned here as to whether these rules and regulations meet the test of the perfectionist. We are, however, vitally concerned with whether they meet the practical requirements of our present social structure.

The advertising agencies, comparatively few in number, wield a tremendous power through the expenditures they control and which they place with media such as newspapers, magazines, radio, and television—all organs of publicity, news, and propaganda. It is because of the influence which the media exert on public opinion, on our economy, and the public welfare that we must inquire into the federal regulations which affect them and the adequacy or insufficiency of such laws.

Chapter 4

CONSTITUTIONAL SOURCES OF FEDERAL REGULATORY POWER

One of the aims of the preceding chapters has been to demonstrate that modern national advertising, as a major factor in our economy and social existence, is of comparatively recent origin. Advertising was as unknown to the framers of the Constitution as the railroad, radio, television, or the direct primary election.

In the examination of the constitutional sources of power upon which federal regulation of advertising is based, one must always remember that our constitutional system has relied for its strength not so much on the particular provisions of the Constitution as in their adaptation to the new, always changing, and ever more complex conditions of American life. The courts have held that the constitutional sources of federal power "keep pace with the progress of the country, and adapt themselves to the new developments of time and circumstances." [1] As the Supreme Court recently expressed it:

> We may assume that the framers of the Constitution in adopting that section, did not have specifically in mind the selection and elimination of candidates for Congress by the direct primary any more than they contemplated the application of the commerce clause to interstate telephone, telegraph, and wireless communication, which are concededly within it. But in determining whether a provision of the Constitution applies to a new subject matter, it is of little significance that

[1] *Pensacola Telegraph Co. v. Western Union*, 96 U.S. 1, 3, 24 L. Ed. 708 (1878).

> it is one with which the framers were not familiar. For in setting up an enduring framework of government they undertook to carry out for the indefinite future and in all the vicissitudes of the changing affairs of men, those fundamental purposes which the instrument itself discloses. Hence we read its words, not as we read legislative codes which are subject to continuous revision with the changing course of events, but as the revelation of the great purposes which were intended to be achieved by the Constitution as a continuing instrument of government.[2]

Prior to the Civil War our economy was predominantly agricultural, characterized in the main by small rural communities, with manufacturing in the simpler stages of organization and with consumer consumption limited to a small selection of goods. Advertising fully reflected this condition. A typical issue of the *Saturday Evening Post* in 1863 showed a magazine of eight pages, with an advertising section of about two-thirds of a page featuring:

> Five patent medicines, including Perry Davis' Pain Killer, Swayne's Syrup, and Brandeth's Pills, some of them including testimonials; Four hair growers, restorers, or dyes; One quack doctor; One medical book; One cattle powder; One preparation for Keeping Cider Sweet; One patent arm and leg; One microscope; One fur; One book; One stock broker.[3]

The development of the railroads and the great industrial organization that sprang up in the last two decades of the nineteenth century brought the American economy into national scope, with industry and commerce most closely intertwined. By the turn of the twentieth century the country had developed a highly advanced industrial economy in which large-

---

[2] *United States v. Classic*, 313 U.S. 299, 316, 61 S. Ct. 1031, 85 L. Ed. 1368 (1941).

[3] G. B. Hotchkiss, *An Outline of Advertising* (New York: The Macmillan Co., 1950), p. 49.

scale producers of an amazing variety of products were to seek national markets through national advertising.

The growth of periodical advertising revenue from $7.6 million in 1865 to $96 million in 1900 may seem modest by today's standards of advertising revenue measured in billions, but it was a good indication of the position which advertising was to occupy in our economy in the future.

As previously shown, no precise date can be assigned for the beginning of national advertising. The basis for it was established early in the nineteenth century when factory production by machinery began to supplant the older methods of handicraft. The concentration of industry in large units, made possible by machinery and power, was of limited value until it became feasible to market production on a national basis. The development of the railroads, national circulation of magazines, and rapid improvement in the techniques of printing, mechanical production, and advertising agency service enabled modern advertising to assume its role in mass distribution.

To Frank Presbrey, the development of modern national advertising in the 1890's is the story of America's great strides in technological and economic progress. After pointing out that large-scale advertising by department stores and a few manufacturers of household articles had demonstrated that extensive advertising could be used by others as well as the sellers of patent medicines, he stated:

> Quantity production had definitely arrived. Transmission of power and the invention of specialized machinery had made manufacture easy. Capital invested in manufacturing had grown from $2,790,000,000 in 1879 to $6,525,000,000 in 1889 and the decade of the '90's was adding $3,000,000,000 more. Development of railroad express and telephone, and wide use of business-quickening devices such as the typewriter had so speeded up distribution that getting the goods into even out-of-the-way places was no longer a problem. With an overcapacity to produce, the need was to get people to buy

> articles which they had not habitually been buying. Progress of industry became dependent upon the making of new consumers. The family of John Smith, who were accustomed to using laundry soap in their ablutions, must be induced to buy toilet soap for that purpose.[4]

In 1916 an American automobile manufacturer gained distinction by being the first to invest a million dollars in national magazine advertising in a single year. In 1929 fifteen different manufacturers invested more than a million dollars each in magazines, in addition to vast sums expended on radio, newspapers, car cards, outdoor posters, and other media. In 1950 forty-five titans of the agency business billed $1,334,500,000, a startling fact indeed, when it is recalled that there are more than 2,000 recognized advertising agents. Advertising is now recognized as a means of mass distribution, and hence an almost indispensable adjunct of mass production.

It took our judiciary many years, however, to grasp the significance of advertising in the economic and social spheres. As late as 1920 the Supreme Court ruled, in the case of *Blumenstock Bros. Advertising Agency v. Curtis Publishing Co.*,[5] that the placement of advertising contracts by an Illinois advertising agency with the Curtis Publishing Company in Pennsylvania, which publishes the *Saturday Evening Post, Ladies' Home Journal*, and *Country Gentleman*, was not interstate commerce. Since a detailed discussion of this case in connection with the interstate commerce clause follows later in this chapter, it will suffice at this point to cite the following comment by the Court:

> It may be conceded that the circulation and distribution of such Publications throughout the country would amount

---

[4] Frank Presbrey, *History and Development of Advertising* (New York: Doubleday, Doran Co., Inc., 1929), pp. 337–38.

[5] 252 U.S. 436, 40 S. Ct. 385, 64 L. Ed. 649 (1920).

> to interstate commerce, but the circulation of these periodicals did not depend upon or have any direct relation to the advertising contracts which the plaintiff offered and the defendant refused to receive except upon the terms stated in the declaration. The advertising contracts did not involve any movement of goods or merchandise in interstate commerce, or any transmission of intelligence in such commerce. . . .

It is significant to note that, in the opinion of the Supreme Court in 1920, the circulation of these periodicals did not depend upon or have any direct relation to the advertising contracts which they received, because these contracts did not involve the movement of goods or merchandise in interstate commerce or the transmission of intelligence in such commerce. Apparently the Court was totally unaware that without advertising most publications would soon cease to exist and so would cease to circulate in interstate commerce. The long list of newspapers and magazines which have disappeared from the scene because of lack of advertising provides an adequate answer to the Court's argument.

In this chapter, then, the constitutional provisions upon which Congress bases its power to regulate advertising are considered before discussing the regulatory bureaus and the methods employed for regulation in subsequent chapters.

The Postal Power

The federal control of the postal service is based on Article I, Section 8 of the Constitution which provides that Congress shall have the power "to establish post offices and post roads." According to W. W. Willoughby:

> No other constitutional grant seems to be clothed in words which so poorly express its object, or so feebly indicate the particular measures which may be adopted to carry out its design. To establish post offices and post roads is the form

of the grant; to create and regulate the entire postal system of the country is the evident intent.[6]

Yet, by a broadened construction of the constitutional provisions the postal system of the country was established. In the case of *Lewis Publishing Company v. E. M. Morgan*,[7] the Supreme Court commented as follows:

> Under that six-word grant of power the great postal system of this country has been built up, involving an annual revenue and expenditure of over five hundred millions of dollars, the maintenance of 60,000 post offices, with hundreds of thousands of employees, the carriage of more than fifteen billions of pieces of mail matter per year, weighing over two billions of pounds, the incorporation of railroads, the establishment of the rural free delivery system, the money-order system by which more than half of a billion of dollars a year is transmitted from person to person, the postal savings bank, the parcel post, an aeroplane mail service, the suppression of lotteries, and a most efficient suppression of fraudulent and criminal schemes, impossible to be reached in any other way.

In 1872 Congress authorized the Postmaster General to forbid delivery of registered letters and payment of money orders to persons or companies found by the Postmaster General to be conducting an enterprise to obtain money by false pretenses through the use of the mails.[8] By the same statute, Congress also made it a crime to place letters, circulars, and advertisements in the mail for the purpose of carrying out such fraudulent schemes. In 1889 Congress declared as "non-mailable, "letters and other matter sent to help perpetrate frauds; [9] and in 1895 the Postmaster General's fraud order powers were extended to cover all letters or other matter sent by mail.[10]

---

[6] W. W. Willoughby, *Constitutional Laws of the United States* (2d ed., New York: Baker, Voorhis & Co., Inc., 1935), p. 438.

[7] 229 U.S. 288, 291, 33 S. Ct. 867, 57 L. Ed. 1190 (1912).

[8] 17 *Stat.* 322–323, 39 *U.S.C.* Sec. 732.

[9] 25 *Stat.* 874, 39 *U.S.C.* Sec. 256.

[10] 28 *Stat.* 964, 39 *U.S.C.* Sec. 259.

The Securities Exchange Act [11] and the Federal Trade Commission Act, as amended,[12] were also enacted to protect people against fraudulent use of the mails.

The constitutionality of the congressional delegation of authority to the Postmaster General to determine, without the aid of the courts, whether printed matter or advertising of any kind can be excluded from the mails, because fraudulent or in the nature of a lottery, was sustained in the case of *Public Clearing House v. Coyne.*[13]

An important feature of postal regulations which affects advertising is the classification of periodicals as second-class mail. The low mailing rate which this classification grants has been of great importance to periodicals and newspapers because it enables them to have a wider circulation, better advertising rates, and hence a greater sphere of influence. The grant of this privilege was explained and justified by the Supreme Court in the case of the *United States v. Burleson* [14] where the Court said:

> The extremely low rate charged for second-class mail—to carry it, was said, in argument, to cost seven times the revenues which it yields—is justified as a part of "the historic policy of encouraging by low postal rates the dissemination of current intelligence." It is a frank extension of special favors to publishers because of the special contribution to the public welfare which Congress believes is derived from the newspapers and other periodical presses.

Congress has set up four conditions upon which a publication may be admitted to the second class.[15] Relevant for our purpose here is the fourth condition, reading as follows:

---

[11] 48 *Stat.* 77, 906, 15 *U.S.C.* Sec. 77(e).
[12] 52 *Stat.* 114, 15 *U.S.C.* Sec. 52.
[13] 194 U.S. 497, 24 S. Ct. 789, 45 L. Ed. 1092 (1903).
[14] 255 U.S. 407, 408, 41 S. Ct. 352, 65 L. Ed. 704 (1921).
[15] *Classification Act of* 1879, 29 *Stat.* 358, 48 *Stat.* 928, 39 *U.S.C.* Sec. 14, 226, 39 *U.S.C.A.* Sec. 226.

> . . . Fourth. It must be originated and published for the dissemination of information of a public character, or devoted to literature, the sciences, arts, or some special industry, and having a legitimate list of subscribers. *Nothing herein contained shall be so construed as to admit to the second class rate regular publications designed primarily for advertising purposes, or for free circulation, or for circulation at nominal rates.*[16]

A publication can obtain the second-class mail privilege through a permit issued by the Postmaster General after a hearing and upon a showing that it will contain only "mailable" matter.[17]

The privilege of second-class mail may be revoked by the Postmaster General where the publication is so edited that it contains other than "mailable" matter.[18] Under the postal law, Congress has also provided that newspapers and periodical publications must file copies with the Postmaster General and the postmaster at the place where "entered," and must publish a sworn statement showing the average circulation, the names of the editors, publisher, owner, stockholders, principal creditors, and to mark all paid reading matter "advertisement."[19] The constitutionality of this law was upheld in the previously cited *Lewis Publishing Company v. E. M. Morgan*, and a detailed discussion of this and the related cases will follow in the chapter dealing with postal regulations of advertising.

The Taxing Power and General Welfare Clause

Article I, Section 8, Paragraph 1 of the Constitution of the United States reads: "The Congress shall have power to lay and collect Taxes, Duties, Imposts and Excises, to pay the

---

[16] Italics supplied.
[17] *Houghton v. Payne*, 194 U.S. 88, 24 S. Ct. 599, 48 L. Ed. 888 (1903).
[18] *Smith v. Hitchcock*, 226 U.S. 53, 33 S. Ct. 6, 57 L. Ed. 119 (1912).
[19] 37 *Stat.* 553, Chap. 389, Sec. 2.

Debts and provide for the common Defense and general Welfare of the United States: but all Duties, Imposts and Excises shall be uniform throughout the United States. . . ."

Theoretically, the national government has no general police power to legislate for the health, morals, and welfare of the nation. It is by now well established, however, that in the exercise of its constitutional powers Congress functions exactly as a state does when employing its police power. In the language of the Supreme Court:

> . . . It is no objection to the assertion of the power to regulate interstate commerce that its exercise is attended by the same incidents which attend the exercise of the police power of the states.[20]

Since the turn of the century, Congress has sought through its commerce and tax powers to adjust and regulate a variety of social and economic conditions. The Supreme Court has sustained a whole series of laws as constitutional even though the obvious intent of Congress was to protect the health, morals, and public welfare of the nation. On the other hand, it balked at some legislation, insisting on its right to inquire into the purpose and motives of Congress. The resulting confusion made it evident:

> . . . that federal police statutes using taxation as an instrument of control now also rested on a somewhat uncertain constitutional foundation. A slight shift in personnel or opinion of the Court might well send taxation as a police device into the constitutional discard.[21]

Despite such uncertainty as to the Court's attitude, there are enough decisions by the Court to warrant the hope that a vast area of federal social and economic controls has been per-

---

[20] *United States v. F. W. Darby*, 321 U.S. 100, 61 S. Ct. 451, 85 L. Ed. 609 (1941).

[21] A. H. Kelly and W. A. Harbison, *The American Constitution* (New York: W. W. Norton & Co., Inc., 1948), p. 591.

manently opened. As yet, Congress has not utilized the power of taxation to regulate advertising, but there can be little doubt as to the existence of such power. The full scope of such controls and their application to advertising can be evaluated and understood by an examination of the attitude of the Supreme Court toward the exercise of the taxing power of Congress.

The Supreme Court, in the case of *McCray v. United States*,[22] sustained a federal police statute involving the use of an excise tax, the primary purpose of which was not to raise revenue. In 1902, Congress had passed a law increasing the tax on artificially colored oleomargarine to ten cents per pound as against only one-quarter of a cent per pound on oleomargarine free from coloring. The law was attacked in the courts on the ground that its true purpose was not taxation but rather regulation of manufacturing, and therefore such a law invaded the reserved powers of the states. The Court refused to inquire into the motive or intent of Congress, saying:

> The decisions of this court from the beginning lend no support whatever to the assumption that the judiciary may restrain the exercise of a lawful power on the assumption that a wrongful purpose or motive has caused the power to be exerted.

The Court's attitude toward this type of social legislation—whether through the commerce or taxation power—was indicated in the case of *Hoke v. United States*: [23]

> Our dual form of government has its perplexities, state and nation having different spheres of jurisdiction, as we have said; but it must be kept in mind that we are one people; and the powers reserved to the states and those conferred on the nation are adapted to be exercised, whether independently or concurrently, to promote the general welfare, material and moral.

---

[22] 195 U.S. 27, 24 S. Ct. 769, 49 L. Ed. 78 (1904).
[23] 227 U.S. 308, 33 S. Ct. 281 (1913).

In *United States v. Doremus* [24] the Supreme Court sustained the Harrison Narcotic Drug Act which employed the taxing power to regulate and suppress illicit drug traffic. On its face, the Act was a tax law, and the Court refused to look for hidden motives.

> . . . And from an early day the court has held that the fact that other motives may impel the exercise of federal taxing power does not authorize the courts to inquire into that subject. If the legislation enacted has some reasonable relation to the exercise of the taxing authority conferred by the Constitution, it cannot be invalidated because of the supposed motives which induced it. . . .
>
> The act may not be declared unconstitutional because its effect may be to accomplish another purpose as well as the raising of revenue. If the legislation is within the taxing authority of Congress—that is sufficient to sustain it.

To surmount the constitutional difficulties which the Court had raised against the use of the federal commerce power to regulate child labor,[25] Congress sought to regulate the employment of children through the taxing power.[26] The law laid a tax of 10 per cent upon the net profits of any firm employing child labor. Now, however, the Court went behind the declared purpose of the Act and found that the "hidden motive" was the regulation of child labor, and therefore the Act was not a proper exercise of the taxing power.[27] The Court pointed out that it had sustained many acts of Congress which had an *incidental* purpose to regulate, but whose *primary* purpose was the securing of revenue. However, when regulation is the primary and revenue the incidental purpose of a tax law, the Court will intervene and hold that the law is *not* properly a

---

[24] 249 U.S. 86, 39 S. Ct. 214, 80 L. Ed. 477 (1919).

[25] *Hammer v. Dagenhart,* 247 U.S. 251, 38 S. Ct. 529, 62 L. Ed. 1101 (1918).

[26] *Child Labor Act of* 1919, 40 *Stat.* 1057, 1138.

[27] *Bailey v. Drexel Furniture Co.,* 259 U.S. 20, 42 S. Ct. 449, 66 L. Ed. 817 (1922).

revenue measure but an act of confiscation. This is so unless Congress has the constitutional power to regulate the subject matter involved, in which case the taxing power may be used to effect that legitimate end. In *Veazie Bank v. Fenno* [28] the Court had sustained a prohibitory 10 per cent tax on state bank notes on the ground that Congress could, under its currency power, drive such notes out of circulation—the end was legitimate. In the child labor cases, however, the end was not legitimate—Congress did not have the constitutional power to regulate child labor under either the commerce or the taxing power. Following the same reasoning, the Court held invalid the Futures Trading Act which imposed a penalty tax on sales of grain for future delivery; [29] again in 1936 in *Carter v. Carter Coal Co.*,[30] the so-called excise tax of 15 per cent on the sales price of coal at the mine was held to be a penalty and not a tax.

Shortly thereafter, the "constitutional revolution in Federalism," i.e., the attitude of the Supreme Court toward the exercise of federal powers, had undergone quite a change. In the case of *Sunshine Anthracite Coal v. Adkins* [31] the Court accepted the Bituminous Coal Act of 1937 which Congress had passed to replace the one held invalid in the Carter case. The 19½ per cent penalty tax levied upon producers who failed to comply with the provisions of the law was held constitutional, since Congress could lawfully "impose penalties in aid of the exercise of any of its enumerated powers." The reasoning of the Court as expressed by Mr. Justice Douglas was as follows:

---

[28] 8 Wall. 533 (1869).

[29] *Hill v. Wallace*, 259 U.S. 44, 42 S. Ct. 453, 66 L. Ed. 822 (1922). A subsequent enactment, known as the *Grain Futures Act*, 1922, c. 369, 42 *Stat.* 998, 7 *U.S.C.A.* Secs. 1–17, was upheld as a valid regulation of interstate commerce in *Board of Trade of City of Chicago v. Olsen*, 262 U.S. 1, 43 S. Ct. 470, 67 L. Ed. 839 (1923).

[30] 298 U.S. 238, 56 S. Ct. 855, 80 L. Ed. 1160 (1936).

[31] 310 U.S. 381, 60 S. Ct. 907, 84 L. Ed., 1263 (1940).

> Clearly this tax is not designed merely for revenue purposes. In purpose and effect it is primarily a sanction to enforce the regulatory provisions of the Act. But this does not mean that the statute is invalid and the tax unenforcible. Congress may impose penalties in aid of the exercise of any of its enumerated powers. The power of taxation, granted to Congress by the Constitution, may be utilized as a sanction for the exercise of another power which is granted to it. . . . It is so utilized here.

The Court apparently was now willing to let Congress be the judge of the wisdom of legislative enactments where the economic and social conditions required them.

It was suggested in Chapter 1 that advertising has reached the proportions of an economic force so great that its unrestrained and unregulated use during an emergency, economic crisis, or a threat of inflation or deflation could defeat the national purpose. If the national powers are needed to regulate advertising through the medium of taxation, what attitude will the Court adopt toward such legislation? The change in attitude on the part of the Court, as noted in the preceding pages, is, therefore, important as a guide to legislation in the future.

Advertising was taxed briefly in our history. In 1765, an effort was made to apply in the colonies the stamp tax on newspapers and advertising, similar to that which was being levied in England. This tax was at the rate of two shillings on each advertisement regardless of what was paid for the advertisement or the circulation given it. Repeal of this stamp tax in 1766 was a powerful victory for an independent press and for advertising. A tax on advertising was levied during the five years of the Civil War decade. One of the war taxes was a 3 per cent levy on advertisements.[32] At the present time adver-

---

[32] According to the returns the income of publishers from advertising for the last fiscal year of the tax, ending June 30, 1867, was $9,609,326. The revenue to the government in that year was $288,009. During the five years

tising receives the benefit of a tax exemption under the Internal Revenue Code, in that reasonable and normal advertising expenditures are considered part of the operating expenses and are deductible.[33] To what extent such deductions are to be permitted and how they are to be integrated into the national welfare will be the subject of further discussion. One thing is certain: this force can be harnessed only by invoking the national power. There is abundant evidence of the existence of such power. As Mr. Justice Holmes expressed it:

> . . . It is not lightly to be assumed that, in matters requiring national action, "a power which must belong to and somewhere reside in every civilized government" is not to be found. . . . What was said . . . with regard to the powers of the States applies with equal force to the powers of the nation in cases where the States individually are incompetent to act. . . . With regard to that we may add that when we are dealing with words that also are a constituent act, like the Constitution of the United States, we must realize that they have called into life a being the development of which could not have been foreseen completely by the most gifted of its begetters. It was enough for them to realize or to hope that they had created an organism; it has taken a century and has cost their successors much sweat and blood to prove that they created a nation.[34]

---

tax was paid on newspaper and periodical advertising valued at $32,766,427, or an average of $6,553,285 a year. Presbey, *op. cit.*, pp. 150–51, 259.

[33] *Internal Revenue Code*, Sec. 23(a).

[34] *Missouri v. Holland*, 252 U.S. 416, 418, 40 S. Ct. 382, 84 L. Ed. 681 (1920). See also *Stewart Machine Co. v. Davis*, 301 U.S. 548, 57 S. Ct. 883, 81 L. Ed. 1279, where, by a five-to-four decision, the Supreme Court held valid an unemployment excise tax upon employers and unemployment grants to states enacting satisfactory unemployment compensation laws. In a ringing nationalistic defense of the taxing power, the Court, through Justice Cardozo, said:

". . . The fact developed quickly that the states were unable to give the requisite relief. The problem had become national in area and dimensions. There was need of help from the nation if the people were not to starve. It is too late today for the argument to be heard with tolerance that in a crisis so extreme the use of the moneys of the nation to relieve the unemployed and their dependents is a use for any purpose narrower than the promotion of the general welfare."

Interstate Commerce

The national power to regulate interstate commerce is found in Article I, Section 8, Clause 3 of the Constitution. It provides that "Congress shall have power . . . to regulate commerce with foreign nations, and among the several states, and with the Indian tribes."

> It is principally under this authority that Congress has assumed control over trusts, railroads, express companies, telephones and telegraphs, corporations, pure food, etc. . . . The moment corporate or private business engages in interstate commerce it becomes subject to the commerce power of the national government.[35]

Such regulatory bodies as the Federal Trade Commission, the Securities and Exchange Commission, and the Federal Communications Commission, all of which deal to some extent with advertising, have been created under the authority of the commerce power.

By judicial constructions and affirmative federal legislation, the commerce power has been converted into the most effective instrument for the integration and control of the American economy. While the original purpose of the "commerce clause" was to eliminate trade rivalries among the states, the federal government has derived from this grant of power over interstate commerce the authority to regulate rates, wages, and hours of labor, to dissolve monopolies, annul contracts, prescribe rules for the sale of securities and commodities, regulate advertising, and control radio and television: in brief, to establish a many-sided and effective control over every business enterprise in interstate commerce. All this was achieved without recourse to constitutional amendment, but rather by

---

[35] Rinehart J. Swenson, *The National Government and Business* (New York and London: The Century Co., 1924), p. 190.

means of judicial adaptation of the Constitution to meet an expanding and increasingly interdependent national economy.

The vast potentialities of the "commerce clause" were revealed for the first time by Mr. Chief Justice Marshall in *Gibbons v. Ogden.*[36] The case involved the validity of a New York law which gave to Robert R. Livingston and Robert Fulton the exclusive right of navigating the waters of that state by steamboat. Competing steamboat owners of New Jersey claimed the right to navigate New York waters by virtue of a federal license issued pursuant to an act of Congress. In freeing steamboat navigation from the restraints of state-created monopolies John Marshall stated:

> Commerce, undoubtedly, is traffic, but it is something more: it is intercourse. . . . This power, like all others vested in Congress, is complete in itself, may be exercised to its utmost extent, and acknowledges no limitations, other than are prescribed in the Constitution. . . . If, as has always been understood, the sovereignty of Congress, though limited to specified objects, is plenary as to those objects, the power over commerce with foreign nations, and among the several States, is vested in Congress as absolutely as it would be in a single government. . . .

The development of the United States as a coherent economic unit and its future as a great nation demanded a liberal and broad interpretation of the power of Congress over interstate commerce. Such was the interpretation made by Marshall's opinion which, his biographer claims, "has done more to knit the American people into one indivisible nation than any one force in our history, except only war."[37] The decision in *Gibbons v. Ogden* is a salient example of the adaptability of constitutional law to dominant economic trends.

---

[36] 9 Wheat. 1, 6 L. Ed. 23 (1824).

[37] Albert J. Beveridge, *The Life of John Marshall* (Boston: Houghton Mifflin Co., 1919), Vol. IV, p. 452.

For half a century after Marshall's death the decisions of the Supreme Court under the "commerce clause" rarely dealt with questions of what Congress might do in the exercise of its granted power under this clause. Its chief concern was with state activity which, many claimed, discriminated against or burdened interstate commerce. As the Court said in *Wickard v. Filburn*:

> . . . During this period there was perhaps little occasion for the affirmative exercise of the commerce power, and the influence of the Clause on American life and law was a negative one, resulting almost wholly from its operation as a restraint upon the powers of the states. In discussion and decision the point of reference instead of being what was "necessary and proper" to the exercise by Congress of its granted power, was often some concept of sovereignty thought to be implicit in the status of statehood. Certain activities such as "production," "manufacturing," and "mining" were occasionally said to be within the province of state governments and beyond the power of Congress under the Commerce Clause.[38]

It was with the enactment of the Interstate Commerce Act in 1887 that the interstate commerce power began to exert a posi-

---

[38] *Wickard v. Filburn,* 317 U.S. 111, 63 S. Ct. 82, 87 L. Ed. 122 (1942). See also *Cooley v. Board of Wardens,* 12 Howard 299, 13 L. Ed. 996 (1851), where the Court upheld a Pennsylvania statute regulating pilotage in the Port of Philadelphia on the theory of "selective exclusiveness." In *Peik v. Northwestern Railway,* 94 U.S. 164, 24 L. Ed. 97 (1876), the Court upheld a Wisconsin statute saying: ". . . Until Congress acts in reference to the regulations of this Company in interstate commerce, it is certainly within the power of Wisconsin to regulate its fares, etc., so far as they are of domestic concern. . . . But certainly until Congress undertakes to legislate for those who are without the state, Wisconsin may provide for those within, even though it may indirectly affect those without."

But in the case of *Wabash St. Louis Pacific Railway v. Illinois,* 118 U.S. 557 (1886), the Court did not follow its ruling in the *Peik* case but instead gave the commerce clause a nationalistic interpretation, saying: ". . . And it would be a very feeble and almost useless provision . . . if at every stage of the transportation of goods and chattels through the country, the State within whose limits a part of the transportation must be done could impose regulations concerning the price, compensation or taxation, or any other restrictive regulation interfering with or seriously embarrassing this commerce."

tive influence on American life. This was followed in 1890 by the Sherman Antitrust Act, and after the turn of the century, by the Pure Food and Drug Act, the Federal Trade Commission Act, and many others. These acts called upon the Court to interpret the commerce clause in the light of positive legislation by Congress in the field of interstate commerce. When the Court first dealt with this new legislation, it allowed but little scope to the power of Congress.[39] Often the Court resorted to the terms "direct," "substantial," "material," or "indirect" as a guide to the determination of what was and was not subject to the congressional power of regulating interstate commerce.[40]

---

[39] *United States v. E. C. Knight Co.*, 156 U.S. 1, 15 S. Ct. 249, 39 L. Ed. 325 (1895), where the Court drew a distinction between "direct" and "indirect" effects upon commerce, and held that the sugar trust did not violate the Sherman Antitrust Law, saying: ". . . Contracts, combinations or conspiracies to control domestic enterprise in manufacture, agriculture, mining, production in all its forms, or to raise or lower prices or wages, might unquestionably tend to restrain external as well as domestic trade, but the restraint would be an indirect result, however inevitable and whatever its extent . . ."

But compare this with *In re Debs*, 158 U.S. 564, 591, 15 S. Ct. 900, 39 L. Ed. 1092 (1895), where the Sherman Act was held to apply to labor union activities. The Court, using the nationalistic doctrine, said: ". . . The Constitution has not changed. The power is the same. But it operates to-day upon modes of interstate commerce unknown to the fathers, and it will operate with equal force upon any new modes of such commerce which the future may develop."

The Sherman Act was also held to apply to agreements between competitive railroads tending to restrain trade, and to corporations engaged in the same business but limiting competition in certain areas. See *United States v. Trans-Missouri Freight Association*, 166 U.S. 290, 17 S. Ct. 540, 41 L. Ed. 1007 (1897); *Addyston Pipe & Steel Co. v. United States*, 175 U.S. 211, 20 S. Ct. 96, 44 L. Ed. 136 (1899).

In *Swift & Co. v. United States*, 196 U.S. 375, 398, 25 S. Ct. 276, 49 L. Ed. 518 (1905), the Court, through Mr. Justice Holmes, in sustaining the exercise of the national power over intrastate activities of the beef trust, said that "commerce among the states is not a technical legal conception, but a practical one, drawn from the course of business."

[40] In *Shreveport Rate Cases*, 234 U.S. 342, 351, 34 S. Ct. 853, 58 L. Ed. 1341 (1914), the Court found federal intervention constitutionally authorized because of "matters having such a close and substantial relation to interstate

While the principles Marshall had announced in *Gibbons v. Ogden* were not openly repudiated, the mechanical applications of legal formulae to a dynamic national economy often produced conflicting judicial decisions, largely because they reflected the social and economic viewpoints of the judges.

In the case of *Champion v. Ames* [41] the Court upheld a federal law which forbade the shipment of lottery tickets in interstate commerce. The real purpose of the law was not the regulation of commerce but the control of gambling, a matter that was held to be within the sphere of the state police power. Yet, Mr. Justice Harlan, in commenting upon the supreme power of Congress in the field of interstate commerce, said:

> The power to regulate commerce among the several states is vested in Congress as absolutely as it would be in a single government. . . . If lottery traffic, *carried on through interstate commerce,* is a matter of which Congress may take cognizance and over which its power may be exerted, can it

---

traffic that the control is essential or appropriate to the security of that traffic, to the efficiency of the interstate service, and to the maintenance of the conditions under which interstate commerce may be conducted upon fair terms and without molestation or hindrance."

In *Santa Cruz Co. v. Labor Board,* 303 U.S. 453, 366, 367, 58 S. Ct. 656, 660, 82 L. Ed. 954 (1938), Chief Justice Hughes said: ". . . 'direct' has been contrasted with 'indirect,' and what is 'remote' or 'distant' with what is 'close and substantial.' Whatever terminology is used, the criterion is necessarily one of degree and must be so defined. This does not satisfy those who seek for mathematical or rigid formulas. But such formulas are not provided by the great concepts of the Constitution such as 'interstate commerce,' 'due process,' 'equal protection.' "

[41] *Champion v. Ames,* 188 U.S. 321, 23 S. Ct. 321, 67 L. Ed. 472 (1903); see also *Hipolite Egg Co. v. United States,* 220 U.S. 45, 31 S. Ct. 364, 55 L. Ed. 364 (1911), where the Court sustained the Pure Food and Drug Act without regard to the intent or purpose of Congress in enacting the law; in *Hoke v. United States,* 227 U.S. 308, 33 S. Ct. 281, 57 L. Ed. 523 (1913), the Court held the Mann Act constitutional, saying: "Our dual form of government has its perplexities, state and nation having different spheres of jurisdiction, as we have said; but it must be kept in mind that we are one people; and the powers reserved to the states and those conferred on the nation are adapted to be exercised, whether independently or concurrently, to promote the general welfare, material and moral."

be possible that it must tolerate the traffic, and simply regulate the manner in which it may be carried on?

Nevertheless, the Supreme Court, in *Hammer v. Dagenhart,* invalidated the first Child Labor Law. The law, in the Court's opinion, was not a regulation of interstate commerce but an outright regulation of production, and therefore it was void. Furthermore, the Court distinguished between *regulation* and *prohibition* of commerce. The power to regulate interstate commerce was limited to the *promotion,* not the prohibition of such commerce, except that Congress could prohibit the transportation in interstate commerce of goods in themselves objectionable or dangerous to the public welfare. In the judgment of the Court, products of child labor were harmless and their movement in commerce was also harmless. Said the Court:

> In our view the necessary effect of this act is, by means of a prohibition against the movement in interstate commerce of ordinary commercial commodities, to regulate the hours of children in factories and mines within the States, a purely state authority.[42]

The Court's decision in this case left the constitutional status of the federal police legislation uncertain and confused.[43]

---

[42] *Hammer v. Dagenhart,* 247 U.S. 251, 38 S. Ct. 529, 62 L. Ed. 1101 (1918). Mr. Justice Holmes, however, with the concurrence of three more dissenters, argued that ". . . It is not for this Court to pronounce when prohibition is necessary to regulation . . . to say that it is permissible as against strong drink but not as against the product of ruined lives."

[43] "The distinction made between things harmful in themselves and things merely producing harmful results lacked even metaphysical reality. Moreover, since 1903 the Court had repeatedly rejected the old Madisonian doctrine that Congress could regulate commerce but could not prohibit any phase of commerce outright. Finally, revival of the old issue of congressional purpose, emphatically rejected in *Champion v. Ames,* 188 U.S. 321, 23 S. Ct. 321, 67 L. Ed. 472 (1903), promised endless judicial complications and confusion, since it implied that the Court would inquire into the constitutionality of congressional purpose every time Congress enacted any regulation of commerce, however correct in form.

In the 1920's there seemed to be two streams of constitutional thought upon the issue of national power. The selection made by the Court did not seem to be based on any fixed constitutional principle as much as on the social and economic implication of the particular case.[44] The country, during the twenties, moved on through a period of gigantic industrial, commercial, and financial development. Advertising, now an important factor in national distribution, marketing, and merchandising, kept pace with the national prosperity and development.[45] There were but few effective controls upon the national economy. The dizzy whirl of frenzied finance, speculation, and promotion was edging the country closer to the brink of the abyss—the catastrophic economic collapse of October, 1929.

The New Deal legislation under President Franklin D. Roosevelt, after March 4, 1933, sought to establish unprecedented controls over banking, finance, labor, agriculture, and manufacturing. But the Supreme Court struck down most of these laws[46] in rapid order and so precipitated the

---

"In short, the Court, in *Hammer v. Dagenhart* broke sharply with the seemingly well-established liberal tradition, and returned to the spirit of strict construction and dual federalism." Kelly and Harbison, *op. cit.*, p. 590.

[44] Compare *Hammer v. Dagenhart*, 247 U.S. 251, 38 S. Ct. 529, 62 L. Ed. 1101 (1918), with *Brooks v. United States*, 267 U.S. 432, 45 S. Ct. 345, 69 L. Ed. 699 (1925); which sustained the *Motor Vehicle Theft Act of 1919* (59 *Stat.* 536, 18 *U.S.C.A.* 2311–2313); and *United States v. E. C. Knight Co.*, 156 U.S. 1, 15 S. Ct. 249, 39 L. Ed. 325 (1895), with *Bedford Cut Stone Co. v. Journeymen Stone Cutters' Association*, 274 U.S. 37, 47 S. Ct. 522, 71 L. Ed. 916 (1927), where the Court recognized the effect of production on interstate commerce.

[45] The increase in periodical advertising revenue from $528,000,000 in 1919 to $1,120,000,000 in 1929 strikingly illustrates the point.

[46] *Panama Refining Co. v. Ryan*, 293 U.S. 388, 55 S. Ct. 241, 79 L. Ed. 446 (1935); *Schechter v. United States*, 295 U.S. 495, 55 S. Ct. 837, 79 L. Ed. 1570 (1935). Here the Court held that: "When industries organize themselves on a national scale, making their relation to interstate commerce the dominant factor in their activities, how can it be maintained that their industrial labor relations constitute a forbidden field into which Congress may not enter when it is necessary to protect interstate commerce from the paralyz-

President's Court reorganization plan of 1936, the net result of which was to cause a majority of the Court to face about and to support re-enacted New Deal legislation. In April, 1937, the National Labor Relations Act was sustained in defiance of the ruling in *Carter v. Carter Coal Co.*, and in 1941, *Hammer v. Dagenhart* was formally overruled when the Fair Labor Standards Act of 1938 was upheld. A chastened reorganized Court now held:

> . . . the motive and purpose of the regulation of interstate commerce are matters for the legislative judgment upon the exercise of which the Constitution places no restrictions and over which the Courts are given no control.[47]

In another series of important decisions, the Court validated far-reaching federal controls upon agricultural produc-

---

ing consequences of industrial war? We have often said that interstate commerce itself is a practical conception. It is equally true that interferences with that commerce must be appraised by a judgment that does not ignore actual experience." *Louisville Bank v. Radford*, 295 U.S. 555, 55 S. Ct. 854, 79 L. Ed. 1593 (1935); *United States v. Butler*, 297 U.S. 1, 56 S. Ct. 312, 80 L. Ed. 477 (1936); *Carter v. Carter Coal Co.*, 298 U.S. 238, 56 S. Ct. 855, 80 L. Ed. 1160 (1936). Here the Court applied the *Schechter* case doctine in these words: "The only perceptible difference between that case and this is that in the *Schechter* case, the federal power was asserted with respect to commodities which had come to rest after their interstate transportation; while here, the case deals with commodities at rest before interstate commerce has begun. That difference is without significance. The federal regulatory power ceases when interstate commercial intercourse ends; and, correlatively, the power does not attach until interstate commercial intercourse begins."

[47] *United States v. Darby*, 312 U.S. 100, 105, 61 S. Ct. 451, 85 L. Ed. 609 (1941); see also *A. B. Kirchbaum v. Walling*, 316 U.S. 517, 62 S. Ct. 1116, 86 L. Ed. 1138 (1942), where building employees in the maintenance and operation of a loft building in which tenants produced garments for interstate commerce were held subject to the Fair Labor Standard Act because they were "necessary to production"; the Court applied this law to operation of oil-well drilling rigs in *Warren Bradshaw Co. v. Hall*, 317 U.S. 88, 63 S. Ct. 125 (1942); to night watchmen in a veneer plant in the case of *Walton v. Southern Packing Corp.*, 320 U.S. 540, 64 S. Ct. 320, 88 L. Ed. 298 (1944); and to porters, elevator operators, and watchmen in a New York office build ing in the case of *Borden Co. v. Bordella*, 325 U.S. 679, 65 S. Ct. 1223 (1945).

tion, and for all practical purposes thereby swept *United States v. Butler* into the discard.[48] The case of *Wickard v. Filburn*[49] sustained the federal power to regulate production not intended in any part for commerce but wholly for consumption on the farm. In a forceful opinion, Mr. Justice Jackson not only repudiated the old distinction between "direct" and "indirect" effects on commerce but also swept away the distinction between commerce and production as a constitutional touchstone. In the words of the Court:

> Once an economic measure of the reach of power granted to Congress in the Commerce Clause is accepted, questions of federal power cannot be decided simply by finding the activity in question to be "production" nor can consideration of its economic effects be foreclosed by calling them "indirect." . . . But even if appellant's activity be local and though it may not be regarded as commerce, it may still, whatever its nature, be reached by Congress if it exerts a substantial economic effect on interstate commerce and this irrespective of whether such effect is what might at some earlier time have been defined as "direct" or "indirect."

The reasoning of the Court in *Wickard v. Filburn* is particularly important in its application to the present and potential scope of federal regulations of advertising. The Court examined carefully the economics of the wheat industry and found that commerce among the states in wheat was "large and important"; that the wheat industry had been a problem

---

[48] *Mulford v. Smith,* 307 U.S. 38, 59 S. Ct. 648, 83 L. Ed. 1092 (1939); *United States v. Rock Royal Cooperative,* 307 U.S. 533, 59 S. Ct. 992, 83 L. Ed. 1446 (1939); *Hood v. United States,* 307 U.S. 588, 60 S. Ct., 111, 84 L. Ed. 492 (1939), where the Court held that since most of the milk sold eventually crossed state lines the local sales were the beginning of interstate commerce and hence subject to federal control. See also *United States v. Wrightwood Dairy,* 315 U.S. 110, 62 S. Ct. 523, 86 L. Ed. 726 (1942), where it was held that the price of milk sold wholly inside state lines and not commingled with interstate milk could be regulated by the federal government because of its effect on interstate commerce.

[49] 317 U.S. 111, 63 S. Ct. 82, 87 L. Ed. 122 (1942).

industry for many years: and that in the absence of regulation the price of wheat would be much affected by world conditions. After examining the effect of consumption of home-grown wheat on interstate commerce, the Court said:

> The maintenance by government regulation of a price for wheat undoubtedly can be accomplished as effectively by sustaining or increasing the demand as by limiting the supply. . . . One of the primary purposes of the Act in question was to increase the market price of wheat and to that end to limit the volume thereof that could effect the market. It can hardly be denied that a factor of such volume and variability as home-consumed wheat would have a substantial influence on price and market conditions. This may arise because being in marketable condition such wheat overhangs the market and if induced by rising prices tends to flow into the market and check price increases.

The willingness of the Court to recognize the impact of production and consumption on our national economy and welfare as a justification for federal regulation of industry, business, or agriculture warrants the belief that any Congressional attempt to regulate advertising by tying it in with the national purpose to combat either inflation or deflation would be sustained by the Courts. This, of course, is based on the premise that the Courts understand advertising and its role in our economy.

Advertising and Interstate Commerce

To what extent is there a judicial recognition of the magnitude and scope of advertising? An examination of the cases dealing with advertising may help provide the answer.

One of the early cases pertaining to advertising, albeit indirectly, was the oft-cited case of *International Text-Book Co. v. Pigg*,[50] where the Court readily conceded that the correspond-

[50] 217 U.S. 91, 30 S. Ct. 481, 54 L. Ed. 678 (1910).

ence school maintained by the plaintiff was a business "of a somewhat exceptional character." In other words, it dealt with intangibles, as does advertising, and required the Court to determine whether it was therefore in interstate commerce.

> The Court first described the business of the plaintiff, a Pennsylvania Corporation engaged in imparting instruction by correspondence; it pointed out this involved the solicitation of students in Kansas by local agents, who were also to collect and forward to the home office the tuition fees, and the systematic intercourse by correspondence between the company and its students and agents, wherever situated, and the transportation of the needful books, apparatus, and papers. The Court then said: "Intercourse of that kind, between parties in different states—particularly when it is in execution of a valid contract between them—is as much intercourse in the constitutional sense, as intercourse by means of the telegraph—'a new species of commerce,' to use the words of this court in *Pensacola Teleg. Co. v. Western U. Teleg. Co.*, 96 U.S. 1, 9, 24 L. Ed. 708, 710." [51]

The case of *Charles Ramsay Co. v. Associated Bill Posters of United States and Canada* [52] presented to the Court the old problem of "direct" or "incidental" effect on interstate commerce. Without delving too deeply into the problem of advertising, it overruled the lower court's contention that once the posters arrived at their destination the posting was a purely local service. The Court, without citing any authorities, held that the defendants were engaged in interstate commerce within the meaning of the Constitution and hence subject to the antitrust laws. Said the Court:

> Advertising by posters has become common, and in most of the larger cities and towns throughout this country and

[51] This decision was cited and applied in *Federal Trade Commission v. Civil Service Training Bureau, Inc.* 79 F. (2d) 113 (1935), the Court holding that a correspondence school selling a "service" rather than commodities was engaged in interstate commerce.

[52] 260 U.S. 501, 43 S. Ct. 167, 67 L. Ed. 368 (1922).

> Canada one or more local concerns follow the business of displaying them. Usually advertisers contract with a lithographer directly or through agents (solicitors), such as plaintiffs, for the manufacture or purchase of posters, and with the local billposter for displaying them. Often the lithographer does business in a different state from the advertiser and both operate in different states from those where most of the billboards are located. Some posters are prepared for the exclusive use of an advertiser and some ("stock" or "sample" ones) for general use. Nearly all are put out by six or eight lithographers.
>
> Plaintiffs were solicitors of advertising for customers in many States. They prepared, designed, purchased and sold posters and caused them to be displayed by local operators in many cities and towns throughout the United States and Canada. They contracted with their customers and received pay for the entire service of preparing, designing, purchasing and posting the advertisements and were engaged in interstate commerce.

Here is to be seen the first faint glimmer of recognition of advertising. Without such an understanding and full appraisal it will be impossible to harness or regulate this great force and integrate it into our social and economic structure to serve the national interest.

The Supreme Court was confronted squarely with the problem of advertising contracts between agencies and publications in the case of *Blumenstock Bros. Advertising Agency v. Curtis Pub. Co.*[53] This case has been cited so often for and against some problem related to advertising[54] that a detailed discussion of the case is in order.

---

[53] 252 U.S. 436, 40 S. Ct. 385, 64 L. Ed. 649 (1920).

[54] See *Indiana Farmer's Guide Pub. Co. v. Prairie Farmer Pub. Co.*, 293 U.S. 268, 55 S. Ct. 182, 79 L. Ed. 356 (1934), where the Court held: "The business that is here alleged to have been damaged is the publication and circulation of these farm papers. That business includes the obtaining of advertising, the transportation between States of electrotypes sent respectively to petitioner and respondents by their customers to be used in setting up advertisements, and the transportation of substantial quantities of the papers

The suit was brought by an advertising agency against the Curtis Publishing Company to recover treble damages under section 7 of the Sherman Antitrust Act. The plaintiff was a Missouri corporation and the defendant a Pennsylvania corporation. The complaint was dismissed in the lower court for want of jurisdiction and was brought before the Supreme Court on a writ of error. After an analysis of the complaint [55]

---

in interstate commerce. Advertising at compensatory rates is an essential element. The opinion in *Blumenstock Bros. Advertising Agency v. Curtis Pub. Co., supra,* assumed that a publishing business such as that now under consideration would amount to interstate commerce. There is no ground for the contention that the evidence in this case is not sufficient to go to the jury on the question of interstate commerce."

In *United States v. South Eastern Underwriter's Assn.*, 322 U.S. 533, 64 S. Ct. 1162, 88 L. Ed. 1440 (1943), Mr. Justice Stone, in a dissenting opinion, cited the *Blumenstock* case as follows: "But it is quite another matter to say that the contracts are themselves interstate commerce or that restraints in competition as to their terms or conditions are within the Sherman Act, in the absence of a showing that the purpose or effect is to restrain competition in the marketing of the goods or services to which the contracts relate."

In *Sunbeam Corp. v. Wentling*, 185 F. (2d) 903 (1951), the Court held that the *Blumenstock* case was no longer authoritative.

[55] The client, agency, and media relationship, clearly set forth in the complaint, justify a lengthy quotation: "That the plaintiff is engaged at Chicago in conducting an advertising agency. That when customers or principals desire to place advertisements in the magazines and periodicals of the trade they make plaintiff their agent, and plaintiff contracts with the defendant and other publishers and distributors of magazines; that plaintiff had many customers for/with whom it placed advertisements in the periodicals published and distributed by the defendant and in other periodicals of other publishers, all of which were distributed throughout the United States and the several states thereof; that the defendant was the owner and publisher of three periodicals sold and distributed throughout the United States known as the Saturday Evening Post, the Ladies' Home Journal, and the Country Gentleman; that the business of the defendant in publishing, selling, and distributing said periodicals was interstate commerce. The character of each of the several publications is described, and a large circulation is attributed to each of them; and it is stated that in publishing and distributing said periodicals defendant held itself out as desirous of taking, receiving, printing, publishing, and distributing throughout the United States its publications and advertisements to persons, firms, and corporations concerning their business and occupation; that in the course of the business the defendant dealt with the plaintiff and other advertising agencies; that the defendant in the regular course of its business dealt with not only advertisers, but with advertising agencies such as the plaintiff, and it is alleged that such dealings were transactions of interstate commerce, and that

the Court was called upon to determine whether the dealings between the parties were transactions in interstate commerce. After paying its respect to *Gibbons v. Ogden*, the Court said:

---

the business of editing, publishing and distributing throughout the United States the advertising matter contained in said publications, pursuant to contracts made with its customers and advertising agencies was interstate commerce; that such commerce is dependent for its operation and growth upon advertising facilities offered by magazines and periodicals such as those of the defendant, and that such publications constitute the chief method of presenting to the buying public the articles held out for sale; that the advertising facilities were necessary to dealers, merchants, and manufacturers in order to bring their products to the notice and attention of purchasers; that the defendant's periodicals, particularly 'The Saturday Evening Post,' have an important position among such publications, and are largely read throughout the United States; that 'The Saturday Evening Post' is the most necessary of such advertising mediums to the customers of the plaintiff; that the defendant's periodicals, together with certain other magazines, periodicals and publications owned by persons other than the defendant, had, to a certain extent, exclusive control of a certain field of advertising; that the magazines and other publications which control and do all the advertising business of the field in question are few in number; that for the advertising of goods and merchandise offered for sale in commerce there were no adequate facilities except those offered by the defendant and other publishers of similar magazines; that the defendant was desirous of using its preponderant position in this special field of advertising as a means of acquiring for itself and its publications, especially for 'The Saturday Evening Post,' a monopoly of the publication and distribution of advertising matter in this restricted field of advertising throughout the United States in violation of the Anti-Trust Act that the defendant refused without any reasonable cause to accept proper and ordinary advertising matter or copy offered in the usual way to the defendant by the plaintiff and other advertising agencies unless the plaintiff, and other advertising agencies, would agree to allow the defendant to increase its preponderance in said advertising field by permitting it to control and limit and reduce, at the will of the defendant, the amount of advertising given by the plaintiff and other advertising agencies to the owners and publishers of other magazines, journals, periodicals, and other publications aforesaid, which were competing with the defendant in the field of advertising mentioned and described; that by reason of the illegal and wrongful acts, done by the defendant in pursuance of its attempt and scheme to create a monopoly for its own benefit in, and to monopolize the advertising business, plaintiff lost the business of its customers for whom it had been acting as agent in placing of advertisements with defendant's and other publications, and was prevented from making further contracts for the placing of advertising matter in publications of the defendant, and in consequence thereof, in any other publication of a like or similar character, to the damage of the plaintiff in the sum of $25,000." 252 U.S. 436, 437, 40 S. Ct. 385, 64 L. Ed. 649 (1920).

In the present case, treating the allegations of the complaint as true, the subject-matter dealt with was the making of contracts for the insertion of advertising matter in certain periodicals belonging to the defendant. It may be conceded that the circulation and distribution of such publications throughout the country would amount to interstate commerce, but the circulation of these periodicals did not depend upon or have any direct relation to the advertising contracts which the plaintiff offered and the defendant refused to receive except upon the terms stated in the declaration. The advertising contracts did not involve any movement of goods or merchandise in interstate commerce, or any transmission of intelligence in such commerce.

This case is wholly unlike *International Text-Book Co. v. Pigg,* 217 U.S. 91, 30 Sup. Ct. 481, 54 L. Ed. 678, 27 L.R.A. (N.S.) 493, 18 Ann. Cas. 1103, wherein there was a continuous interstate traffic in text-books and apparatus for a course of study pursued by means of correspondence, and the movements in interstate commerce were held to bring the subject-matter within the domain of federal control, and to exempt it from the burden imposed by state legislation. This case is more . . . within that line of cases in which we have held that policies of insurance are not articles of commerce, and that the making of such contracts is a mere incident of commercial intercourse. *Paul v. Virginia,* 8 Wall. 168, 19 L. Ed. 357; *Hooper v. California,* 155 U.S. 648, 15 Sup. Ct. 207, 39 L. Ed. 297; *N. Y. Life Ins. Co. v. Deer Lodge County,* 231 U.S. 495, 34 Sup. Ct. 167, 58 L. Ed. 332.

The Court closed its eyes to the realities of advertising practice in reaching this conclusion. An advertising agency does not just place a contract with a publication and then stop further activity. The contract must be followed up by mailing to the publication the mechanical requirements, such as copy, electrotypes, or photoengravings; and the publication must accept the contract and mail to the agency "proofs" of the advertisement and "checking" copies of the magazine. After publication the magazine is sold nationally, and the products advertised are sold and bought on a national scale. If such dealings are not interstate commerce, it is difficult to conceive what could constitute such commerce. As for the contention that the circulation of the periodicals did not depend or have any direct relation to advertising contracts, it is sufficient to point to what has been stated heretofore that it has been proved that the best publications cannot exist without advertising revenue.

The more liberal interpretation of the commerce clause since 1937 has reflected itself in the judicial attitude toward advertising as being "in commerce." The Federal Trade Commission was given greater latitude, and a stricter yardstick was applied to truth in advertising.

The most realistic judicial approach to advertising and its role in our economy is to be found in the case of *Ford Motor Company v. Federal Trade Commission.*[56] It was urged upon the court that the 6 per cent plan and the advertising relate solely to the financing of payments on time sales of cars sold by its dealers to their customers and are matters with which the Ford Motor Company was not concerned; and that sales by dealers of cars to customers are purely intrastate transactions. It became important therefore to determine just what part advertising plays in selling and distribution. The Court, in ruling that the transaction constituted interstate commerce, said:

> Advertising goes hand in hand with volume of production and retail distribution. It operates to increase the demand for and availability of goods and to develop quickly consumers' acceptance of the manufactured products. Expressed another way, it breaks down consumers' resistance, creates consumers' acceptance, and develops consumers' demand. . . . All of those things which stimulate or decrease the flow of commerce, although not directly in its stream, are essential adjuncts thereto and the Congress has power to confer on

[56] 120 F. (2d) 175 (1941). Petition for certiorari denied in 314 U.S. 668, 62 S. Ct. 130 (1941).

the Federal Trade Commission their regulation (*Stafford v. Wallace*, 258 U.S. 495, 516).

The use of advertising as an aid to the production and distribution of goods has been recognized so long as to require only passing notice. The economy of mass production is just as well known and the effects of advertising may be described as mass selling without which distribution would be lessened and a fortiori production correspondingly decreased. The present advertisement of the method for financing the purchase of petitioner's cars on credit was an integral part of their production and distribution.

The sale on credit of petitioner's cars by its local dealers, when separately considered, may be intrastate in character but when the activities of petitioner's local agencies are weighed in the light of their relationship to the petitioner, and its financing sales of cars, it is at once apparent that there is such a close and substantial relationship to interstate commerce that the control of such activities is appropriate to its protection.

When the Supreme Court in the case of *United States v. South Eastern Underwriters Association* [57] overturned precedents maintained for 75 years to the effect that insurance was not interstate commerce, it based its decision on a realistic appreciation of the growth and development of the insurance business.

The modern insurance business holds a commanding position in the trade and commerce of our Nation. Built upon the sale of contracts of indemnity, it has become one of the largest and most important branches of commerce. Its total assets exceed $37,000,000,000, or the approximate equivalent of the value of all farm lands and buildings in the United States. Its annual premium receipts exceed $6,000,000,000, more than the average annual revenue receipts of the United States Government during the last decade. Included in the labor force of insurance are 524,000 experienced workers, almost as many as seek their livings in coal mining or auto-

[57] 322 U.S. 533, 64 S. Ct. 1162, 88 L. Ed. 1440 (1944).

> mobile manufacturing. Perhaps no modern commercial enterprise directly affects so many persons in all walks of life as does the insurance business. Insurance touches the home, the family, and the occupation or the business of almost every person in the United States.
>
> This business is not separated into 48 distinct territorial compartments which function in isolation from each other. Interrelationship, interdependence, and integration of activities in all the states in which they operate are practical aspects of the insurance companies' methods of doing business. A large share of the insurance business is concentrated in a comparatively few companies located, for the most part, in the financial centers of the East.

The growth of advertising since the turn of the century has been depicted in earlier chapters. All that the Court said about the effects of insurance on the home, the family, and the business or occupations of all of us is equally applicable to advertising. It was not surprising, therefore, when the District Court in the *Ford* case overturned the decision in the *Blumenstock* case and held that advertising contracts are per se interstate commerce.

In the case of *Sunbeam Corporation v. Wentling,*[58] the Court summed up its present position on this subject as follows:

> Some at least of the defendant's business is interstate commerce. That point seems to us abundantly clear, but since the parties seemed to have some dispute about it we will stop on it for a moment. First, the purchase of advertising space in a publication published in another state and of national circulation is interstate commerce. . . . To the extent that *Blumenstock Bros. Advertising Agency v. Curtis Publishing Co.*, 1920, 252 U.S. 436, 40 S. Ct. 385, 64 L. Ed. 649, can be construed as holding to the contrary we think it is no longer authoritative in the light of more recent cases.

---

[58] 185 F. (2d) 903 (1951).

The preceding pages have shown in bare outline that the history of the federal system since 1789 is, to a great degree, the history of the constantly expanding importance and authority of the national government under the Constitution. The trend in the cases cited has indicated that the original provisions of the Constitution have been found adequate to cope with the enormous increase in interstate commerce transactions, including advertising. Thus, a broadened interpretation of the Constitution has made it possible for the nation to cope with vital social and economic problems, which the framers of the Constitution could not possibly have foreseen.

Chapter 5

ADVERTISING AND THE MAINTENANCE OF COMPETITION–THE FEDERAL TRADE COMMISSION

Legislative History

Of all federal regulatory bodies concerned with advertising, the Federal Trade Commission (FTC) has the widest jurisdiction. The Federal Communications Commission, the Securities and Exchange Commission, the Alcohol Tax Unit, the Post Office Department, and others, of which more will be said later, are restricted respectively to radio and television, stocks and securities, alcoholic beverages, and the mails. But the Federal Trade Commission is concerned with advertising in general and is not limited to any particular medium, commodity, or service. The jurisdiction of the Federal Trade Commission, which will be discussed in some detail, covers any advertising practice that is unfair or deceptive and is in commerce. Though other regulatory agencies concern themselves with advertising, they are limited in the scope of their operation. Therefore, the principal role of the federal government in the regulation of advertising is played by the Federal Trade Commission. To understand the role is to appreciate the performer.

Legislation that is corrective or regulatory by nature is predicated upon the belief that some practice or situation is in need of correction or regulation. Judges have long felt that their function in the government required them to question the constitutional propriety of legislation and then, having established the propriety, to interpret and apply the legislation in the light of the legislature's intentions. Thus, the early judicial history of any novel enactment will reflect the judiciary's opinion as to what Congress intended. The Federal Trade Commission Act is, on its face, a corrective and regulatory measure; and to understand its purposes, we must know not only the history of the enactment but also the judicial interpretation of the congressional intention.

The background of the Federal Trade Commission, in the light of its present activities, is paradoxical. Today, one of the Commission's principal activities is the regulation of advertising. Originally, however, the evil to be corrected by its enactment was "that competition which is resorted to for the purpose of destroying competition, of eliminating a competitor, and of introducing monopoly." [1] It is clear that in 1914 the interest of the consumer, for purposes of federal regulation, was deemed limited to the continuance of free, competitive enterprise. Since the preceding decades were concerned with monopoly as the principal problem confronting the American economy, we can see why the protection of the consumer from deception was not considered essential.

Unfettered by legal restraints and spurred by industrialization, American business and industry developed rapidly in the years following the Civil War. Between 1850 and 1880, invested capital increased from $533 million to $2.8 billion, or 424 per cent.[2] This increase was marked by insistent and successful efforts among entrepreneurs toward combination and consolidation, sometimes approaching monopoly. Railroad rebate practices and corporate price restraints imposed serious burdens on unorganized competitors and consumers. Although

---

[1] *Congressional Record*, 63d Cong., 2d Sess. (1914), Vol. LI, Part 11, p. 11104.

[2] Louis M. Hacker, *The Triumph of American Capitalism* (New York: Simon & Schuster, Inc., 1940), p. 437.

the competitor had common law rights of action based on diversion of patronage because of "unfair" competition, he was required to prove damages.[3]

In addition to difficulties entailed in meeting the burden of proof, the expense involved in litigation prevented effective legal action by a small business against the organized and wealthy forces of the "trust." Nor was the consumer in a better position. He had a right to sue for fraud; but since the individual consumer had too little at stake to make litigation worth while and not enough money to hire expensive legal talent to support the litigation, his remedies also were of little value.

In the absence of public or private legal restraints, business methods became so unsavory in the last quarter of the nineteenth century that monopoly was thought to be inevitable. The business world was recognized as being a "Darwinian jungle" with only the strongest surviving, but it was soon apparent that a test of survival-fitness produced commercial ruthlessness and monopoly rather than productive efficiency. As a result, the public became apprehensive and alarmed, expressing fear at the dangerous economic and social tendencies of the business combines. In 1878 the New York Chamber of Commerce demanded an investigation of railway abuses, and by 1890 six states had passed antitrust laws. But the great diversity in state laws and their inapplicability to interstate transactions made state regulation ineffective. One result of this was a marked similarity between Republican and Democratic platforms in 1888, both opposing "all combinations of capital, organized trusts or otherwise, to control arbitrarily the condition of trade." [4]

---

[3] *American Washboard Co. v. Saginaw Manufacturing Co.*, 103 Fed. 201 (1900).

[4] T. H. McKee, *The National Convention and Platforms of All Political Parties*, 1789–1904 (Baltimore: Lord Baltimore Press, 1906), p. 241.

In response to political and economic agitation Congress enacted the Sherman Antitrust Law of 1890.[5] The Sherman Act, as written, was comprehensive and tough; and it was hoped at the time that a remedy had been found to stop the wave of monopolistic control.[6] However, only a few years passed before it was realized that the Sherman Act fell short of its purpose. This failure has been attributed to:

> 1) the discouragement of the Department of Justice over the results of its efforts to enforce the law, and therefore its failure to enforce it with sufficient energy and persistence; 2) the failure of the courts to understand the enormous damage that could and did result to the public interest from the strangulation of normal business by great combinations, and the fear of the results of enforcement (*United States v. U. S. Steel Corporation*, 251 U.S. 417, 40 Sup. Ct. 293, 64 L. Ed. 343 (1920); and lastly, the ability through legal skill of defendant's counsel and the great resources at hand to befog cases and extend records to such a degree that juries were bewildered.[7]

The Sherman Act lost much of its effectiveness through judicial construction when the Supreme Court held that only "unreasonable" restraint of trade and competition was proscribed,[8] and that mere "bigness" did not constitute a prohibited monopoly, even when the corporation involved was

---

[5] Act of July 2, 1890, 26 Stat. 209 (1890), 15 *U.S.C.A.* Sec. 1 (1934).

[6] The Sherman Act was the first regulation of commercial activities to rest on the commerce clause of the Constitution. Prior to 1890 the commerce clause had been confined almost exclusively to railroads. Myron W. Watkins, *Public Regulation of Competitive Practices*, 3d ed. (New York: National Industrial Conference Board, 1940), chaps. ii and iii. See also Alfred H. Kelly and Winifred A. Harbison, *The American Constitution* (New York: W. W. Norton & Co., 1948), p. 548.

[7] Huston Thompson, "Highlights in the Evolution of the Federal Trade Commission," 3 *George Washington Law Review* (1940), p. 258.

[8] *Standard Oil Co. v. United States,* 221 U.S. 1, 31 S. Ct. 502, 55 L. Ed. 619 (1911); *United States v. American Tobacco Co.*, 221 U.S. 109, 31 S. Ct. 632, 55 L. Ed. 663 (1911).

capitalized at $110 million and its cash on hand exceeded the total capitalization of its nearest competitor.[9]

Even before these important decisions, business combinations had become great threats; and in the hope of investigating and publicizing the organization and conduct of these combinations, the Bureau of Corporations, as a part of the Department of Commerce and Labor, was established in 1903. It was hoped by President Theodore Roosevelt that the publicity resulting from these investigations would be in itself remedial so as to cure the disease and permit and enable the making of appropriate recommendations to Congress. However, this proved to be a vain hope.

The inability of the Bureau of Corporations to curb combinations, and the setbacks received by the Sherman Act in the steel, oil, and tobacco cases, facilitated continuing business abuses. The reaction of these abuses was inevitable, and once again both the Republican and Democratic parties in the 1912 campaign condemned the growth of monopoly and called for new legislation. In 1913, when the Democrats and Woodrow Wilson came into office, there were two schools of thought on the relationship of business to government and to the public welfare. One school maintained that business combinations should be permitted to incorporate under a federal act, which would control them. The other school, to which Wilson adhered, believed that federal legalization of combinations would result eventually in control of the government by the combinations. This group maintained, therefore, that the only solution was legislation which would stop combinations at their inception rather than permit trusts to form, as they did in spite of the Sherman Act, before the government could intervene.

---

[9] *United States v. United States Steel Corporation,* 251 U.S. 417, 40 S. Ct. 293, 64 L. Ed. 343 (1920).

In response to public demand, particularly by small business, President Wilson recommended to Congress the creation of an Interstate Trade Commission.[10] The problem facing the Congress in its deliberation about the proposed legislation was principally how to nip monopolistic organizations in the bud. Therefore, rather than being punitive in nature as in the case of the Sherman Act, the new legislation, to be effective, was to be primarily preventive—in the nature of a "prophylactic" measure.[11] The purpose of the bill, as reported to the Congress, was to stop "unfair competition" before such practices became illegal within the proscriptions of the Sherman Act.[12]

Congress was convinced that the "rule of reason," created by the Supreme Court in applying the Sherman Act, represented an assumption by the judiciary of the legislative prerogatives of Congress. The "rule of reason," it was felt, meant that the courts would undertake to define the business practices or market policies that made a trust permissible or not. It was not the intention of Congress to permit the courts to exercise such a lawmaking power.[13]

The principal point of disagreement in Congress was the meaning of "unfair competition." Some Congressmen believed that the term was limited to monopoly and to restraint of trade and practices which had been recognized as deceptive and fraudulent prior to 1914. As a matter of fact, there were almost as many views as to the meaning of "unfair competition" as there were members of Congress participating in the

---

[10] The President stressed the need for the commission as an instrumentality where the process of the courts or extralegal forces of correction were inadequate to cope with the situation. *Congressional Record,* 63d Cong., 1st Sess. (1913), Vol. LI, pp. 1962–64.

[11] *Federal Trade Commission v. Gratz et al.,* 253 U.S. 421, 426, 40 S. Ct. 572, 64 L. Ed. 993 (1920).

[12] *Congressional Record,* 63d Cong., 2d Sess. (1914), Vol. LI, p. 11455.

[13] *Senate Report 1326,* 63d Cong., 3d Sess. (1914).

debates. The following indicates the variety of meanings expressed in the debates: [14]

1. Every act of passing off one's business or goods for another's.
2. All methods of competition tending to restraint of trade or monopoly which have been forbidden by the Sherman Law.
3. Substantially all violations of the antitrust laws, including even wrongs arising from interlocking directorates and allied incorporate directorships.
4. All unfair methods of stifling competition.
5. All other acts which the "commission . . . decides . . . may lead to monopoly or restraint of trade" though not now forbidden by the Sherman Act.
6. All other acts affecting a competitor for which "a remedy lies either at law or in equity."
7. All other acts which either affect a competitor and are "against public morals," or in anyway interfere with economic "efficiency," though heretofore quite lawful and not forbidden by the Sherman law or by any other law.
8. All other acts comprehended within the meaning which "unfair competition" has today in common parlance and in literature.

In view of the variety of meanings assigned to the term "unfair competition," it is clear that Congress was coping with an evil that could not be defined satisfactorily. Enumeration of the practices to be acted against was impracticable since business always could devise new methods of competition. On the other hand, to avoid a restrictive interpretation based on the limits of the common law, it was decided to substitute "unfair methods of competition" for "unfair competition." Thus changed, the bill was passed in 1914 and the Federal Trade Commission was organized early in the following year.

---

[14] G. H. Montague, "Unfair Methods of Competition," 25 *Yale Law Journal* (1915), pp. 20, 29–30.

As established by statute, the Federal Trade Commission was a body of five commissioners holding office for seven years but with their terms so arranged that only one would end in any year. The Commission absorbed the personnel and functions of the Bureau of Corporations and was given broad investigatory powers. On application from the Attorney General, or on its own initiative, the Commission could investigate the effectiveness of antitrust decrees, and upon request by a court act as a master in chancery in recommending the frame of new decrees after successful prosecution.

The Commission also shared with the Department of Justice responsibility for enforcing the four specific prohibitions of the Clayton Act of 1914, a companion piece to the Federal Trade Commission Act and an amendment to the Sherman Law. Section 2 of the Clayton Act forbade price discrimination among purchasers where the effect "may be to substantially lessen competition or tend to create a monopoly in any line of commerce," except for discrimination on account of difference in grade, quality or quantity, difference in transportation costs or "in good faith to meet competition." Section 3 outlawed exclusive dealing arrangements or tying contracts and price concessions where the effect "may be to substantially lessen competition or tend to create a monopoly in any line of commerce." Section 7 forbade intercorporate stock acquisitions, except among railroads, where the effect "may be to substantially lessen competition" between the corporation concerned or tend to create a monopoly within any line of commerce. Section 8 of the Clayton Act prohibited interlocking directorates among banks with over $5 million in capital or among competing industrial corporations with over $1 million in capital.

It is to be observed that the Commission came into being largely as a protest against nefarious trade practices grouped under the headings of monopoly, restraints of trade, and practices that were fraudulent prior to 1914. A reading of the congressional debates leads to the conclusion that the Congress was concerned with the maintenance of competition and the preservation of small, unorganized businesses. Nowhere in the debates is there mention of advertising. Montague's list of the various meanings assigned to the term "unfair competition" by the legislators does not include advertising, except perhaps indirectly, as in the case of "passing off." But, even in that situation, the primary consideration was the protection of the competitor. It would seem that so long as free competition was maintained the consumer's interest was protected. Strictly interpreted, it follows that a deceptive practice carried on by all competitors and, therefore, not damaging to competition would be permissible even though the consumer was deceived and misled, no matter from whom he purchased a product. How then did the Federal Trade Commission become concerned with advertising and the protection of the consumer? An analysis of Commission cases will provide the answer.

"Unfair Methods of Competition in Commerce"

The principal difficulty confronting the Commission in its formative years was that it had to operate under a general and broad mandate—the control of "unfair methods of competition." Though generality and adaptability in a legislative provision may be desirable because it is broad enough to close loopholes for escape and not too narrow so as to work injury to legitimate purposes, a lack of particularity also may be a weakness. General standards are a source of legislative strength only if given flexible interpretation. But the generality of Section 5 of the Federal Trade Commission Act in formulating the legal and regulatory powers of the Commission reflected the confusion of the legislators, rather than a workable statement of policy. Because of such confusion in the meaning of "unfair methods of competition," the attempts of the Commission in its early years to derive a formula for its activities were frustrated by the judiciary.[15]

Under the original Act, the Commission was required to secure an enforcement order from a Circuit Court when a corporation or person refused to accede to a cease and desist order of the Commission. In addition, the corporation or person could protest an order from the Commission by a petition to review in a Circuit Court. The first case in which the Commission, as a party, had its authority tested in a Circuit Court, followed the latter procedure.[16] The case involved an order by the Commission directing Sears, Roebuck (1) to stop advertising, in its catalog distributed in interstate commerce, that it could sell sugar at lower prices than its competitors because of large purchases and quick turnover; (2) to stop selling or offering to sell sugar below cost; (3) to stop advertising that competitors did not deal fairly with consumers; (4) to stop advertising that it had a representative in Japan who supervised the picking of choice teas, when such was not the case; and (5) to stop advertising that it purchased the coffee it sold from the best plantations in the world.

Sears, Roebuck, petitioning to review the FTC's order, argued that it was invalid for these reasons: (1) the petitioner had discontinued the practices complained of and had no intention of resuming them; (2) the Act was void because of indefiniteness, and unconstitutional because of the delegation of legislative power to the Commission; and (3) even if the Act were constitutional, it was not infringed by petitioner's practices. In meeting these arguments, the court pointed out that the cessation of the practices by the peti-

---

[15] M. W. Watkins, "An Appraisal of the Work of the Federal Trade Commission," 32 *Columbia Law Review* (February, 1932), pp. 272–89.

[16] *Sears, Roebuck & Co. v. Federal Trade Commission*, 258 Fed. 307 (1919).

tioner did not preclude the order, for there was no assurance other than statements by the petitioner that the practices would not be resumed if the Commission stopped its proceedings. But the more important arguments regarding lack of definite standards, unconstitutionality because of improper delegation of the legislative power, and denial that the petitioner's practices were "unfair methods of competition," presented a somewhat more difficult problem. The court made the point that "unfair methods of competition" is no more indefinite than "due process of law" or other legislative phrases of a similarly broad nature. Although the court's holding that "unfair methods of competition" was not too indefinite might seem a total victory for the Commission, this impression was quickly dissipated by the court when it said: "This statute is remedial, and orders to desist are civil . . . thus leaving the *courts* free to condemn new and ingenious ways that were unknown when the statutes were enacted." [17] Though the court pointed out that the Commission, representing the government as *parens patriae,* was to exercise its common sense in stopping trade practices injurious to competition, the point was also made that the Commission's orders were merely provisional and subject to review by the courts. It is to be observed that this case, which was the first review of a Commission order by a Circuit Court, dealt with advertising; and even though the Commission's order was substantially affirmed, the result of the case was a diminution of the Commission's powers.

The case is important for three reasons. First, the constitutionality of the Act was sustained. Second, the court held, in effect, that since the Commission's order was subject to judicial review the problem of determining what constituted "unfair methods of competition" was for the courts

---

[17] 258 Fed. at 311. Italics supplied.

and not the Commission. Third, the representations made by the petitioner were enjoined because it had the capacity or tendency to injure or discredit competitors. This would seem to indicate that deceptive advertising was subject to control only where competition was injured; and in the absence of such injury to competition, mere deception of the consuming public was not enough to support a proceeding by the Commission. A decision which, on the one hand, sustained the order and, on the other, reserved the final power for the courts was obviously confusing as to the Commission's standing in the courts. However, this confusion was short-lived, for in 1920, in its first appearance before the Supreme Court, the Commission's activities were limited severely.

Federal Trade Commission v. Gratz et al.[18] concerned a petition to review an order of the Commission directing Gratz to refrain from compelling the purchase of bagging as a prerequisite to the purchase of cotton. The Circuit Court had annulled the Commission's order, and the Supreme Court affirmed the judgment of the lower court. In discussing the condemnation by the Commission of Gratz's practices as an "unfair method of competition," the Court, speaking through Mr. Justice McReynolds, said:

> The words "unfair methods of competition" are not defined by the statute and their exact meaning is in dispute. *It is for the courts, not the commission,* ultimately to determine as a matter of law what they include. They are clearly inapplicable to practices never heretofore regarded as opposed to good morals because characterized by deception, bad faith, fraud or oppression, or as against public policy because of their dangerous tendency unduly to hinder competition or create monopoly.[19]

By declaring that the determination of an "unfair method of competition" was for the courts and that the courts re-

[18] 253 U.S. 421, 40 S. Ct. 572, 64 L. Ed. 993 (1920).
[19] 253 U.S. at 428 (1920). Italics supplied.

stricted the term so as to include only monopolistic practices or pre-1914 frauds, the Supreme Court nullified the breadth of the legislative standard in the Act and its capacity for development. In addition, the judgment of the court was held to be superior to that of an expert and highly specialized administrative tribunal. Though the *Gratz* case was not concerned with advertising directly, it seemed to suggest that advertising practices could not be regulated except where there was a question of utilizing advertising to further a monopoly or combination.

> All questions of monopoly or combination being out of the way, a private merchant, acting with entire good faith, may properly refuse to sell, except in conjunction, such closely associated articles as ties and bagging.

The *Gratz* case, while stripping the Federal Trade Commission of its essential function, the power to determine what was an "unfair method of competition," held out some hope for the Commission. The dissenting opinion of Mr. Justice Brandeis was a portent of things to come.[20] In distinguishing between "acts" of unfair competition, within the terms of the Sherman Law, and "methods" of unfair competition Brandeis pointed out that:

> . . . it is necessary to bear in mind the nature of the proceeding under review. The proceeding is not punitive. The complaint is not made with a view to subjecting the respondents to any form of punishment. . . . The proceeding is strictly a preventative measure taken in the interest of the general public. And what it is brought to prevent is not the commission of *acts* of unfair competition, but the pursuit of unfair *methods*.[21]

Although the majority opinion declared "unfair methods of competition" to be a matter of law, Mr. Justice Brandeis

[20] *Federal Trade Commission v. Algoma Lumber Co.*, 291 U.S. 67, 54 S. Ct. 315 78 L. Ed. 655 (1934), which will be discussed in detail.

[21] 253 U.S. at 432. Italics supplied.

made the point clear that, for practical purposes, "unfair methods of competition" must be a matter of fact. Since Congress refused to define what methods are unfair, and since Congress also established a Commission to correct such unfair methods, then the Act left the determination to the Commission and not the courts.[22] To continue in the words of Brandeis:

> Experience with existing laws had taught that definition being necessarily rigid, would prove embarrassing, and, if rigorously applied, might involve great hardships. Methods of competition which would be unfair in one industry, under certain circumstances, might, when adopted in another industry, or even in the same industry under different circumstances, be entirely unobjectionable. Furthermore, an enumeration, however comprehensive, of existing methods of unfair competition must necessarily soon prove incomplete, as with new conditions constantly arising novel unfair methods would be devised and developed.

The majority opinion, limiting "unfair methods of competition" to monopolistic practices, seemed to preclude the inclusion of newly devised competitive practices, such as advertising. In addition, if determination of "unfair methods of competition" was a matter of law, Section 5 of the Federal Trade Commission Act, which in part provided that the findings of the Commission as to the facts, if supported by testimony, shall be conclusive, had no significance. But if certain advertising practices were ever to come within the meaning of "unfair methods of competition," the Commission had to establish its authority as a fact-finding agency and on that basis show conclusively that such practices were unfair.

The hostility shown the Commission by the courts is demonstrated by the fact that of the first five orders of the

[22] Senate Committee on Interstate Commerce, *Senate Report* 597, 63d Cong., 2d Sess. (1914), p. 13.

Commission reviewed by the Circuit Courts, four were set aside.[23] A further demonstration of the Commission's frustration by the judiciary is found in an examination of the Commission's record before the Supreme Court. In the eight cases involving the Commission which were determined from 1920 to 1924 by the Supreme Court, the Commission was victorious in only three.[24] The *Gratz* case, as already mentioned, limited the term "unfair methods of competition" to include only monopolistic, price-restraining, or such other practices as were fraudulent prior to 1914. The *Curtis Publishing Co.* case, concerning the refusal of the respondent to sell its publications to newsdealers unless they stopped handling the publications of certain competitors, relied on the *Gratz* decision; and as Mr. Chief Justice Taft pointed out in his "doubting" opinion, the Court ignored the obvious intention of Congress that the Commission be the fact-finding body.[25] In the *Sinclair* case, the Commission sought to restrain the practice of leasing gasoline tanks on the condition that they be used only for gasoline supplied by the lessor.

---

[23] These four cases were *Federal Trade Commission v. Gratz,* 258 Fed. 314 (1919), the affirming opinion of the Supreme Court has been discussed; *Ward Baking Co. v. Federal Trade Commission,* 264 Fed. 330 (1920), prohibiting free deals; *New Jersey Asbestos Co. v. Federal Trade Commission,* 264 Fed. 509 (1920), commercial bribery; and *Beech-Nut Packing Co. v. Federal Trade Commission,* 264 Fed. 885 (1920), retail price maintenance. The fifth case, discussed previously, was *Sears, Roebuck and Co. v. Federal Trade Commission,* 258 Fed. 307 (1919), but even in this case, the Commission's victory was questionable.

[24] *Federal Trade Commission v. Gratz,* 253 U.S. 421, 40 S. Ct. 572, 64 L. Ed. 993 (1920); *Federal Trade Commission v. Beech-Nut Packing Co.,* 257 U.S. 441, 42 S. Ct. 150, 66 L. Ed. 307 (1922); *Federal Trade Commission v. Winsted Hosiery Co.,* 258 U.S. 483, 42 S. Ct. 384, 66 L. Ed. 729 (1922); *Federal Trade Commission v. Curtis Publishing Co.,* 260 U.S. 568, 43 S. Ct. 210, 67 L. Ed. 408 (1922); *Federal Trade Commission v. Sinclair Refining Co.,* 261 U.S. 463, 43 S. Ct. 450, 67 L. Ed. 746 (1923); *Federal Trade Commission v. Raymond Brothers Clark Co.,* 263 U.S. 565, 44 S. Ct. 162, 68 L. Ed. 448 (1924); *Federal Trade Commission v. American Tobacco Co.,* 264 U.S. 298, 44 S. Ct. 336, 68 L. Ed. 696 (1924).

[25] 260 U.S. at 583.

Once again the Commission's order was set aside, the Court taking unto itself, as in the *Gratz* case, the power of evaluating the respondent's practices. The Commission suffered still another defeat in the *Raymond Brothers* case. Its order to the respondent to cease delaying the delivery of "competitor's" goods which passed through the Raymond Brothers channels in a pool car shipment, was set aside on the grounds that, in the Court's opinion, the practices complained of disclosed no element of monopoly or oppression. Since the Supreme Court in the *Gratz* case limited the term "unfair methods of competition" to include only monopoly or oppression, the Commission's order was held improper. In the *American Tobacco Co.* case, the Court again assumed the prerogative of evaluating facts under the guise of interpreting law.

Since not one of these five cases is concerned with advertising, why are they included in a discussion of advertising regulations? The answer is that inasmuch as the Federal Trade Commission is the government instrumentality most concerned today with advertising, it is vitally necessary to understand the evolution of the Commission's powers. To bring advertising under the jurisdiction of the Commission, deceptive or fraudulent advertising practices had to be found to be "unfair methods of competition." Such inclusion, as a result of the five cases mentioned, was precluded.

Gradual Acceptance of FTC Jurisdiction over Advertising

Two of its early cases before the Supreme Court in which the Commission was victorious were the *Beech-Nut Packing Co.* case and the *Winsted Hosiery Co.* case.[26]

---

[26] In the case of *Mishawaka Woolen Manufacturing Co. v. Federal Trade Commission*, 260 U.S. 748, 43 S. Ct. 247, 67 L. Ed. 494 (1923), the Commission was sustained per curiam, on the basis of the decision in the *Beech-*

The *Beech-Nut Packing Co.* case[27] involved a scheme of retail price maintenance, and not advertising. The Commission's order, directing the Beech-Nut Packing Co. to refrain from requiring its dealers to sell at prices fixed by the company, was sustained. The Court said:

> That act [Federal Trade Commission Act] declares unlawful "unfair methods of competition" and gives the Commission authority after hearing to make orders to compel the discontinuance of such methods. What shall constitute unfair methods of competition denounced by the act is left without specific definition. Congress deemed it better to leave the subject without specific definition, and *to have each case determined upon its own facts,* owing to the multifarious means by which it is sought to effectuate such schemes.

Perhaps the Commissioners experienced a moment of elation in the hope that when Mr. Justice Day alluded to the determination of each case upon its *facts,* he would hold that since the Commission deemed the Beech-Nut Co. practice an unfair method of competition as a matter of fact and since the Commission's finding is conclusive when supported by evidence, the Court had no choice but to go along with the Commission. But the Court proceeded to re-emphasize the holding in the *Gratz* case that "unfair methods of competition" were a matter of law and for the courts to decide. Thus, although the Court sustained the Commission's order, such affirmation was predicated on the fact that in the Court's opinion the Beech-Nut Co. practices, as a matter of law, were "unfair methods of competition."

Nut Packing Company case. Therefore, discussion of the *Mishawaka* case is omitted.

[27] *Federal Trade Commission v. Beech-Nut Packing Co.*, 257 U.S. 441, 42 S. Ct. 150, 66 L. Ed. 307 (1922). Italics supplied in the following quotation.

The *Winsted Hosiery Company* case,[28] which the Commission also won, was important principally because it involved branding and labeling, which are much akin to advertising. The Commission had attacked the respondent's practice of labeling underclothing as wool when it seldom contained more than 10 per cent wool. Upon petition of the Winsted Company to the Circuit Court, the Commision's order directing the respondent to cease false and misleading labeling was set aside. The Supreme Court observed that the Commission's findings of fact as to practices in the knit underwear industry were supported by evidence and therefore could not be doubted; that the labels, being literally false, were calculated to and did deceive part of the purchasing public, thereby attracting customers by this fraud and diverting trade from producers who truthfully labeled their goods; and that:

> . . . a method inherently unfair does not cease to be so because those competed against have become aware of the wrongful practice. Nor does it cease to be unfair because the falsity of the manufacturer's representation has become so well known to the trade that dealers, as distinguished from consumers, are no longer deceived . . . and trade-marks which deceive the public are deemed protection, although members of the trade are not misled thereby. As a substantial part of the public was still misled by the use of the labels which the Winsted Company employed, the public had an interest in stopping the practice as wrongful.

Although the Supreme Court's decision in favor of the Commission did not serve to overrule the *Gratz* holding that the determination of what was an "unfair method of competition" was a matter of law for the courts to decide, the case, for purposes of advertising, was important for several

[28] *Federal Trade Commission v. Winsted Hosiery Co.*, 258 U.S. 483, 42 S. Ct. 384, 66 L. Ed. 729 (1922).

reasons. First, by condemning manufacturers' representations as capable of being "unfair methods of competition," the Court paved the way for the regulation of advertising, which is, in essence, representation. The dicta in the case of *New Jersey Asbestos Company v. Federal Trade Commission* had expressly excluded advertising from the Commission's regulatory powers.[29] Thus, an important result of the *Winsted* case was that it settled, once and for all, the Commission's power to control advertising practices which were unfair methods of competition. In addition, the Court, in declaring that a practice does not cease to be unfair because the falsity of representations is known in the trade, suggested that perhaps protection of the consumer from deception may be enough in itself to justify action by the Commission, although the Court did not indicate this interpretation explicitly.[30]

The Commision's role in advertising was basically weak. The ruling in the *Gratz* case required that for an advertising practice to be enjoined, it was necessary to show that the practice tended to further monopoly or restraint of trade and the courts were the final arbiters of whether the practice would have such a result. The Commission was caught between two fires—on the one hand, it had to consider the legislative standards prescribed by Congress and on the other hand, the judicial standards prescribed by the Courts.

---

[29] "So broad a construction of the statute [Federal Trade Commission Act] would bring within the disposition of the commission a vast number of subjects and controversies which in their nature belong to the legislative and judicial departments of the Government. For instance, advertising is a method of selling goods which, without increasing their merits, increases their costs; . . . *though we suppose no one would say that the act gives the commission a right to regulate these matters.*" 264 Fed. at 511. Italics supplied.

[30] That this came to pass and that the need to show injury to competition before the Commission could proceed against deceptive advertising was dispensed with, will be discussed later.

As a result of the *Winsted* case, which had established that false labeling and advertising was an unfair method of competition, the Commission proceeded to take action against a myriad of advertising practices. Among these were attempts to induce the public into believing that a baking powder contained "cream of tartar" rather than "phosphate"; [31] that the government was a regular and continual purchaser of a salt-block for livestock when such was not the case; [32] or that a breed of hogs possessed certain qualities which it did not possess.[33] The Commission also attacked the use of a corporate name in advertising that was similar to that of a competitor whose product was of a better quality and sold at a higher price.[34] Many other practices were attacked, ranging from deceptive advertising of reissued films to the false advertising of products as containing radium when such was not the truth.[35]

---

[31] *Royal Baking Powder Company v. Federal Trade Commission*, 281 Fed. 744 (1922).

[32] *Guaranty Veterinary Co. v. Federal Trade Commission*, 285 Fed. 853 (1922). Although the Commission's order was affirmed, that part of the Act declaring that a finding of fact by the Commission is conclusive if based on the evidence was reduced so as to apply only to findings as to the falsity of the advertising and not as to whether the false advertising was an "unfair method of competition." The *Gratz* case was still good law.

[33] *L. B. Silver Co. v. Federal Trade Commission*, 289 Fed. 985 (1923). In this case the court exercised its power to modify the Commission's order, and affirmed, as modified, that the order was worthless. The court, in getting around the *Winsted* case, held that advertising, to be condemned, must be palpably and literally false and must tend to lessen competition or create monopoly. It held that an advertisement, based on conflicting expert opinions, could not be palpably false. The effect of this was to deny the Commission its fact-finding role.

[34] *Juvenile Show Company v. Federal Trade Commission*, 289 Fed. 57 (1923). This was a clear case of passing off goods as those of a competitor with a diversion of trade from the competitor. The case was based almost entirely on injury to competition and would seem to come within even the most narrow construction of Section 5.

[35] *Fox Film Corp. v. Federal Trade Commission*, 296 Fed. 353 (1924). Reissued motion pictures were advertised under new names, leading the public into believing them to be new films. *Federal Trade Commission v. Pure Silk*

Most of the cases were governed by the mandate of the *Gratz* case that "unfair methods of competition" was a matter of law for the courts. However, these decisions also followed the rule of the *Winsted* case in declaring that deceptive labeling or advertising was, as a matter of law, an "unfair

---

Hosiery Mills, Inc., 3 F. (2d) 105 (1925). This case concerned the use of the term "mills" in the corporate name of an organization that did not manufacture the product. Such advertising tended to lead the public into believing that they were saving on the price because middlemen and jobbers were eliminated. *Chicago Portrait Co. v. Federal Trade Commission*, 4 F. (2d) 759 (1925). This case concerned the leading of the purchasing public to believe that the price of the article was much higher than that which they were paying. The Commission's order was vacated on the grounds that there was no tendency to injure any competitor, even though the purchaser was deceived. *John C. Winston Co. v. Federal Trade Commission*, 3 F. (2d) 961 (1925). The company advertised that the purchaser was getting three items for the price of two, whereas actually the cost of the third item was included in the entire price. Again the Commission's order was vacated, the court pointing out that the advertiser had offered to stipulate not to resume his practices. The court's unrealistic attitude toward advertising was demonstrated when the court said: "It is conceivable that a very stupid person might be misled by this method of selling books, yet measured by ordinary standards of trade and by ordinary standards of the intelligence of traders, we can not discover that it amounts to an 'unfair method of competition' within the sense of the law." *Procter and Gamble Co. v. Federal Trade Commission*, 11 F. (2d) 47 (1926). The company advertised soap as containing naphtha to make it an effective cleanser when such was not the case. *Ostermoor and Co. Inc. v. Federal Trade Commission*, 16 F. (2d) 962 (1927). The company sponsored pictorial advertising which grossly exaggerated the thickness and resiliency of mattresses. The Commission's order was set aside because the respondent did less than 1 per cent of all the mattress business in the country and its competitors used similar advertising. The court denied that competition was being injured and declared that the practices complained of were permissible "puffing" even though a segment of the public, albeit small, was misled. *Federal Trade Commission v. Balme*, 23 F. (2d) 615 (1928). Balme used a brand name and package similar to that of a competitor, i.e., passing-off. Some indication that perhaps public interest extended beyond mere injury to competition is found in the opinion, when the court said that the test of unfair competition is ". . . whether the natural and probable result of the use by a respondent of a label which is deceptive to the ordinary purchaser makes him unwittingly, under ordinary conditions, purchase that which he did not intend to buy." *Indiana Quartered Oak Co. v. Federal Trade Commission*, 26 F. (2d) 340 (1928). The company advertised wood as mahogany when it was not, and following the rule of the *Winsted* case, the court suggested that an advertising practice, which possessed

method of competition." The principal uncertainty concerned the definition of "public interest" and whether the courts or the Commission was to determine that a proceeding was in the "public interest." This confusion was resolved by the *Klesner* (*Shade Shop*) case.[36]

The facts of the *Klesner* case are quite simple. Two concerns had been in the window-shade business in Washington, D. C. for many years, one of which did business under the name of "Shade Shop," although both used the same premises on a sublease and subcontracting basis. A dispute having arisen, the party that used the name "Shade Shop" moved out and the remaining party (Klesner) began advertising itself as the "Shade Shop." The Commission sought to stop the use of the "Shade Shop" name by Klesner on the grounds that such use constituted "passing off." The Court of Appeals dismissed the Commission's suit to enforce its order. The principal problem facing the Supreme Court was whether the proceeding against Klesner was in the nature of a private administrative remedy in favor of the original owner of "Shade Shop," or a proceeding in the public interest. The

---

the tendency to deceive the public was enough to invoke the jurisdiction of the Commission. However, since the facts involved competition in the lumber industry, the case cannot be said to rest squarely on deception per se. *Masland Duraleather Co. v. Federal Trade Commission*, 34 F. (2d) 733 (1929). The practice of using the name "Duraleather" on a product which was imitation leather was condemned. The court apparently believed the property interest in a trade-mark was paramount over public interest, for the court modified the Commission's order so as to permit the respondent to continue using the false name for six months so that it might develop a new name. *Federal Trade Commission v. Kay*, 35 F. (2d) 160 (1929). The court affirmed the Commission's order that respondent stop advertising that its product contained radium when such was not the case. *Lighthouse Rug Co. v. Federal Trade Commission*, 35 F. (2d) 163 (1929). The use of the term "Lighthouse" was held properly condemned because the term had acquired a secondary meaning, i.e., products labeled "Lighthouse" implied that they were made at institutions for the blind.

[36] *Federal Trade Commission v. Klesner*, 280 U.S. 19, 50 S. Ct. 1, 74 L. Ed. 138 (1929).

Court cited the Act which provided, in part, that a complaint may be filed by the Commission only "if it shall appear to the Commission that a proceeding by it in respect thereof would be to the interest of the public." Thus, even though the Commission may act in a "passing off" situation so as to enforce a private right, such enforcement is merely incidental to the protection of the public. In analyzing the problem, the Court, through Mr. Justice Brandeis, observed:

> In determining whether a proposed proceeding will be in the public interest, the Commission exercises a broad discretion. But the mere fact that it is to the interest of the community that private rights shall be respected is not enough to support a finding of public interest. *To justify filing a complaint, the public interest must be specific and substantial.* Often it is so, because the unfair method employed threatens the existence of present or potential competition. Sometimes, because the unfair method is being employed under circumstances which involve flagrant oppression of the weak by the strong. Sometimes, because, although the aggregate of the loss entailed may be so sinuous and widespread as to make the matter one of public consequence, no private suit would be brought to stop the unfair conduct, since the loss to each of the individuals affected is too small to warrant it.[37]

Although the mandate of the statute, in speaking of public interest, reads, "if it shall appear to the *Commission*," the Court paid only lip service to the command of the legislature.

> Its [the Commission] preliminary determination that institution of a proceeding will be in the public interest, while not strictly within the scope of that provision, will ordinarily be accepted by the courts. But the Commission's action in authorizing the filing of a complaint, like its action in making an order thereon, is subject to *judicial review*. The specific facts established may show, *as a matter of law* that the proceeding which it authorized is not in the public interest, within the meaning of the Act.

---

[37] 280 U.S. at 28. Italics supplied; also, in the next excerpt.

The judgment of the Court was that since the proceeding was not in the public interest, the Commission's order was improper. The result of the case was that the Court arrogated to itself the determination of whether proceedings by the Commission were in the public interest. Thus, what was originally intended to be directional language was given jurisdictional effect.

As of 1929, the Commission's powers with respect to advertising were small indeed. In the *Gratz* case the Commission had been divested of its authority to determine what constituted an unfair method of competition. It seemed that before advertising could be regulated, the courts had to find it to be an "unfair method of competition." By virtue of the *Klesner* case, the Commission had been stripped also of its authority to determine whether a proceeding was in the public interest. A Commission order directed against advertising would have to meet standards imposed by the court and not by the Commission. The Commission's only remaining function was the fact-finding duty with respect to whether or not an advertisement was false.[38] Only the *Winsted* case favored the Commission, and even that case left one question open. The case stood for the point that a false advertisement was an unfair method of competition. However, the question as to whether injury to competition or a tendency to so injure was necessary before false advertising could be attacked, remained unanswered. If the answer were in the affirmative, the problem of preventing false advertising would be magnified and the Commission's remaining effectiveness destroyed. This, no less, was the result of the decision in *Federal Trade Commis-*

[38] But even this has been somewhat limited by *L. B. Silver v. Federal Trade Commission*, 289 Fed. 995 (1923), which held that where there was conflicting opinion as to the veracity of a claim and where such conflicting opinion was known to the public, the advertisement was not necessarily false, even though the Commission thought it so.

sion v. Raladam.[39] The case concerned the advertising of a patent medicine, an obesity cure, and in the advertisement the respondent claimed that the drug was effective and harmless, though as a matter of fact it contained ingredients that could be dangerous if taken without medical supervision. The Court of Appeals reversed the Commission and vacated the order. The Supreme Court, in reviewing the case, said:

> If the necessity of protecting the public against dangerously misleading advertising of a remedy sold in interstate commerce were all that is necessary to give the Commission jurisdiction, the order could not successfully be assailed. But this is not all.
>
> By the plain words of the act, the power of the Commission to take steps looking to the issue of an order to desist depends upon the existence of three distinct prerequisites: (1) That the methods complained of are *unfair*; (2) That they are methods of *competition* in commerce; and (3) That a proceeding by the Commission to prevent the use of the methods appears to be in the *interest of the public*. We assume the existence of the first and third of these requisites, and pass at once to the consideration of the second.

The Court continued by pointing out that the Sherman Act, the Clayton Act, and the Federal Trade Commission Act all sought to protect the public from abuses in interstate competition and foreign trade. Though "unfair methods of competition" is broader than "unfair competition," the Court maintained that the former term was not so broad as always to include all unfair methods:

> It is obvious that the "competition" imports the existence of present and potential competitors, and the unfair methods must be such as injuriously affect or tend thus to affect the business of these competitors—that is to say, the trader whose methods are assailed as unfair must have present or potential

[39] 283 U.S. 643, 51 S. Ct. 587, 75 L. Ed. 1324 (1931).

> rivals in trade whose business will be, or is likely to be, lessened or otherwise injured. It is that condition of affairs which the Commission is given power to protect, and it is against that condition of affairs, and not some other, that the Commission is authorized to protect the public.

Having thus imposed the requirement that the Commission show affirmatively that the deceptive advertising injured or tended to injure competitors, the Court affirmed the lower court on the grounds that:

> Findings of the Commission justify the conclusion that the advertisements naturally would tend to increase the business of respondent; but there is neither finding nor evidence from which the conclusion legitimately can be drawn that these advertisements substantially injured or tended thus to injure the business of any competitor or competitors generally, whether legitimate or not . . . one of the facts necessary to support jurisdiction to make the final order to cease and desist, is the existence of competition, and the Commission cannot, by assuming the existence, if in fact there be none, give itself jurisdiction to make such an order. If, as a result of the inquiry, it turn out that the preliminary assumption of competition is without foundation, jurisdiction to make that order necessarily fails, and the proceeding must be dismissed by the Commission.

Thus the *Raladam, Gratz,* and *Klesner* cases reduced the Commission's power over advertising to a mere shadow. The courts had deprived the Commission of the power to evaluate what was unfair, what was in competition, and what was in the public interest. The only power left to the Commission was its authority to determine whether or not an advertisement was false or deceptive. Thus after seventeen years of existence, the Commission had been stripped progressively of its power, leaving it little more than a token of authority. But just as three opinions had effectively crippled the Commission, two new opinions quickly restored a good part of the

Commission's authority. These were the *Algoma* and *Keppel* cases.[40]

The facts of the *Algoma* case were very much like those of the previously cited *Indiana Quartered Oak* case. The respondent and thirty-eight other manufacturers of lumber products advertised their goods as "California white pine" when, in fact, they were a species of yellow pine. White pine is much superior to yellow pine, and the deception inherent in advertising an inferior product as a superior one, was the practice attacked by the Commission. The lower court held that the Commission's finding had no support in the evidence. Upon appeal by the Commission, the Supreme Court observed that some retail dealers believed they were receiving white pine and selling it as such, while others knew the wood was inferior but sold it to the public as the better product. In discussing the lower court's ruling on the Commission's finding that respondents competed unfairly, Mr. Justice Cardozo observed:

> The findings of the Commission as to facts, if supported by testimony, shall be conclusive. 15 *U.S.C.A.* Sec. 45. The Court of Appeals, though professing adherence to this mandate, honored it, we think, with *lip service only*. In form the court determined that the finding of unfair competition had no support whatever. In fact, what the court did was to make its own appraisal of the testimony, picking and choosing for itself among uncertain and conflicting inferences. Statute and decision (*Federal Trade Commission v. Pacific States Paper Trade Association,* 273 U.S. 52, 61, 63) *forbid that exercise of power.*[41]

In arguing that the proceeding was not in the public interest, respondent claimed that the sale of the "California

---

[40] *Federal Trade Commission v. Algoma Lumber Co.,* 291 U.S. 67, 54 S. Ct. 315, 78 L. Ed. 655 (1934); *Federal Trade Commission v. R. F. Keppel and Brothers, Inc.,* 291 U.S. 304, 54 S. Ct. 423, 78 L. Ed. 814 (1934).

[41] 291 U.S. at 73. Italics supplied.

white pine" at a price cheaper than that of genuine white pine represented a saving to the consumer. The Court, in meeting the argument, said:

> But a saving to the consumer, though it be made out, does not obliterate the prejudice. Fair competition is not attained by balancing a gain in money against a misrepresentation of the thing supplied. The courts must set their faces against a conception of business standards so corrupting in its tendency. The consumer is prejudiced if upon giving an order for one thing, he is supplied with something else. *Federal Trade Commission v. Royal Milling Co.*, 288 U.S. 212, 216; *City of Carlsbad v. W. T. Thackeray & Co.*, 57 Fed. 18. In such matters *the public is entitled* to get what it chooses, though the choice may be dictated by caprice or by fashion or perhaps by ignorance . . . *The careless and unscrupulous must rise to the standards of the scrupulous and diligent.* The Commission was not organized to drag the standard down.[42]

Thus, by adopting this view, the Court gave the Commission much support and encouragement. First, the Act had to be obeyed. This meant that when the Commission made a factual determination and when there was evidence to support the determination, the finding was conclusive upon the courts. Second, the Court suggested that the public must get what it desires, irrespective of the motive for its choice. This would indicate an awakening by the judiciary to the fact that the public interest extended far beyond the maintenance of unfettered competition. The Commission's stature was improving, and it was given further aid by the *Keppel* case.

The *Keppel* case did not concern advertising. However, the principle for which it stands is so closely related to the advertising problem, that an examination of the case is important. The case involved "break and take" candy packages. This was a device whereby candy, sold by individual pieces,

---

[42] 291 U.S. at 78–79. Italics supplied.

was so arranged that the price of the candy depended on the piece chosen. In a box of 120 pieces, sold at one cent each, four had a penny in their wrappers, thereby returning the cost of the candy if that piece was selected. Another assortment contained sixty pieces. Ten candies had slips marked at one cent, ten at two cents, and forty at three cents. Still another assortment contained candies with variously colored fillings. A prize might be won if candies with a filling of a particular color were chosen. The Commission found that this system represented the sale of the candy by lottery or gambling, that accompanying display cards enticed the participation of children, and that a substantial amount of trade was diverted from candy manufacturers who maintained normal sale methods.

The lower court held that the Commission's proceeding was improper. The court also held that since competitors could resort to the same device they were not injured, and that the practice did not create or tend to create monopoly or deceive the public and was not, therefore, an unfair method of competition. This was the position that respondent took before the Supreme Court. The Court first disposed of any doubt whether the practice in question was of public concern:

> Sales of the break and take package by respondent aggregate about $234,000 per year. The proceeding involves more than a mere private controversy. A practice so generally adopted by manufacturers necessarily affects not only competing manufacturers but the far greater number of retailers to whom they sell. Thus, the effects of the device are felt throughout the penny candy industry. A practice so widespread and so far reaching in its consequences is of public concern if in other respects within the purview of the statute.

Having thus affirmed that the proceeding was in the public interest, the Court stated that the decisive question was whether this practice was unfair and, therefore, within the jurisdiction of the Commission. The Court refused to sustain the argument that the practice could not be condemned since it did not fall within any class of practices that the Court held subject to the Commission's prohibition. The Court said:

> But we cannot say that the Commission's jurisdiction extends only to those types of practices which happen to have been litigated before this Court. . . .
>
> Neither the language nor the history of the Act suggests that Congress intended to confine the forbidden methods to fixed and unyielding categories. . . . It would not have been a difficult feat of draftsmanship to have restricted the operation of the Trade Commission Act to those methods of competition in interstate commerce which are forbidden at common law or which are likely to grow into violations of the Sherman Act, if that had been the purpose of the legislation.
>
> It is unnecessary to attempt a comprehensive definition of the unfair methods which are banned, even if it were possible to do so. . . .

Thus far the Court had declared the proceeding to be in the public interest. It had declared also that "unfair methods of competition" was a phrase broad enough to encompass many practices which had not already been litigated. It is to be remembered that the *Gratz* doctrine, which had rendered "unfair methods of competition" a matter of law for the courts to determine, was one of the principal limitations on the jurisdiction of the Commission. The Court, in commenting on this, said through Mr. Justice Stone:

> While this court has declared that it is for the courts to determine what practices or methods of competition are to be deemed unfair, *Federal Trade Commission v. Gratz, supra,* in passing on that question, *the determination of the Commission is of weight.* It was created with the avowed purpose of lodging the administrative functions committed to it in a "body specially competent to deal with them by reason of information, experience, and careful study of the business and economic conditions of the industry affected," and it was organized in such a manner, with respect to the length and

expiration of the terms of office of its members as would "give to them an opportunity to acquire the expertness in dealing with these *special questions* concerning industry that comes from experience." [43]

Although the *Keppel* case did not expressly overrule the *Gratz* decision, its effect has been so to weaken the *ratio decidendi* of the *Gratz* case that the latter was overruled in effect. The Commision had the power at last to determine, within the limits of evidence alone, whether a practice was an unfair method of competition. In addition, the *Algoma* case required that more than lip service be accorded fact-findings of the Commission where supported by evidence. The *Klesner* case of 1929 still retained its vitality, but its effect was only to exclude mere private rights from the "public interest." This was not an overly harsh requirement.

The only serious legal barrier remaining in the way of the Commission was the *Raladam* case. It will be remembered that the case required that injury or the tendency to injure competition be present before false advertising could be an "unfair method of competition." The affirmative burden of proving injury or the tendency to injure, as imposed upon the Commission, was onerous and often so hard to sustain that a patently misleading advertisement would be beyond the Commission's reach. This obstacle was the last to be removed and it was overcome by the Wheeler-Lea Amendments of 1938.

The Wheeler-Lea Amendments

The Wheeler-Lea Amendments made several vitally important changes in the Federal Trade Commission Act, all enhancing the Commission's authority over advertising. The

---

[43] 290 U.S. at 314. Italics supplied.

first of these changes altered the substantive meaning of Section 5. The Commission's jurisdiction in the original Act was limited to "unfair methods of competition." The amendment extended the jurisdiction to include "unfair or deceptive acts or practices." This provision overcame the limiting effects of the *Raladam* decision. The Commission's duty to serve the public interest remained the same as under the original Act,[44] the amendment enabled the Commission to proceed against unfair or deceptive acts or practices in commerce which injuriously affected the public interest, whether or not these acts or practices affected competition.

The second change effected by the amendment was procedural, and altered the manner of enforcing Commission orders. It will be recalled that under the original Act the Commission was required to petition for a judicial enforcement order when its preliminary order to cease and desist was disobeyed. Under the amendment, the Commission was no longer required to go to court for the enforcement of its order. A Commission order to cease and desist assumed a quasi-judicial nature in that it became automatically a final order sixty days after issuance. Thus, if a respondent-advertiser did not appeal from the order within sixty days and did not comply with the order, the Commission, upon a showing of noncompliance, could move the court to declare the respondent in contempt of the order and subject him to a civil monetary penalty. This produced a marked change with respect to false advertising. Since an advertising campaign can sell a lot of goods and deceive many persons in a matter of a few months, and since the original enforcement procedure required the Commission to seek enforcement in the courts, thereby consuming a great deal of time, it was possible for an advertiser to disobey the order and continue his false

---

[44] *Scientific Manufacturing Co. v. Federal Trade Commission*, 124 F. (2d) 640 (1941).

advertising until a court ordered him to desist. Though it did not stop false advertising, the new procedure reduced to two months the advertiser's time of continuing his nefarious practices and imposed the threat of a penalty if he continued beyond that time.

The third change of importance Sections 12 and 13, related, directly to advertising, and declared that a false advertisement inducing or likely to induce the purchase of foods, drugs, cosmetics, or devices was unfair and deceptive within the meaning of Section 5. Thus, advertising was specifically mentioned for the first time in the amended Federal Trade Commission Act, but the Commission's jurisdiction over false advertising, as such, was limited to certain commodities. Inasmuch as advertising had not been mentioned in the legislation before, why was it now? The answer to the question is so closely related to pure food and drug legislation that a brief history of the latter is necessary in order to understand what prompted the enactment of Sections 12 and 13.

As indicated in an earlier chapter, a large amount of advertising in the last decades of the nineteenth century was patent medicine advertisements. Public indignation had been aroused over frauds committed by patent medicine and food manufacturers. Even the government had fallen victim to such frauds, for food and other army supplies purchased during the Spanish-American War proved to be not only inferior but often dangerous and harmful. Pure food bills had been introduced as early as 1890, because even before the Spanish-American War frauds the public had long been deceived and cheated. But all of the early attempts at corrective legislation were to no avail. The efforts of lobbyists, particularly the Proprietary Association of America in cooperation with Southern Democrats, were most successful in sidetracking this needed legislation. Their obstructionism was overcome by the slow process of public education, led by Dr. Harvey Wiley of the Department of Agriculture. Wiley's "poison squad" conducted chemical analyses of various drug and food products, and the result of such experimentation, publicized in books and magazine articles on the subject, produced public excitement and an irresistible demand for congressional action.

Action took form in the Pure Food and Drug Act and the Meat Inspection Act, both of 1906. The basic provision of the Pure Food and Drug Act prohibited the shipment in interstate commerce of adulterated and misbranded food and drugs. Misbranding, which is false labeling, included affirmative falsity and the failure to state the quantity of ten enumerated dangerous drugs. Other provisions of the Act, relating to adulteration, are omitted from this discussion because they bear no relation to the problem of advertising.

With respect to the labeling provisions, two observations are in order. First, the requirement of accurate labeling was limited to situations where the law required a label. The Act was inherently weak because food and drugs sold under brand names were exempt from any disclosures of ingredients. Second, the Act did not extend to advertising of food and drugs. The result was that a sufficient amount of deceptive and fraudulent advertising could be employed to build up a strong market position on the basis of consumer deception. In addition, the deceptive advertising often sold the product so well that the average consumer was too lax to inspect the label where one was required. Finally, the prohibition of false and fraudulent representation, in connection with labeling, imposed a difficult burden of proof on enforcement officers, since fraud requires proof of knowledge and intent.

The inherent weaknesses in the Act were such that it fell far short of its intended purpose, and fraudulent practices continued. For twenty-five years the Pure Food and Drug Administration complained of its limited powers, but the complaints fell on deaf ears until there was a resurgence of interest in consumer protection during the depression years. Legislation was proposed as early as 1933, but the well-organized forces of manufacturing and advertising interests were successful in overcoming the more numerous, but unorganized, consumer forces. The principal controversy centered about false advertising provisions, and as late as 1936 it was very doubtful whether any legislation at all would be passed. But just when the hopes of the consumer groups were at their lowest, an event occurred which precipitated the enactment of the needed legislation. One hundred persons were killed through the use of a drug called "elixir sulfanilamide." Public indignation reached such heights that many drug manufacturers and advertisers stopped opposing legislation for the correction of evils in the distribution of goods widely used by the public. The result was the enactment of the Pure Food, Drug, and Cosmetic Act of 1938.

The most important change in the new Act was one which made the failure to reveal material facts on a label an element of misbranding. But the opponents of the bill, so they believed, were not without victory. The Act, as passed, had eliminated all provisions relating to advertising. The opposition to the inclusion of such provision was not based on an attempt to exclude any prohibition of false advertising, for such a position would have been impossible to sustain. The opposition was based, instead, on the desire to exclude false advertising from the control of the Pure Food and Drug Administration, which was believed to be too strong as a result of the new Act. The lobbyists for business and advertising were aware that the Federal Trade Commission's standing in the courts was weak as a result of the *Raladam* case. Accordingly, they maintained that control over false advertising of food and drugs should be placed, if at all, in the hands of the agency already active in the advertising field, namely, the Federal Trade Commission, hoping thereby to secure a not too vigorous enforcement of the Act. It was thus that Sections 12 and 13 came to be included in the amendments to Federal Trade Commission Act, and the irony of the situation is that the Commission acquired this new power because it was deemed too weak to exercise it effectively.

To recapitulate, the basic changes relating to advertising which the Wheeler-Lea Amendments brought about were:

1) The Commission's jurisdiction was extended to include unfair or deceptive acts or practices in commerce, in addition to unfair methods of competition. This served to dispense with the requirement, imposed by the *Raladam* decision, that injury or the tendency to injure competition be shown before bad advertising could be assailed.
2) The Commission's orders to cease and desist were self-executory within sixty days of issuance, thereby eliminating an action by the Commission to secure a judicial enforcement order.
3) The Commission was given specific jurisdiction over the false advertising of food, drugs, cosmetics, and devices. This included not only false representations but also the failure to reveal material facts. Not only was the advertiser liable if he told a deliberate falsehood, but he was also responsible for deception by omission.
4) In the case of falsely advertising a commodity, where use of the commodity as a result of the advertisement might be injurious to health, the Commission was empowered to bypass the usual procedure of complaint and hearing before issuing a cease and desist order. In such a situation where injury to health might result, the Commission had authority, upon a proper showing, to seek a temporary injunction pending the formal hearing. Failure to obey the injunction subjects the advertiser to criminal penalties.

As a result of the Wheeler-Lea Amendments, and the *Winsted* and *Keppel* cases, the Commission has made extensive use of the authority given it. This is evidenced by the wide range of bad advertising practices that the Commission has acted against. These cover false and misleading advertising in many situations, such as the advertiser's business status and advantages;[45] disparagement of competitor and his product;[46] falsely advertising the composition,[47] condition,[48] content,[49] nature,[50] quality,[51] price,[52] safety,[53] or ori-

[45] *Air Conditioning Training Corp.*, D. 4182, 6 F.R. 1840 (1941); *Grand Rapids Exchange Inc.*, D. 3703, 6 F.R. 3314 (1941); *Weaver Real Estate Appraisal Training Service*, D. 4353, 6 F.R. 3632 (1941); *Ideal Mail Order Co.*, D. 5246, 12 F.R. 4173 (1947); *The Blind Weavers Inc.*, 22 F.T.C. 145 (1936); *Silver Mfg. Co.*, D. 3211, 4 F.R. 3369 (1939); *Universal Industries, Inc.*, D. 3822, 9 F.R. 1462 (1944); *Parfum L'Orle Inc.*, D. 4511, 8 F.R. 3247 (1943); *Federal Military Equipment Corp.*, D. 5096, 12 F.R. 3171 (1947); *Webster University*, D. 5171, 10 F.R. 3130 (1945); *Gallant Trading Co.*, D. 4780, 8 F.R. 4752 (1943); *Stevens Clothing Mfg.*, D. 5240, 11 F.R. 4146 (1946); *Myndall Cain House of Beauty*, D. 5466, 12 F.R. 4905 (1947); *Globe Trading Co.*, D. 5098, 10 F.R. 10074 (1945); *Kodize Process Corp.*, D. 5206, 10 F.R. 5498 (1947).

[46] *Univis Lens Co.*, D. 5351, 13 F.R. 8216 (1948); *Supercold Corp.*, D. 4904, 12 F.R. 6969 (1947); *Mirra Chemical Laboratories*, D. 5301, 10 F.R. 14891 (1945).

[47] *Retonga Medicine Co.*, D. 5519, 13 F.R. 6370 (1948); *Wm. R. Warner & Co.*, D. 4770, 13 F.R. 5677 (1948); *Jackson Research Laboratories*, D. 5493, 13 F.R. 4869 (1948); *Shepherd Knitwear Co.*, D. 5336, 13, F.R. 4791 (1948); *Sunway Vitamin Co.*, D. 5224, 13 F.R. 4185 (1948).

[48] *Eunice Mail Order House*, D. 5170, 13 F.R. 2160 (1948); *American Sales Co.*, D. 5331, 12 F.R. 2472 (1947); *Beau Peep Products*, D. 5345, 11 F.R. 13480 (1946).

[49] *Hillman Periodicals, Inc.*, D. 5440, 13 F.R. 2160 (1948); *Margood Publishing Corp.*, D. 5413, 12 F.R. 6757 (1947).

[50] *Fleming and Sons*, D. 5264, 13 F.R. 6748 (1948); *Alberty Food Products*, D. 5101, 13 F.R. 2129 (1948); *Oxford Products, Inc.*, D. 5388, 11 F.R. 8077 (1946); *United Watch Co.*, D. 4653, 11 F.R. 5283 (1946).

[51] *Everett Foot Cushion Laboratories*, D. 5285, 13 F.R. 5564 (1948); *American Chemical Paint Co.*, D. 5135, 13 F.R. 4869 (1948); *Excelsior Laboratory Inc.*, D. 5394, 13 F.R. 4380 (1948); *Artra Cosmetics, Inc.*, D. 4930, 13 F.R. 4277 (1948); *Market Drug*, D. 5478, 13 F.R. 3183 (1948); *American Dietaids Co., Inc.*, D. 5070, 13 F.R. 1985 (1948); *Parker Pen Co.*, D. 4338, 13 F.R. 2091 (1948); *General Motors Co.*, D. 4724, 13 F.R. 1645 (1948); *Hammacher Schlemmer & Co.*, D. 5410, 13 F.R. 400 (1948); *Frontier Asthma Co., Inc.*, D. 3935, 11 F.R. 12127 (1946).

[52] *Memorial Granite Co., Inc.*, D. 4214, 7 F.R. 7879 (1942); *Theophilus J. Craig*, D. 4600, 8 F.R. 1054 (1943); *Fox Studios*, D. 4807, 8 F.R. 1054 (1943); *Silver Service Corp.*, D. 3654, 5 F.R. 2716 (1940); *Plaza Luggage and Supply Co.*, D. 4857, 13 F.R. 1663 (1948); *Averbach Co., Inc.*, D. 3342, 9 F.R. 13800 (1944); *Simon Ackerman Mfctrs. & Tailors, Inc.*, D. 5109, 11 F.R. 6818 (1946); *Ford Motors Co.*, D. 3174, 6 F.R. 5561 (1941); *Western Auto Supply Co.*, D. 4054, 6 F.R. 3320 (1941).

[53] *D. J. Lane Co.*, D. 5252, 13 F.R. 2405 (1948); *Clark's Drugs and Sundries*, D. 4968, 12 F.R. 7857 (1947); *Schulte Laboratories*, D. 5382, 12 F.R. 3987 (1947).

gin [54] of the product or the manner in which it is manufactured, the terms and conditions under which it is sold,[55] and the results to be expected from its use.[56] The Commission has also sought to curb the use of fictitious affidavits,[57] fictitious or misleading guaranties,[58] fictitious endorsements and testimonials,[59] fictitious "free" offers [60] or trials,[61] and misleading offers to refund, repair, or replace.[62] Still some other advertising practices prohibited by the Commission include falsely advertising government approval,[63] promising jobs or

---

[54] *Universal Laboratories*, D. 5069, 13 F.R. 4690 (1948); *Dr. H. A. Petri Co.*, D. 5146, 10 F.R. 2680 (1945); *Gallant Trading Co.*, D. 4780, 8 F.R. 4752 (1943).

[55] *Gold Star Novelty House*, D. 3449, 10 F.R. 4531 (1945); *Texas Tasty Co.*, D. 3487, 10 F.R. 4413 (1945); *Kaiden-Kax-Anjian Studios*, D. 4812, 8 F.R. 3077 (1943); *Copper Roofs Corp.*, D. 4651, 8 F.R. 293 (1942); *Nu-Way Mfg. Co.*, D. 3852, 6 F.R. 1017 (1941).

[56] *Jung Arch Brace Co.*, D. 4767, 10 F.R. 6642 (1945); *Ultra-Violet Products, Inc.*, D. 4407, 9 F.R. 11789 (1944); *Philip R. Park, Inc.*, D. 4504, 9 F.R. 4803 (1944); *Brooks Appliance Co.*, D. 5072, 9 F.R. 1641 (1944); *Charboy Products Inc.*, D. 4756, 9 F.R. 1087 (1944); *Chemicals of the South*, D. 4999, 8 F.R. 17035 (1943).

[57] *Progress Tailoring Co.*, D. 3747, 8 F.R. 10395 (1943).

[58] *Sales Stimulators*, D. 4982, 13 F.R. 8215 (1948); *Parker Pen Co.*, D. 4338, 13 F.R. 2091 (1948); *Elgin Razor Corp.*, D. 4458, 12 F.R. 6356 (1947); *The Camera Man*, D. 5386, 11 F.R. 7656 (1946); W. A. *Sheaffer Pen Co.*, D. 4337, 10 F.R. 6168 (1945).

[59] *American Chemical Plant Co.*, D. 5135, 13 F.R. 4869 (1948); *Staffin Johns Co.*, D. 5120, 13 F.R. 4100 (1948); *Manhattan Brewing Co.*, D. 4572, 11 F.R. 6174 (1946); *R. L. Swain Tobacco Co.*, D. 4981, 10 F.R. 15062 (1945); *Hearst Magazines, Inc.*, D. 3872, 6 F.R. 2646 (1941).

[60] *Harold S. Schwartz*, D. 5245, 13 F.R. 5208 (1948); *Central Merchandise Co.*, D. 5257, 13 F.R. 3229 (1948); *Lee Products*, D. 5215, 13 F.R. 2424 (1948); *Paradise Seed Co.*, D. 5499, 13 F.R. 1580 (1948); *Farmers' Mail Order House*, D. 5461, 12 F.R. 8228 (1947).

[61] *J. A. Stransky Mfg. Co.*, D. 1612, 8 F.R. 6078 (1943).

[62] *Bockenstille's Blue Ribbon Farms*, D. 4537, 11 F.R. 5595 (1946); *Fairmount Merchandise Co.*, D. 4665, 7 F.R. 4289 (1942); *Motor Retread Co., Inc.*, D. 4325, 6 F.R. 3719 (1941); *Howard Sales Co.*, D. 3514, 5 F.R. 2714 (1940).

[63] *McKinley-Roosevelt, Inc.*, D. 5272, 12 F.R. 5299 (1947); *Commonwealth Training Institute*, D. 4880, 9 F.R. 6937 (1944); *U.S. Ordinance Engineers, Inc.*, D. 2484, 4 F.R. 2705 (1939); *Home Diathermy Co., Inc.*, D. 4901, 9 F.R. 1202 (1944); *Emmet J. Smith and Daughter*, D. 5159, 12 F.R. 4261 (1947); *Century Travel Service, Inc.*, D. 5229, 11 F.R. 13627 (1946); *Erdley Hatcheries*, D. 4696, 8 F.R. 4231 (1943).

employment,[64] advertising an old or used item as new,[65] and deceiving the public through the deceptive use of scientific facts and claims.[66]

Knowledge of the widely varying advertising practices acted against by the Commission is important if its role in the advertising field is to be understood. But even more important is an awareness of the underlying policies which dictate the taking of action by the Commission. The basic premise upon which the Commission acts is the protection of the consuming public. Although the sale of products by the use of false and misleading statements and representations necessarily injures competition,[67] maintenance of free trade and competition is not the essential element upon which the public interest is predicated. The law is quite clear that a respondent who is guilty of false and misleading advertising can no longer rely on a defense, "Everybody else is doing it, why can't I?" [68] This rule of law, considered in the light of the fact that injury to competition is impossible if all manufacturers in the same field employ misrepresentation, indicates that protecting the public from deception is of itself

---

[64] *National Secretaries Assn.*, D. 5003, 10 F.R. 5030 (1945); *DeForest's Training Inc.*, D. 4441, 8 F.R. 12259 (1943); *Press Radio Service*, D. 4783, 7 F.R. 10834 (1942).

[65] *American Corp.*, D. 5085, 13 F.R. 4893 (1948); *American Sales Co.*, D. 5331, 12 F.R. 2472 (1947); *Westville Refinery Inc.*, D. 4370, 8 F.R. 4152 (1943); *Saks & Co.*, D. 8456, 6 F.R. 2120 (1941).

[66] *American Viscose Corp.*, D. 4862, 13 F.R. 7463 (1948); *Isabelle Beautetics Co.*, D. 5010, 13 F.R. 613 (1948); *Supercold Corp.*, D. 4904, 12 F.R. 6969 (1947); *R. B. Semler Inc.*, D. 4773, 11 F.R. 7458 (1946); *Rightway Institute*, D. 3158, 4 F.R. 1653 (1939).

[67] *Federal Trade Commission v. Good-Grape Co.*, 45 F. (2d) 70, 72 (1930); *Federal Trade Commission v. Winsted Hosiery Co.*, 258 U.S. 483, 494 (1922); *Federal Trade Commission v. Artloom Co.*, 69 F. (2d) 36, 38 (1934); *Consolidated Book Publishers v. Federal Trade Commission*, 53 F. (2d) 942, 945 (1931), cert. denied 286 U.S. 553 (1932).

[68] *Royal Baking Powder Co. v. Federal Trade Commission*, 281 Fed. 744, 752 (1922); *Butterick & Co. v. Federal Trade Commission*, 4 F. (2d) 910, 912 (1925); *Federal Trade Commission v. Standard Education Society*, 86 F. (2d) 692, 695 (1936).

an important part of the Commission's policy. Does this mean that in a proceeding based on false advertising, the Commission must call witnesses from the general public who will testify that they were deceived? The answer is in the negative, for the Commission's jurisdiction is not restricted to those situations where there has been actual deception of purchasers.[69] If an advertisement is misleading and has the tendency to deceive, the Commission will go into action; and the question confronting the Commission is the meaning of the advertisement itself. This is a question of fact, not of law, and the advertisement itself is all the evidence that is required.[70] Inasmuch as the meaning of an advertisement is a question of fact, the Commission's judgment as to its meaning and its false and deceptive character, is conclusive unless palpably wrong.[71] Thus, because the meaning of an advertisement is a question of fact that requires skill and knowledge, the Commission's findings are construed liberally in support of an order to cease and desist.[72]

---

[69] *Sears, Roebuck & Co. v. Federal Trade Commission*, 258 Fed. 307, 311 (1919); *Charles of the Ritz v. Federal Trade Commission*, 143 F. (2d) 676 (1944); *Herzfeld v. Federal Trade Commission*, 140 F. (2d) 207, 208 (1944); *Bockenstille v. Federal Trade Commission*, 134 F. (2d) 369, 371 (1943); *Pep Boys v. Federal Trade Commission*, 122 F. (2d) 158, 161 (1941); *Federal Trade Commission v. Hires Turner Glass Co.*, 81 F. (2d) 362, 364 (1935); *Brown Fence and Wire Co. v. Federal Trade Commission*, 64 F. (2d) 934, 936 (1933); *Masland Duraleather Co. v. Federal Trade Commission*, 34 F. (2d) 733, 737–38 (1929); *Federal Trade Commission v. Balme*, 123 F. (2d) 615, 621 (1928), cert. denied 272 U.S. 598 (1928).

[70] *Liggett & Myers Tobacco Co. v. Finzer*, 128 U.S. 122, 184, 9 S. Ct. 40, 32 L. Ed. 369 (1888); *Aronberg v. Federal Trade Commission*, 132 F. (2d) 165 (1942), 138 F. (2d) 388, 393 (1943).

[71] *Brougham v. Blanton Manufacturing Co.*, 249 U.S. 495, 496–500, 39 S. Ct. 363, 63 L. Ed. 725 (1919); *Houston v. St. Louis Independent Packing Co.*, 249 U.S. 479, 484, 39 S. Ct. 332, 63 L. Ed. 717 (1919); *Farley v. Simmons*, 99 F. (2d) 343, 346 (1938); *Aronberg v. Federal Trade Commission*, 132 F. (2d) 165 (1942); *Sebrone Co. v. Federal Trade Commission*, 135 F. (2d) 676, 678–79 (1943); *Federal Trade Commission v. Civil Service Training Bureau*, 79 F. (2d) 113, 114–15 (1935).

[72] *Allied Paper Mills v. Federal Trade Commission*, 168 F. (2d) 600, 606 (1948), cert. denied 336 U.S. 918 (1949); *Triangle Conduit and Cable Co.*

The more important question concerns the standards employed by the Commission in determining whether or not an advertisement is false. That a graduate chemist could recognize the deceptive use of a scientific fact in an advertisement needs no elaboration. A psychologist, even though an amateur, would have no difficulty in seeing through the copy appeals employed in advertising. It seems obvious then that advertisements, if they are to sell products, must be directed at those persons who may read or hear and be convinced. The Commission is aware of this, and in determining the meaning of advertisements they are read as they would be read by those to whom they are addressed.[73] That the courts are also aware of this was demonstrated when Justice Black said:

> The fact that a false advertisement may be obviously false to those who are trained and experienced does not change its character, nor take away its power to deceive others less experienced. There is no duty resting upon a citizen to suspect the honesty of those with whom he transacts business. Laws are made to protect the trusting as well as the suspicious. The best element of business has long since decided that honesty should govern competitive enterprises, and that the rule of *caveat emptor* should not be relied upon to reward fraud and deception.[74]

Because of the realization that the maxim of *caveat emptor* has no place in our interdependent society, the Commission and the courts have both agreed that even advertisements which are merely ambiguous and create a false impression, al-

---

v. Federal Trade Commission, 168 F. (2d) 175, 179 (1948), aff'd 336 U.S. 956 (1949).

[73] *Aronberg v. Federal Trade Commission*, 132 F. (2d) 165, 167–68 (1942); *DDD Corp. v. Federal Trade Commission*, 125 F. (2d) 679, 681–82 (1942); *Consolidated Book Publishers v. Federal Trade Commission*, 53 F. (2d) 942, 944 (1931), cert. denied 286 U.S. 553 (1932).

[74] *Federal Trade Commission v. Standard Education Society*, 302 U.S. 112, 116, 58 S. Ct. 113, 82 L. Ed. 141 (1937).

though literally true, are unlawful.[75] Therefore, to protect the most ignorant or unsuspecting purchaser, the Commission may insist upon a representation being meticulously worded.[76]

To indicate how far the courts have come in recognizing the economic and social implications of advertising, it is necessary to consider briefly two cases. The first case, *Ford Motor Co. v. Federal Trade Commission* [77] concerned the advertising of an automobile purchase finance plan. The advertisements, though literally true, conveyed the impression that the rate of interest was only 6 per cent, when it was actually a great deal more. The company opposed the action of the Commission on the grounds that first, the advertising employed did not affect interstate commerce because only the local dealer used the advertising, and his sales were to people in the same state; and second, the method of advertising used was not unfair or deceptive because it was literally true. In commenting upon the first argument, the Court took a realistic and practical view when it said:

> Advertising goes hand in hand with the volume of production and retail distribution. It operates to increase the demand for and availability of goods and to develop quickly consumers' acceptance of the manufactured products. Expressed another way, it breaks down consumers' resistance, creates consumers' acceptance, and develops consumers' demand. . . . The use of advertising as an aid to the production and distribution of goods has been recognized so long as to require only passing

---

[75] *United States v. Ninety-Five Barrels*, 265 U.S. 438, 442–43, 44 S. Ct. 529, 68 L. Ed. 1094 (1924); *Ford Motor Co. v. Federal Trade Commission*, 120 F. (2d) 175, 182 (1941), cert. denied 314 U.S. 668 (1941).

[76] *Progress Tailoring Co. v. Federal Trade Commission*, 153 F. (2d) 103, 106 (1946); *Charles of the Ritz v. Federal Trade Commission*, 143 F. (2d) 676, 680 (1944); *Aronberg v. Federal Trade Commission*, 132 F. (2d) 165, 167 (1942); *General Motors Corp. v. Federal Trade Commission*, 114 F. (2d) 33, 36 (1940); *Jacob Siegal Co. v. Federal Trade Commission*, 327 U.S. 608, 614, 66 S. Ct. 758, 90 L. Ed. 888 (1946).

[77] 120 F. (2d) 175 (1941), cert. denied 314 U.S. 668 (1941). Italics supplied in the following excerpts.

notice. The economy of mass production is just as well known and the effects of advertising may be described as mass selling without which distribution would be lessened and a fortiori production would correspondingly decrease. The present advertisement of the method for financing the purchase of petitioner's cars on credit was an integral part of their production and distribution.

The sale on credit of petitioner's cars by its local dealers, when separately considered, may be intrastate in character but when the activities of petitioner's local agencies are weighed in the light of their relationship to the petitioner, and its financing sales of cars, it is at once apparent that there is such a close and substantial relationship to interstate commerce that the control of such activities is appropriate to its protection.

Though the Court stated that the connection between advertising and production has long been recognized, this marked the first time that advertising's role in the national economy was enunciated so clearly in a case involving the Federal Trade Commission. The second argument, concerning literal truth as a defense, was dispensed with as follows:

The *average individual* does not make, and often is incapable of making minute calculations to determine the cost of property purchased on the deferred payment plan. Mechanization, industrialization, and urbanization have transformed the structure of our society and raised to the proportions of a major social problem, the protection of the installment purchaser against *his own* ignorance and the pressure of his need.

The present advertisement must be considered from the view of the prospective purchasers of petitioner's cars and, in determining its capacity or tendency to mislead, *must be judged from its general fabric, not its single thread.*

However, the second case to be considered is even more explicit in speaking of the need to devise laws and regulations that can be employed to protect the average citizen. This case, *P. Lorillard Co. v. Federal Trade Commission,*[78] dealt with the

[78] 186 F. (2d) 52 (1950).

advertisement of Old Gold cigarettes which claimed that the cigarette contained less irritating substances and was therefore less harmful to the throat than any of the six other leading brands of cigarettes. The advertising campaign in question was based on chemical analyses, reported in *Reader's Digest* magazine, which indicated that Old Gold cigarettes did contain less irritating substances. However, the same tests showed that the difference in content of these irritants was negligible and there could be absolutely no difference in the physiological effect upon the smoker. In commenting upon the company's contention that they had merely claimed what had been truthfully stated in the magazine, Judge Parker said:

> An examination of the advertisements, however, shows a perversion of the meaning of the *Reader's Digest* article which does little credit to the company's advertising department—a perversion which results in the use of the truth in such a way as to cause the reader to believe the exact opposite of what was intended by the writer of the article.

After discussing the content of the article, which mentioned the fact that the difference among the various brands of cigarettes was negligible, Judge Parker continued:

> The company proceeded to advertise this difference as though it had received a citation for public service instead of a castigation from the *Reader's Digest*. . . .
>
> The fault with the advertising was not that it did not print all that the *Reader's Digest* article said, but that it printed a small part thereof in such a way as to create an entirely false and misleading impression, not only as to what was said in the article, but also as to the quality of the company's cigarettes. Almost anyone reading the advertisements or listening to the radio broadcasts would have gained the very definite impression that Old Gold cigarettes were less irritating to the throat and less harmful than other leading brands of cigarettes because they contained substantially less nicotine, tars, resins, and that the *Reader's Digest* had established this fact in impartial laboratory tests; and few would have troubled to look up the *Reader's Digest* to see what it really had said. . . . To

tell lesss than the whole truth is a well-known method of deception; and he who deceives by resorting to such method cannot excuse the deception by relying upon the truthfulness per se of the partial truth by which it has been accomplished.

The ambitions of the crusaders against deceptive practices had at long last been realized, and the reward for their zealous activities cannot be expressed better than it was by Judge Parker:

> In determining whether or not advertising is false or misleading within the meaning of the statute, regard must be had, not to the fine-spun distinction and arguments that may be made in excuse, but to the effect which it might reasonably be expected to have upon the general public. "The important criterion is the *net impression* which the advertisement is likely to make upon the general populace." *Charles of the Ritz Dist. Corp. v. Federal Trade Commission,* 143 F. (2d) 676, 679–680. As was well said by Judge Coxe in *Florence Manufacturing Co. v. J. C. Dowd & Co.,* 178 F. 73, 75, with reference to the law relating to trade-marks: "*The law is not made for the protection of experts, but for the public—that vast multitude which includes the ignorant, the unthinking and the credulous,* who in making purchases do not stop to analyze, but are governed by appearance and general impressions." [79]

It is to be hoped that when the courts, in general, adopt the attitude of Judge Parker, as expressed in the Old Gold case, the social and ethical battle with the less well-meaning forces of advertising will have been won.

Administrative Procedure

Thus far the legislative history of the Commission and its case-wise evolution through the courts have been dealt with in some detail. However, that is but half the story because

---

[79] 186 F. (2d) at 55. Italics supplied.

other activities of the Commission play just as important a part in its work in advertising. The Commission appears in court only when a respondent, who has been ordered to cease and desist, appeals to a circuit court for review of a Commission order within sixty days of its issuance; or when the Commission seeks a civil violation (under Section 5) or criminal penalty (under Section 12) because a respondent disobeys an order. But such appearances in court occur only in a very small number of Commission cases. False advertising material coming to the attention of the Commission is usually settled administratively by a letter, which often produces compliance, by means of a stipulation, trade practice conference, or a formal hearing resulting in an order which is obeyed.

A proceeding originates when a false, deceptive, or misleading advertisement comes to the attention of the Commission. This is done in several ways. The Commission has a Division of Investigation which is a unit of the Bureau of Antideceptive Practices and which, on its own initiative, maintains a continuing survey of national advertising. Through the cooperation of publishers and broadcasters this division is supplied, upon request, with current magazines, newspapers, farm and trade journals, mail order catalogs, and radio and television commercial continuities. The frequency with which a magazine, newspaper, or other periodical is requested will depend upon the periodical itself. Most periodicals are examined approximately three times each year. Periodicals with the bulk of their circulation among groups with little education, and which frequently print advertisements of questionable character, are called upon more often. There is no scheduled frequency of examination of radio and television continuities.[80]

---

[80] The Division also examines the commercial portions of all electrical transcription recordings made each month. The Division's activities in the television field are of recent origin, naturally. Commercial scripts, continuities, and films are received from television stations, networks, and film producers.

National and regional radio networks, which necessarily reach a greater number of homes, are examined on a continuous, weekly basis; and large and powerful urban stations, not affiliated with any network, are also subject to frequent examination. Smaller, less powerful urban and rural stations are examined less frequently, as is the case of less widely circulated periodicals. This does not suggest that the smaller radio stations and periodicals are less likely to be the channels of advertising abuses. Less frequent examination is dictated by two reasons. First, the Commission's appropriations have never been sufficient to provide for a staff large enough to conduct a more frequent survey of advertising, and therefore some selectivity is necessary. Second, in keeping with its obligation to protect the public, the Commission must exhaust its funds and staff on an examination of those media which reach the greatest segment of the public. Therefore, the large periodicals, stations, and networks receive more detailed attention.

In maintaining its continuing survey, the Division employs expert knowledge and ability. The samples of the various advertising media are distributed to examiners, who read and check the advertisements.[81] The problem facing the examiner is not to permit his own judgment to be the sole guide as to the falsity of an advertisement. He must read each advertisement from the viewpoint of an ordinary member of the public and must be aware of the weakness in the consumer's psychological makeup. Although the examiner may see through the inherent deception in an advertisement that may be literally true, his job is to evaluate the advertisement as though he were a farm hand, factory worker, or office stenographer.

[81] Advertisements advancing pseudoscientific claims require specialized talents for examination. Thus, several examiners may be experts in the cigarette or cold remedy fields and will concentrate their major efforts on advertisements in the particular field.

In the course of the examination, all advertisements which are of a questionable character are separated from valid advertisements. It should be noted, that when the examiner has any doubt as to the veracity of a claim, he resolves it in favor of the public. The questioned advertisements and continuities are routed to a central office, in the nature of a clearing house, where all such advertisements of the same product or the same advertiser are brought together in one folder. The folder is sent to an attorney in the Division, who examines the advertisements and prepares a memorandum setting forth his recommendations. These recommendations are reviewed by the chief of the Division who makes the final decision. The matter may be dropped under certain conditions. In the event the practice in question is merely "puffing," and not deceptive, the particular folder may be set aside, pending an examination of further advertising by the same manufacturer. However, sometimes a practice that is clearly deceptive is not proceeded against. This is because the Commission's funds and personnel are limited, and the docket of the Commission may be sorely overcrowded. The deceptive practices which are not proceeded against are usually those involving little public interest. In such a situation the product advertised may be one which appeals only to a small segment of the public, or the advertisement has appeared in a small number of publications with limited circulation.

When the Division chief decides that an advertisement is deceptive and concerns the public interest sufficiently to warrant the use of the Commission's limited funds and personnel, he orders an investigation. This is conducted in two ways. First, contact letters are sent to the advertiser, requesting his past advertising history and proof of the claims which the Division deems deceptive. Although this is a purely administrative procedure and the advertiser is not required to answer, the contact letter in many cases will result in the furnishing of the requested information and, often, in complete cessation of the objectionable practices. It is obvious that such a procedure is most efficient and economical for protecting the public. Second, when the contact letter does not elicit the necessary information or voluntary compliance, a field investigation is conducted. At this point the Division of Field Investigation begins to function.[82] This Division maintains field offices in

TABLE 15

PRELIMINARY ADVERTISING SURVEY OF FEDERAL TRADE COMMISSION, 1941–50

Year	Radio	Television	Newspapers	Magazines	Mail Order
			Advertising Examined		
1941	1,826,140		201,401	185,308	22,213
1942	2,005,506		187,265	154,619	14,808
1943	1,815,644		183,474	144,893	9,617
1944	1,428,752		195,479	96,246	9,903
1945	1,260,614		179,300	113,633	15,018
1946	1,308,708		245,628	153,609	14,325
1947	1,427,103		208,554	165,014	12,334
1948	1,198,796	1,480	159,488	132,812	12,391
1949	1,508,323	31,656	170,629	144,582	10,133
1950	1,538,895	55,177	210,482	135,840	15,096
			Marked Questionable		
1941	25,715		13,047	12,455	799
1942	15,307		10,065	9,056	446
1943	24,481		14,310	10,685	757
1944	13,509		14,251	6,438	550
1945	9,811		9,985	5,871	789
1946	7,880		12,959	7,023	295
1947	10,540		8,401	6,921	230
1948	7,861	42	5,730	5,019	344
1949	14,454	643	7,599	7,049	144
1950	13,393	1,040	10,350	6,744	354

Source: Tables 15–17 were prepared for the author by the Federal Trade Commission. The radio and television columns refer to pages of continuities. The newspaper, magazine, and mail order figures refer to individual advertisements.

[82] The Division of Field Investigation is also responsible for original violations. Complaints originating with the public, rather than by survey, or complaints originating with one of the Commissioners, receive preliminary consideration in this Division. The same criteria of examination and recommendation are used here as in the Division of Investigation.

several cities across the country and will investigate the activities of the advertiser at his plant and central points of distribution. The investigation usually reveals the nature of the product, its qualities and properties, the results of using the product, and the effect of its advertising on the public. In addition to the Division of Field Investigation, the Commission has also a Bureau of Medical Opinion which, in cases of violations under Section 12 (foods, drugs, cosmetics, and devices), furnishes the Commission with the necessary scientific information.

TABLE 16

SECONDARY REVIEW BY FEDERAL TRADE COMMISSION OF CASES INVOLVING QUESTIONABLE ADVERTISING, 1941–50

Year	Cases Reported	Investigations Completed
1941	2,691	812
1942	2,441	617
1943	1,779	433
1944	1,558	352
1945	842	246
1946	942	252
1947	1,225	471
1948	1,434	401
1949	2,036	620
1950	2,491	436

Table 15 indicates the advertising examined and marked questionable by the Division of Radio and Periodical Advertising from 1941 to 1950.

After all investigations have been completed, the assembled data are turned over to the legal staff which interprets the facts and the law prior to disposing of the case. This is called secondary review, and the number of cases and investigations that have been subject to such review, from 1941 to 1950, is reported in Table 16.

The attorneys who conduct this secondary review may recommend that the case be handled in one of six manners:

1. *Matters closed.* In the event the investigation reveals that the advertising is not actually misleading and deceptive, or would not induce purchase of the product by misrepresentation, or was an isolated instance and not part of a general advertising scheme, or reaches only a small part of the public, the matter will be dropped. This means that no further action will be taken; but the advertiser's folder is retained in the event of new violations or increased public interest. Table 17 provides data on the disposition of cases after secondary review from 1941 to 1950.

2. *Matters handled administratively.* The Commission has permitted administrative settlement of cases since 1949.[83] The procedure involves the sending of a letter to the advertiser, informing him of the Commission's objections to his advertising. When the advertising practice complained of is not a serious one and it appears that the advertiser's error was made in good faith and will not be repeated, the Commission will accept his promise not to resume the objectionable practices. The administrative settlement is not a matter of public record, and the fact that the advertiser's name does not receive onerous publicity has been a great incentive for his acquiescence. Though the matter has been settled administratively, the Commission will retain a file on the advertiser and check his future advertising for compliance. Twenty-five matters were settled administratively in 1949, and seventy in 1950.

3. *Matters placed on suspense.* This procedure is followed when the secondary review reveals that the advertising practices are objectionable and continuous; but because of the need for additional information and uncertainty as to whether or not a proceeding would be in the public interest, the matter

---

[83] Federal Trade Commission, *Order* of June 29, 1949.

TABLE 17

DISPOSITION OF CASES, INVOLVING FALSE, DECEPTIVE OR MISLEADING ADVERTISING, AFTER SECONDARY REVIEW BY THE FEDERAL TRADE COMMISSION, 1941–50

Year	Matters Closed	Matters Suspended *	Matters Transferred to Other Divisions	Stipulations **		Complaints Recommended
				Recommended	Accepted	
1941	527		27	226	532	32
1942	389		22	164	560	42
1943	272		15	111	280	35
1944	224		15	90	303	23
1945	170		17	45	286	14
1946	146	1	57	40	96	7
1947	209	31	162	65	145	4
1948	227	4	142	31	152	3
1949	364	4	166	56	139	5
1950	101	6	133	98	164	28

* No figures available prior to August, 1946, when the Commission underwent reorganization.

** With respect to stipulations accepted, the figures for 1940–45 include each draft of a stipulation as a separate one. The figure for 1948 includes 53 amended stipulations accepted, and there were 5 in both 1949 and 1950.

is temporarily shelved. Upon acquisition of the additional data and resolution of the public-interest question, the proceeding may then take any of the five other courses.

4. *Matters transferred to other divisions.* Where violations of the Clayton Act, Export Trade Act, Wool Products Labeling Act, Robinson-Patman Act, or Trade-Mark Act of 1948 are involved, the investigations and proceedings are transferred to the divisions which are responsible for the enforcement of those Acts.

5. *Stipulation recommended.* This is an informal, but highly effective procedure. The stipulation procedure is predicated upon an admission by the advertiser that his practices have violated the Act. Therefore, if there is any doubt whatsoever as to the advertiser's guilt in his own mind or in the Commission's interpretation, the stipulation process will not be employed. It is to be noted that this procedure is entirely cooperative and is not in the nature of litigation or judicial proceeding. The Commission recommends and seeks stipulations because it believes that good will exists between itself and the advertiser. Stipulation always will be denied when it appears that the violation by the advertiser was intentional and that the stipulation, therefore, would not be entered into in good faith and could not be effective in preventing continued use of misleading advertising; or when the product advertised is an inherently dangerous food, drug, cosmetic, or device and can be summarily stopped by injunction.

The stipulation hearing is only partly judicial because it is conducted before an attorney-conferee who acts as trial examiner. Although the attorney who represents the Commission must support the Commission's charges at the conference, there are no formal requirements as to who has the burden of proof. All the facts and arguments of both sides are presented in an informal manner without the restricting influence of rules of evidence.[84] If at any time during the conference the conferees reach an impasse, either side may withdraw and the proceeding will go to complaint.

At the conclusion of the conference when all data have been examined and all discussion heard, the attorney-conferee drafts the stipulation. If the respondent agrees to the stipulation and places his signature upon it, the stipulation is sent to the Commissioners with a recommendation that it be accepted. After the stipulation has been agreed to by both the Commission and the advertiser, the latter is required to submit to the Commission a report within sixty days that he has complied with the stipulation. Generally, the advertiser will prepare and submit an affidavit as to manner and nature of compliance and will include also samples of his latest advertising copy.

It should be noted that the agreement by the Commission to stipulate does not technically preclude a subsequent proceeding by complaint or a modification of the stipulation because of a change in Commission policy. However, inasmuch as the stipulation procedure is based on good will, informality, and cooperation, less than 1 per cent of all matters stipulated have gone into complaint.

6. *Complaints recommended.* Where the matter cannot be disposed of by any of the five other methods, complaint is recommended. The complaint is the most formal of all Commission procedures. A formal complaint, enumerating the charges against the respondent, is served upon him; and he must answer this complaint within a certain period of time. Since the matter has not been disposed of previously by some other method, it is more than likely that the respondent's answer will claim that his advertising is not unfair or deceptive,

---

[84] That the stipulation procedure is in no way a litigation proceeding is demonstrated by the fact that the stipulation can be agreed to via the mails.

or that a proceeding by the Commission is not in the public interest, or that the respondent's activities are not in commerce. Upon receipt of the answer the Commission sets a date for hearing, which must be scheduled so as to be convenient for the Commission's attorney, the trial examiner, the respondent and his attorney, and expert and lay witnesses who may be scattered throughout the country.

The hearing itself is conducted before a trial examiner who is employed by the Commission.[85] The Commission must bear the burden of proof that the respondent's advertisements are deceptive or tend to deceive, and must conform to rules of evidence that are standard in administrative proceedings. After all the evidence and testimony have been heard, the trial examiner makes findings of fact as to the character and nature of respondent's practices. The findings of fact are then submitted with recommendations to the Commissioners. If the Commissioners believe that the Commission has not sustained its charges, the proceeding against the respondent is dropped. But if the Commissioners are of the opinion that the burden of proof has been met, an order will be issued against the respondent, directing him to cease and desist from certain of his practices. As indicated previously, this order stands in the shoes of a judicial order, and becomes final if the respondent does not appeal from the order to a Court of Appeals within sixty days of issuance.

Conclusion

Thus far we have observed that the courts, as, for example, in the *P. Lorillard* case, have awakened to the realization that advertising is directed at the "unthinking," and that the Com-

[85] A long-standing complaint against administrative agencies has been that the "judge" (trial examiner) and "counsel" (Federal Trade Commission attorney) are on the same side. Though this be technically true in that both are paid by the federal government, the trial examiner can properly boast of impartiality.

mission has developed a great variety of procedures to cope with an equally great variety of situations. But one general question remains unanswered. Is the Federal Trade Commission sufficiently armed to wage a successful campaign against the forces of bad advertising? The answer is in the negative, for the Commission suffers from many deficiencies which prevent a thorough policing of advertising. Some of them are as follows:

1. The Division of Investigation and the Division of Legal Investigation must, of necessity, bypass a great number of advertisements which are of a questionable nature. Congress has failed to recognize the fact that the Commission, unlike other agencies which are restricted to particular media and commodities, must police the entire field of advertising. Opposed to the legal and technical resources of many thousands of advertisers and advertising agencies, the Commission has a staff of 600 employees, including those in the Commission's branch offices.[86] These include attorneys, economists, accountants, statisticians, and office and administrative personnel who must concern themselves with several other Acts enforced by the Commission in addition to advertising practices. The shortage of personnel must necessarily limit the activities of the Commission to the point where many deceptive practices are permitted to escape.

2. Many matters that have gone to stipulation are neglected in that compliance is not checked beyond the sixty-day period imposed by the regulations. This is the result of not having enough personnel to conduct an active check.

3. The complaint procedure is such that it is relatively ineffective. Experience in the advertising field reveals that a clever and well-executed advertising campaign can deceive a

[86] Federal Trade Commission, *Annual Report, July 1, 1948 to June 30, 1949*, p. 5.

great many people and sell a large quantity of goods in a short time. The minimum time that must elapse from the discovery of a false advertisement to its cessation is about six months. After a deceptive practice has been uncovered by the Commission's survey or a complaint from a competitor or the general public has been received, at least twenty days are required to complete an investigation. Another twenty days will be consumed by an evaluation and interpretation of the data necessary for the preparation and serving of the complaint. The respondent has twenty days in which to answer the complaint.[87] Thus far, at least sixty days have elapsed. After respondent's answer has been received, a hearing must be scheduled. This may consume as much as two months, because a date must be found which is convenient to the witnesses, respondent and his attorney, the Commission's attorney, and the trial examiner's calendar. After the hearing, another week or ten days will elapse until the trial examiner prepares his findings and the Commission issues its order. Even when the hearing is over and the respondent has been ordered to cease and desist, he may continue his advertising for another sixty days, in the event he does not wish to appeal the order, or beyond that time if he does. Therefore, at a minimum, about 180 days have elapsed between the time the advertisement is picked up and the time it is effectively stopped. That advertising can convince and sell very effectively in six months needs no elaboration.[88]

---

[87] The time for answering often extends beyond twenty days because postponements are requested for legitimate reasons, e.g., respondent's attorney is engaged in other matters, more than twenty days is needed to compile the information necessary for the preparation of the answers, etc.

[88] Also, note amendment to Section 5 of the Federal Trade Commission Act by the *Act of March 16, 1950*, Chapter 61, P.L. 459, 81st Cong. "Each separate violation of such an order shall be a separate offense, except that in the case of a violation through continuing failure or neglect to obey a final order of the Commission each day of continuance of such failure or neglect shall be deemed a separate offense." It remains to be seen whether making

4. As part of the formal hearing on complaint, the Commission must sustain the burden of proof as to the falsity of the respondent's advertising. It is believed that this is a harsh requirement to impose upon the Commission for two reasons. First, a proceeding by the Commission is not penal in nature, since no fine ensues until after an order has been disobeyed. Thus, the Commission is charged with a burden of proof analogous to that confronting a prosecutor in a criminal action. Second, the advertiser owns and manufactures or sells the product and is, therefore, in a much better position to know the truth or falsity of the claims made in his advertising.

5. Another obstacle confronting the Commission concerns the hearing after complaint. When the truth or falsity of advertising involves a scientific or technical question, there is a need for expert opinion and testimony. Respondents can command great sums of money to provide transportation, expenses, and fees for experts. The Commission, on the other hand, has a total of two physicians and one biochemist in its Division of Medical Opinion. No matter how industrious or competent these men may be, they are physically unable to handle expeditiously the large amount of work. In addition, Congress has not allowed the Commission funds to provide for additional needed experts.

The foregoing enumeration of the Commission's shortcomings necessarily raises the question as to whether these deficiencies can be overcome. The answer is in the affirmative, and the following recommendations are submitted as possible solutions:

1. Congressional recognition of the important and difficult problems facing the Commission will go a long way toward

each day of the failure to obey such an order as a separate offense will curb violations when continuance may result in a good sales volume and greater profit.

their solution. Increased appropriations should provide additional investigatory personnel, attorneys, examiners, scientists, and witnesses. This will permit a more detailed examination of advertising, especially where limited public interest is involved, closer checks on compliance, more expeditious scientific testing and evaluation, and more expert testimony.[89] Given increased personnel and funds, the Commission will have the tools to attack deceptive advertisements.

2. The law of unfair and deceptive advertising practices has been developed case by case since 1914. Such a myriad of bad practices has been uncovered and condemned that it seems unlikely that many new schemes can be devised. It is recommended, therefore, that the deceptive advertising practices be codified and enacted as penal statutes. The imposition of money penalties per se does not act as a sufficient deterrent to the advertiser who knowingly uses deceptive advertising because he can accomplish his purpose within the time necessary for a cease and desist order to operate effectively.[90] The anticipated complaints of harshness against such penal codification are met by advocating the establishment of an

---

[89] Thus far the Commission has been fortunate in the cooperation which it has received from various professional people, who have been willing to assist it without remuneration.

[90] "Despite the tentative restraining order of a Federal Trade Commission examiner, Dolcin will continue its national advertising as 'an outstanding drug for relieving arthritic and rheumatic pains and discomfort.'

"Piqued over the order, the company says it has no alternative but to appeal to the commission and, if need be, to the courts. Its chief "beef" is that it was not permitted full opportunity to present its principal evidence on the succinate-salicylate formulation's superiority over salicylates alone for the relief of arthritic and rheumatic pains and discomfort.

"The tentative order, the Dolcin Corporation claims, is characteristic of a type frequently issued in proceedings of this kind. It is based altogether on testimony—only opinion testimony—of the Government's witnesses in answering questions put to them by Government counsel. It ignores entirely the respondent's evidence and even ignores some of the significant answers favorable to Dolcin, given by Government witnesses to questions put to them on cross-examination, the company maintains." *New York Times,* Advertising and Marketing News, February 15, 1952.

advisory service. This would permit an advertiser to present his proposed advertising for approval. If the Commission approves the advertising, the advertiser may use it, secure in the knowledge that he will be free from prosecution. If the advertising is disapproved, the advertiser may then use it at the risk of prosecution.

3. Thus far the Commission's power has been corrective. Only after the advertisement has appeared can the Commission go into action. In addition to the codification suggested above, the Commission should be given the power to make rules which will have the force and effect of law. That this is a practicable and workable system is demonstrated by the success of the Securities and Exchange Commission, the Federal Alcohol Administration, and others.

4. It is recommended that the Commission be given effective injunctive power not subject to a sixty-day appeal period. This power should be extended to reach all advertising practices and not be limited to the advertising of food, drugs, cosmetics, and devices. In addition, the courts should be required to give greater effect to the verified pleading and affidavits of the Commission when seeking a preliminary injunction.[91]

---

[91] See *Federal Trade Commission v. Rhodes Pharmacal Co.*, 191 F. (2d) 744 (1951). In this case the Federal Trade Commission brought an action for a temporary injunction restraining the dissemination of false advertisements representing that the defendants' drug product was an effective remedy or treatment for arthritis and other diseases. The United States District Court denied the injunction and dismissed the complaint on the ground that the verified pleadings and the affidavits presented debatable questions which were not resolved by supporting affidavits and the plaintiffs appealed. The Court of Appeals held that the district court had only to resolve whether there was reasonable cause to believe that the alleged violation had taken place, and the dismissal of the complaint was an error. Commenting upon the fact that the Commission may seek a temporary injunction in an effort to protect the public from false advertisements of drugs and foods "upon proper showing," the court said, "it is true that there is nothing in the Act or in its legislative history to indicate what should be considered as a 'proper showing.' We think, however, that it is fair to say that all the Commission had to show was a justifiable basis for believing, derived from reasonable inquiry or other credible information, that such a state of facts probably existed as reasonably would lead the Com-

It is to be hoped that the adoption of all or some of the recommendations and suggestions mentioned above, combined with a realistic attitude by the courts, will give the Commission the necessary authority to meet its responsibilities.

---

mission to believe that the defendants were engaged in the dissemination of false advertisements of a drug in violation of the Act. *Le Baron v. Los Angeles Building & Construction Trades Council, D.C.*, 84 F. Supp. 629. See also *Federal Trade Commission v. Koch*, 3 F.T.C. Statutes & Decisions 720. The District Court was not required to find the charges made to be true, but to find reasonable cause to believe them to be true. Shore, for and on *Behalf of N.L.R.B. v. Building & Construction Trades Council*, 3 Cir., 173 F. (2d) 678, 682, 8 A.L.R. (2d) 731. This is to say, in the instant case, the court had only to resolve the narrow issue of whether there was 'reasonable cause' to believe that the alleged violation had taken place. Compare *Bowles v. Montgomery Ward & Co.*, 7 Cir., 143 F. (2d) 38, 42."

Chapter 6

ADVERTISING AND THE PUBLIC INTEREST—THE FEDERAL COMMUNICATIONS COMMISSION

The massive impact of radio and television upon our way of life has been discussed in Chapter 2. We noted that both these media possess great potentialities for educational and commercial purposes, ranging from the telecasting of a medical operation or a Senate committee hearing to the filmed commercial or personal sales message. Furthermore, the radio or television message can originate in a studio in New York and be received by sets throughout the country. Thus, radio and television transcriptions, carried on air waves that are not the private property of any individual, firm, or corporation, cannot be confined within the boundaries of one state. Radio and television are inherently national in character and must be regulated, if at all, by the federal government, for the separate states are incapable of supervising such a national phenomenon. The federal government has elected to control the use of the nation's air waves for radio and television broadcasting, and the instrumentality to exercise such control is the Federal Communications Commission.

Unlike the Federal Trade Commission, which is concerned with the character and nature of all advertising in commerce, the Federal Communications Commission concerns itself principally with the quantitative aspects of advertising on the radio and on television. But in at least one respect, the Federal Communications Commission parallels the Federal Trade Commission. As previously explained, the Federal Trade Commission was created to control practices that tended to burden free competition, and advertising came under its control through the breadth of the legislative standard in the acts to be administered. The Federal Communications Commission, which regulates some phases of advertising on the radio and television, was also created for different purposes. In order to understand how and why this Commission exercises control over advertising, it is necessary to understand first its history and evolution.

Historical Perspective

The first federal act for the regulation of radio was passed in 1910 and was designed for purposes of marine safety.[1] At that time standard commercial broadcast stations were unknown, and therefore general regulation of radio communications was unnecessary. Two years later the technical problems of radio that were to give rise in the future to extensive regulation made their appearance when radio was beginning to emerge from the purely experimental stage. The increased use of radio by vessels, amateur operators, and governmental installations throughout the world resulted in varying wave emissions, distress signals, and frequency interferences, and so it became necessary, if not urgent, that international radio frequencies be controlled. To fulfill this country's obligations under an international communications treaty, Congress enacted the Radio Communications Act of 1912, which required that a license be obtained from the Secretary of Commerce and Labor before radio apparatus could be operated.[2]

---

[1] 36 *Stat.* 629, 46 *U.S.C.A.* Sec. 484 *et seq.* This act required that a steamer licensed to carry more than fifty persons must be equipped with radio apparatus in charge of a skilled operator before it could leave an American port.

[2] 37 *Stat.* 302, 47 *U.S.C.A.* Sec. 51 *et seq.* The statute allocated certain frequencies for the use of the government and restricted the character of wave emissions and the transmission of distress signals.

The problem of standard broadcast stations did not become important until after the first World War. Standard broadcasting had become practicable by the early 1920's and the recognition of the commercial advantages that might be obtained through broadcasting led to a rapid increase in the number of standard stations. Unlike the general growth of industry and manufacturing, the growth of radio was subject to certain technical limitations. The number of broadcasting frequencies are limited by nature, and therefore when the number of radio stations exceeds the number of broadcast frequencies, interference is inevitable.

Similarly to the rapid expansion of industry in the last quarter of the nineteenth century, the vitality of radio and the confusion within this new field overran the bounds of public control. Between 1921 and 1924 the number of radio stations increased so much that the number of available frequencies was not sufficient to keep pace with the expansion of this new industry. The National Radio Conference, which met in 1923 and 1924, recommended that the Secretary of Commerce establish a policy of assigning specified frequencies to particular stations. Since there were not enough channels to accommodate all the stations, the Secretary attempted to provide for dual use of the same channel by limiting power and hours of station operation. In 1925 every channel in the standard broadcast band was occupied by at least one station. The problem continued to grow and under the regulatory system then existing, solution was impossible.[3]

---

[3] For a history of federal regulation of radio communication, see James M. Herring and Gerald G. Gross, *Telecommunications* (New York: McGraw-Hill Book Co., Inc., 1936), pp. 239–86; U. S. Dept. of Justice, Attorney General's Committee on Administrative Procedure, *Senate Document No. 186*, 76th Cong., 3d Sess. (1940), pp. 828–84; Arthur W. Socolow, *Law of Radio Broadcasting* (New York: Baker Voorhis & Co., Inc., 1939), pp. 38–61; William J. Donovan, "Origin and Development of Radio Law," 2 *Air Law Review* (1931), 107–29, 349–70, 468–71.

The authority of the Secretary of Commerce to deal with the situation had been severely limited. The courts had held that a license could not be denied to a legally qualified applicant for the reason that a proposed station would interfere with existing stations.[4] In addition, the courts had held that the Secretary could not restrict the frequency, power, or hours of operation of a station, nor did the use of an unassigned frequency by a station violate any law.[5]

Stripped of the authority necessary to meet his responsibilities, the Secretary of Commerce abandoned further attempts at regulation. This was followed by a flood of new stations using any frequency, power, or hours of operation they desired. With all the stations on the air simultaneously, none could be heard because of the interference. The situation became so bad that the President of the United States was forced to appeal to Congress for the enactment of a comprehensive radio law. The political temper was such that, in response to demands by the public as well as the radio industry, Congress enacted the Radio Act of 1927, the first comprehensive scheme of control over radio communication.

The Radio Act of 1927 bore the marks of compromise. A Federal Radio Commission was appointed to assign wave lengths and determine the power of output and hours of operation. Although the Act prescribed a maximum of three years for a broadcasting license, the Commission had the power to limit the license to a shorter period. The Act specified that the air waves belonged to the nation in that no licensee could enjoy vested rights. In order to transfer license ownership or to construct a new station, the Commission's consent was necessary. The Commission regulates advertising by virtue of a broad grant of licensing power, the criterion being "the

---

[4] *Hoover v. Intercity Radio Co.*, 52 App. D. C. 339, 286 F. 1003 (1926).
[5] *United States v. Zenith Radio Corp.*, 12 F. (2d) 614 (1926); *opinion of the Attorney General*, 35 Op. Atty. Gen. 126 (1926).

public interest, convenience, or necessity." In the exercise of the power the Commission may not censor or impose positive requirements of broadcast content on stations.

It would appear that the Radio Act of 1927 was an important expansion of federal regulatory powers. Although the Act did not make broadcasting a public utility,[6] it did vest the Commission with authority to determine the future structure and development of broadcasting. However, the Commission did not in its early years employ its authority with vigor, and as a result the broadcasting structure remained chaotic. This may perhaps be explained by the fact that the Commission was created for one year, and until 1930 its life was renewed each year. That such a system produced uncertainty, amounting to timidity on the part of the Commission, cannot be denied.

The heart of the Commission's authority is its licensing power which is to be exercised in the public interest, convenience, or necessity. In one of the Commission's early appearances before the Supreme Court, this standard was held to be more limited than perhaps Congress had intended. Mr. Chief Justice Hughes said:

> The requirement is to be interpreted by its context, by the nature of radio transmission and reception, by the scope, character and quality of services, and, where an equitable adjustment between states is in view, by the relative advantages and services which will be enjoyed by the public through the distribution of facilities. In making such an adjustment, the equities of existing stations undoubtedly demand consideration.[7]

---

[6] "In contradistinction to communication by telephone and telegraph, which the Communications Act recognizes as a common carrier activity and regulates accordingly . . . the Act recognizes that broadcasters are not common carriers and are not to be dealt with as such. . . ." *Federal Communications Commission v. Sanders Bros. Radio Station*, 309 U.S. 470, 474, 60 S. Ct. 693, 84 L. Ed. 869 (1940).

[7] *Federal Radio Commission v. Nelson Bros.*, 289 U.S. 266, 53 S. Ct. 627, 77 L. Ed. 116 (1933).

As in the case of any regulatory body equipped with a broad legislative standard, the Commission was unable to formulate a comprehensive definition of public interest. Like the Federal Trade Commission, the Federal Communications Commission is to decide each case on its particular facts, and the Commission's findings are to be conclusive. Though the Commission was established in 1927, it was not until 1940 that intrusions by the courts into administrative processes were effectively stopped.[8]

At the outset the Commission was faced with the problem of deciding which of several applicants was to receive a license to use a particular frequency in a particular area at a particular time. Prior to the creation of the Commission, commercial broadcasting had appropriated the most desirable channels. Nonprofit broadcasters, on the other hand, with less funds at their disposal were slower to commence broadcasting. As a result, the nonprofit stations were forced to use the undesirable frequencies and at the hours not used by the commercial broadcasters. When a nonprofit broadcaster and a commercial broadcaster each applied to the Commission for a license to use the same facilities, the Commission was required by the court to apply the principle of priority in deciding which of the applicants should be the licensee.[9] This meant that all other considerations being equal, the established station had prior rights, although the Act had expressly denied any licensee a vested interest. As pointed out, it was the commercial broadcaster who had been the first to use these facilities, and therefore it was the commercial broadcaster who secured the license. It is interesting to note that during this early period

---

[8] *Federal Communications Commission v. Pottsville Broadcasting Co.*, 309 U.S. 134, 60 S. Ct. 437, 84 L. Ed. 656 (1940); *Fly v. Heitmayer*, 309 U.S. 146, 60 S. Ct. 443, 84 L. Ed. 664 (1940).

[9] *Chicago Federation of Labor v. Federal Radio Commission*, 41 F. (2d) 422 (1930).

the control of radio advertising had not yet been thought to be in the public interest. The fact that commercial broadcasters received licenses for the best available frequencies, eventually led to radio programming that consisted primarily of commercially sponsored broadcasts. This problem of advertising excesses will be discussed later.

In addition to the principle of priority, the courts imposed on the Commission three other criteria as to the public interest. These were technical qualifications, economic qualifications, and serviceability to the listening public. Technical qualifications referred to engineering standards which were, of course, purely objective. Economic qualifications referred to the applicant's financial standing and adequate commercial support for the station. Obviously, those with strong financial backing could satisfy best this prerequisite. It is quite clear, then, that the commercial broadcaster was favored by this standard, as he was by the principle of priority.

Serviceability to the listening public implied that programs had to be so arranged as to provide interest for all groups in the listening public. It is upon this criterion that the regulation of radio and television advertising has been based. Because of the limitations in the number of channels, the commercial broadcasters were able to secure the best facilities on the theory that sponsored programs were of much wider general interest and therefore served a larger segment of the listening public. It would seem that each of the arguments advanced by the courts, or standards imposed by the Commission, favored advertising. Since original regulation of broadcasting by the federal government served to assign frequencies, eliminate interference, and technically improve broadcasting and since the standards employed by the regulatory body in issuing exclusive licenses favored commercial broadcasting, it is apparent that radio advertising, which opposes government regulation in any form, received its greatest impetus from such regulation.

The "Public Interest, Convenience, or Necessity"

Although the Federal Radio Commission was abolished in 1934 and its powers transferred to the newly created Federal Communications Commission (FCC), few important changes in the radio field were involved.[10] This was because the statutory standards to be administered by the new Commission were largely taken over from the original Radio Act of 1927.

The Act of 1934 included the regulation of telephone, telegraph, and all other forms of electrical communications; but the principal provision relating to radio and television [11] was that which gave the Commission authority to grant or revoke licenses and to make regulations necessary to carry out the provisions of the Act. Thus armed with a legislative mandate to act in the public's interest, convenience, and necessity, the newly organized Commission addressed itself to the problems of the broadcasting industry. The five principal problems confronting the Commission were:

1. *A fair and equitable geographic distribution of facilities.* However worthy a desire to allocate radio facilities geographically may seem, the Commission has often been confronted with a situation where a geographically equal distribution of facilities might work a disservice to the listener. To provide rural listeners with radio, the Act of 1934 provided for unlimited licensing of small stations in rural areas. But the problem has not been solved because of the economic difficulties

---

[10] 48 *Stat.* 1064, 47 *U.S.C.* Sec. 151 *et seq.*

[11] That the Act extends to television as well as radio is beyond doubt. "If there were any doubt respecting the intention of Congress in this respect, it would be set at rest by legislative history. *Senate Report No.* 781 discussing *Senate Bill S.* 3215 which was later enacted as the Federal Communications Act stated: 'The purpose of this bill is to create a communications commission with regulatory power over all forms of electrical communication. . . .' The language employed is so all inclusive as to leave no doubt but that it was the intention of Congress to occupy the television field in its entirety." *Allen B. Dumont Laboratories v. Carroll,* 184 F. (2d) 153, 155 (1950).

facing the rural station licensees. The revenue from advertising, as in the case of newspapers and magazines, is absolutely necessary to the existence of a radio or television station. There is a great deal of competition for station facilities in urban areas because of greater advertising revenue, but for want of advertising income the successful radio station in the sparsely populated regions is somewhat rare.

2. *Avoiding monopoly in the broadcasting industry.* The radio or television network is analogous to the business monoply, and the use of chain broadcasting demonstrates how one or two networks can control stations throughout the country. This situation is particularly undesirable where the only station in a locality is network owned or affiliated. The problem was recognized in the Act of 1934, which gave the Commission authority in Section 154(g) to make regulations applicable to chain broadcasting. But it must be remembered that the Commission licenses stations, not networks, and therefore regulations against chain broadcasting must be directed at the particular station. Theoretically, the Commission's licensing power gives it complete authority to prevent radio monopoly. Whether such theory has been transformed into practice will be discussed later.

3. *Education's place in the broadcasting picture.* The principal problem here is the battle between commercial and educational groups for broadcasting facilities. The Commission has avoided making a definite allocation and, indeed, has recommended that "mutual cooperation" between the opposing camps is the solution of the problem. The results of such mutual cooperation are evident when one observes that the most educational programs on the radio and television are seen and heard during the daytime hours. The evening hours, when the listening audience is much greater, are devoted almost exclusively to commercial broadcasting.

4. *The relationship between program control and censorship.* The Commission's control over radio and television programs is conditioned by two sections of the Act: one provides that the Commission shall have no power of censorship; the other, that where a licensee permits his station to be used by a political candidate, he must afford equal opportunities to all other candidates for the same office.[12] Further discussion of this problem will follow in subsequent pages.

5. *Encouraging wider and more effective use of the radio in the public interest.* The Act specifically provides that the Commission shall "study new uses for radio [and television], provide for experimental use of frequencies, and generally encourage the larger and more effective use of the radio in the public interest." The principal problem confronting the Commission in carrying out this mandate is to determine when new technical developments are ready to be authorized for public use. Standardization that is premature can often result in retarding development, for the setting of standards according to technical developments that are protected by patents may lead to a monopoly by those controlling the patents. The problem was encountered by the Commission when it authorized standard commercial broadcasting by frequency modulation stations and commercial telecasting. The color television controversy is another illustration of this problem.

The problems listed in the foregoing pages have been introduced in this book because these questions and advertising are intertwined. The problem of the geographic allocation of broadcasting and telecasting facilities exists because the need for advertising revenue prevents the development of adequate facilities in rural areas. The problem of monopoly and chain broadcasting is closely connected with advertising in that the network is the instrumentality through which radio advertising

---

[12] 47 U.S.C. Sec. 177 and Sec. 168, respectively.

is used most effectively. The problem of educational time as opposed to commercial time is due entirely to the quest for the advertising dollar. The problem of censorship is concerned often with that of controlling fraudulent advertising on the radio and television. Finally, the problem of encouraging larger and more effective use of these media is part and parcel of the advertising problem, since commercial interests, seeking to attract additional advertising funds, are the first to seek authorization to use new technical methods.

A mere glance at these problems reveals that the Federal Communications Commission is concerned with some of the most important elements of advertising. In keeping with its responsibility to make certain that radio and television are used in the public interest, the Commission must concern itself with the nature of radio and television advertising, that is, fraud, obscenity, deception, and so on. The Commission must also concern itself with another aspect of advertising, namely, whether radio and television are being used excessively for commercial purposes. The qualitative and especially the quantitative aspect of advertising on the radio and television are the responsibilities of the Commission. But before examining how the Commission has sought to meet its responsibilities, one must first understand what the powers of the Commission are.

The Networks Challenge FCC Authority

A comprehensive discussion of the Federal Communications Commission's responsibility and authority in the field of radio may be found in the case of *National Broadcasting Co. v. United States*.[13] The case involved a suit by the leading radio networks to enjoin enforcement of chain broadcasting

---

[13] 319 U.S. 190, 63 S. Ct. 997, 86 L. Ed. 1586 (1943).

regulations which had been formulated by the Federal Communications Commission.[14] The regulations were broad in scope and provided that:

1. No license shall be granted to a standard broadcast station having any contract, arrangement, or understanding, express or implied, with a network organization under which the station is prevented or hindered from, or penalized for, broadcasting the programs of any other network organization.

Investigations made by the Commission had revealed that most networks required an affiliated station to contract not to broadcast the programs of any other network. As a result the affiliated licensees could not exercise their statutory duty of choosing programs which would best serve the needs of their particular community. The Commission's report pointed out that the 1939 World Series, which was broadcast exclusively by the Mutual Network, could not be heard in areas serviced by stations affiliated with other networks. The "exclusive" clause destroyed competition in the radio field because the existing networks had tied up the best stations in the country, and as a result advertising sponsors had to turn to the networks. Even if a new network desired to commence broadcasting and offered better programming in the public interest, it could not obtain station outlets. It was the advertising dollar which made this practice possible, for by securing exclusively affiliated stations, the network could guarantee the advertiser what was tantamount to a "captive audience."

2. No license shall be granted to a standard broadcast station having any contract, arrangement, or understanding, ex-

---

[14] Federal Communications Commission, *Commission Order in Docket No. 5060*. Regulations 3.101–3.108 (1941). For the investigation that preceded the issuance of the regulations, see Federal Communications Commission, *Report on Chain Broadcasting* (Washington, D. C.: U. S. Govt. Printing Office, 1941).

press or implied, with a network organization which prevents or hinders another station serving substantially the same area, from broadcasting the network's programs not taken by the former station, or which prevents or hinders another station serving a substantially different area from broadcasting any program of the network organization.

The evil to be corrected by this regulation was network affiliation agreements whereby a network was bound not to sell programs to any other station in the same area. Many programs, which might be of interest to the listening public, could not reach the public in an area where the affiliated station chose not to broadcast the program. The result of the territorial agreement was the same as if deliberately induced electrical interference had drowned out the program broadcast by a nonaffiliated station.

3. No license shall be granted to a standard broadcast station having any contract, arrangement, or understanding, express or implied, with a network organization which provides, by original term, provisions for renewal, or otherwise for the affiliation of the station with the network organization for a period longer than two years.

The underlying cause for the promulgation of this regulation was that an affiliated station was bound by a contract (usually for five years), even though the policy of the network and the caliber of its programs might deteriorate to the point where they were entirely commercial.

4. No license shall be granted to a standard broadcast station which options for network programs any time subject to call on less than 56 days notice, or more time than a total of three hours within each of the four segments of the broadcast day. . . . 8:00 A.M. to 1:00 P.M., 1:00 P.M. to 6:00 P.M., 6:00 P.M. to 11:00 P.M., 11:00 P.M. to 8:00 A.M.; . . . Such options may not be exclusive as against other network organizations and may not prevent or hinder the station from optioning or selling any or all of the time covered by the option or other time, to other network organizations.

Formerly the practice had been for affiliation agreements to contain optional time clauses. On 28 days' notice the network could require the affiliated station to carry a network program during the optioned time. The optioned time ran from eight and one-half hours a day for some networks to the entire day for others. The result was that the affiliate had little opportunity to build up locally sponsored programs of local interest and service, because regular scheduling was impossible if the network could suddenly require the affiliate to carry a network program. The affiliated station was rendered completely dependent upon the network because it could not enter into a long-term sponsorship contract for a local program. Moreover, the station's service to the local community was diminished because, by exercising the option, local events of importance and interest could be pushed off the air by a network program.

> 5. No license shall be granted to a standard broadcast station having any contract, arrangement, or understanding, express or implied, with a network organization which (a), with respect to programs offered pursuant to an affiliation contract, prevents or hinders the station from rejecting or refusing network programs which the station reasonably believes to be unsatisfactory or unsuitable; or which (b), with respect to network programs so offered or already contracted for, prevents the station from rejecting or refusing any program which, in its opinion, is contrary to the public interest, or from substituting a program of outstanding local or national importance.

Existing affiliation contracts allowed a station the right to reject a network program if the station reasonably believed the program was not in the public interest. It was impossible, however, as a practical matter for a station to determine in advance if a program was not in the public interest on the basis of the skeletal information supplied by the network. In practice the stations were forced to delegate their programming authority to the networks; and the network, in turn, delegated actual program production to an advertising agency. Because the station is licensed to serve the public and since it cannot lawfully delegate that duty to the network or advertising agency, the existing contract clauses violated the purpose of the Act.

> 6. No license shall be granted to a network organization, or to any person directly or indirectly controlled by or under common control with a network organization, for more than one standard broadcast station where one of the stations covers substantially the service area of the other station, or for any standard broadcast station in any locality where the existing standard broadcast stations are so few or of such unequal desirability (in terms of coverage, power, frequency, or other related matters) that competition would be substantially restrained by such licensing.

The Commission's investigation revealed that the majority of the most powerful and best-located stations in the country were network-owned and not merely network-affiliated. As a result the facilities of these stations were denied to competing networks, and, in addition, plural station ownership in the same area by one network often resulted in subverting the station's policies to the network's interest. The network's desire for advertising revenue might result in denying an area important local programs. The statutory duty of a licensee was to the public in his particular community, and that duty could not be met where several stations in the same section of the country were owned and operated by one network. In addition, the network's proprietary interest in a station which it owned, might operate to the disadvantage of a station which was affiliated.

> 7. No license shall be issued to a standard broadcast station affiliated with a network organization which maintains more than one network.

The purpose behind this regulation was to prevent monopoly in the broadcasting industry. Multi-network operation could result in complete control over areas that had more than one operating station. If such control were allowed to develop unhampered, a network organization could dictate the program content for large areas without an awareness of the needs of the local community.

> 8. No license shall be granted to a standard broadcast station having any contract, arrangement, or understanding, express or implied, with a network organization under which the station is prevented or hindered from, or penalized for, fixing or altering its rates for the sale of broadcast time for other than the network's programs.

Most affiliation agreements contained a clause which empowered the network to reduce a station's network rate (i.e., reduce the station's compensation) if the station charged less for non-network advertising than the rate charged for network advertising. In other words, a station could not charge a national advertiser less than the network charged him. Thus the station was unable to compete for national advertising and such inability to bargain, in the Commission's opinion, did not serve the public interest.

The networks attacked the regulations on the grounds that:

1) In formulating the regulations, the Commission exceeded its regulatory powers under the Act.
2) If the Commission did not exceed its authority, then it misconceived the scope of the Act and the regulations were arbitrary and capricious.
3) If the Act authorized the Commission to formulate such regulations, the Act was unconstitutional because it was an improper delegation of legislative power.
4) The regulations violated the First Amendment of the Constitution because they abridged the right of free speech.

The Court observed that the contention of the networks was that the Commission's powers were limited to only the engineering and technical aspects of radio communication. The Court asserted that the argument was specious because the Act provided that the Commission's power was to be governed by the public interest, convenience, or necessity. Speaking for the Court, Mr. Justice Frankfurter said:

> Yet we are asked to regard the Commission as a kind of traffic officer, policing the wave lengths to prevent stations from interfering with each other. But the Act does not restrict the Commission merely to supervision of the traffic. It puts upon the Commission the burden of determining the composition of that traffic. The facilities of radio are not large enough to accommodate all who apply. And since Congress itself could not do this, it committed the task to the Commission.

Thus having established that the regulations were within the scope of the Commission's authority under the Act, the Court considered next the question of whether the Commission had acted in an arbitrary and capricious manner. The Court observed that the Commission had to conform to certain standards when performing its functions.[15] One standard was that of the public interest.[16] Mr. Justice Frankfurter continued:

> The facilities of radio are limited and therefore precious; they cannot be left to wasteful use without detriment to the

---

[15] The question of whether the Commission's authority in the Act had been confined within sufficiently definable standards, had been previously answered by the Supreme Court. *Federal Communications Commission v. Pottsville Broadcasting Co.*, 309 U.S. 134, 60 S. Ct. 437, 84 L. Ed. 656 (1939), held that the public interest, convenience, or necessity was as concrete a criterion as could be devised in a field where the exercise of delegated authority involved such complicated factors. In *New York Central Securities Corp. v. United States*, 287 U.S. 12, 53 S. Ct. 45, 77 L. Ed. 138 (1933), the Court observed that the criterion of public interest is sufficiently definite so that there is no danger of unlimited power being conferred. In *Federal Radio Commission v. Nelson Bros. Bond and Mortgage Co.*, 289 U.S. 266, 53 S. Ct. 627, 77 L. Ed. 116 (1933), the Court held that the requirement of public interest was to be interpreted according to the nature of radio transmission and reception, its scope, character, and quality.

[16] The public interest in the issuing of a license is the ability of the licensee to render the best service possible to the community which is reached by his broadcast. *Federal Communications Commission v. Sanders Bros. Radio Station*, 309 U.S. 470, 60 S. Ct. 693, 84 L. Ed. 869 (1939).

> public interest. . . . The Commission's licensing function cannot be discharged, therefore, merely by a finding that there are no technological objections to the granting of a license.

If the public interest was deemed satisfied because a licensee satisfied certain engineering requirements, then the Commission would be unable to resolve the situation created by the filing of several applications for one channel when all applicants could and did meet the engineering requirements. The Court denied that the meaning of the public interest was so limited, and maintained that the Act was designed to secure for the public the maximum benefits of radio. After citing the sections of the Act applicable to the Commission's authority to encourage more effective use of radio, to regulate stations engaged in chain broadcasting specifically, and to make regulations generally, the Court went on to say:

> These provisions, individually and in the aggregate, preclude the notion that the Commission is empowered to deal only with technical and engineering impediments. . . . Suppose, for example, that a community can, because of physical limitations, be assigned only two stations. That community might be deprived of effective service in any one of several ways. More powerful stations in nearby cities might blanket out the signals of the local stations so that they could not be heard at all. The stations might interfere with each other so that neither could be clearly heard. One station might dominate the other with the power of its signal. *But the community could be deprived of good radio service in ways less crude.* One man, financially and technically qualified, might apply for and obtain the licenses of both stations and present a single service over the two stations, thus wasting a frequency otherwise available to the area. The language of the Act does not withdraw such a situation from the licensing and regulatory powers of the Commission, and there is no evidence that Congress did not mean its broad language to carry the authority it expresses.[17]

---

[17] 319 U.S. at 217, 218; italics supplied.

Thus, the Court demonstrated that even though the Act did not expressly authorize the Commission to deal with inimical network practices, the legislative interest and language were sufficiently broad to cloak the Commission with the authority to protect the public interest, and the regulations in question were issued under that authority. As to whether or not the regulations were arbitrary, the Court pointed out that the distinction between that which is arbitrary and that which is unwise must be preserved. The Court had no authority to question the wisdom of the Acts of Congress or its agents.[18]

In determining whether the regulations in question would further or retard the public interest, Mr. Justice Frankfurter remarked:

> The responsibility belongs to the Congress for the grant of valid legislative authority and to the Commission for its exercise. It would be sheer dogmatism to say that the Commission made out no case for its allowable discretion in formulating these Regulations. Its long investigation disclosed the existence of practices, which it regarded as contrary to the "public interest," . . . The problems with which the Commission attempted to deal could not be solved at once and for all time by rigid rules-of-thumb. . . . In each case that comes before it, the Commission must still exercise an ultimate judgment whether the grant of a license would serve the 'public interest, convenience, or necessity.' If time and changing circumstances reveal that the 'public interest' is not served by application of the Regulations, it must be assumed that the Commission will act in accordance with its statutory obligations.

Having thus disposed of the arguments of unreasonableness and unconstitutional delegation of authority, the Court con-

---

[18] The technical opinion of an administrative agency run by experts in a particular field is superior to that of a court. In addition, most administrative acts divest the courts of authority to question the wisdom of an administrative finding if such finding is based on fact. *Board of Trade v. United States,* 314 U.S. 534, 62 S. Ct. 366, 86 L. Ed. 1132 (1941).

sidered the network's contention that the regulations violated the First Amendment of the Constitution because they abridged the right of free speech. In answer, the Court observed that if the argument was sound, every person denied a license would be denied also his right of free speech. This is a completely untenable argument, because the operation of radio facilities is inherently not available to all. Therefore, unlike other channels of expression, radio transmission must be regulated and some persons who wish to use it must be denied that privilege. In commenting upon this denial the Court said:

> But Congress did not authorize the Commission to choose among applicants upon the basis of their political, economic or social views, or upon any other capricious basis. If it did, or if the Commission by these Regulations proposed a choice among applicants upon some such basis, the issue before us would be wholly different. . . . The licensing system established by Congress in the Communications Act of 1934 was a proper exercise of its power over commerce. The standard it provided for the licensing of stations was the public interest, convenience or necessity. Denial of a station license on that ground, if valid under the Act, is not a denial of free speech.

By denying the petition of the network for enjoinment of the enforcement of the chain broadcasting regulations, the Court clearly defined the Commission's powers over radio (and television). First, the Commission's authority extended far beyond the technical or engineering aspects of radio communication. Second, in employing such authority, the Commission acted in the "public interest, convenience, or necessity," which clearly was definite enough to be constitutional. Third, the core of the Commission's authority was its licensing power and the Commission, within the confines of the Act, could deny the granting or renewal of a license where it would not be in the public interest, convenience, or necessity. For purposes of controlling advertising practices, the Commission's authority lies in its power to determine that certain advertising practices are not in the public interest, convenience, or necessity, and the wisdom of such determination is a matter for the Congress and not the courts.

Advertising Problems of FCC

At this point an examination of the advertising problems confronting the Commission and how its authority may be used to cope with such problems is in order. It is beyond doubt that for both practical and legal reasons the federal government alone is able to regulate advertising on the radio and television. Legal restrictions preclude any state regulation of radio advertising whatsoever, for Congress has fully occupied the field under the commerce clause of the Constitution and the field is not open to state regulation.[19]

As indicated previously, radio and television advertising problems fall into two separate categories. The first is a *qualitative* category and includes advertising that is obscene, profane, fraudulent, or deceptive—all adverse to the public interest, convenience, or necessity. The second is a *quantitative* category and includes only the amount of radio and television time devoted to advertising. Where a radio or television station program log is predominantly commercial, the station licensee may be said to serve commercial rather than the public interest. A separate examination of these categories will serve best to illustrate the Commission's concern with advertising.

The Commission's problem with respect to the first, or qualitative, category is not nearly as difficult as is its problem

---

[19] *Allen B. Dumont Laboratories v. Carroll*, 184 F. (2d) 153, 156 (1950); see also *Hines v. Davidowitz*, 312 U.S. 52, 61 S. Ct. 399, 85 L. Ed. 581 (1940); *Cloverleaf Butter Co. v. Patterson*, 315 U.S. 148, 62 S. Ct. 491, 86 L. Ed. 754 (1941).

with the second category. Although not specifically directed at bad advertising, the Act provides for suspension of the broadcast license of any operator upon proof that radio communication containing profane or obscene words or meaning has been transmitted. This provision has been embodied in the criminal code and provides for punishment by fine and imprisonment.[20] A lingerie commercial on television featuring nudity would be a typical violation. Thus, indecency in advertising on the radio and television is subject to double-barreled punishment. The station operator may lose his license and the person who utters the profanity may be jailed. It is obvious that this dual sanction effectively deters the condemned practices. The practices which are more closely related to advertising, namely, deception and fraud, do not cause the Commission much trouble. As indicated in the previous chapter, the Federal Trade Commission continually monitors radio and television commercials, and the major portion of the deceptive or fraudulent radio and television advertising practices are discovered and acted against by that governmental agency. But the Federal Communications Commission frequently receives letters of complaint from the public about radio and television advertising.

In a situation where only deception is involved, the FCC refers the complaint to the Federal Trade Commission, since the responsibility for most deceptive practices lies with the advertiser, who is subject to the Federal Trade Commission's jurisdiction. Furthermore, the licensee, in the absence of flagrant and obvious misrepresentation, is not in a position to know the truth or falsity of a commercial. If, however, the practice complained of is fraudulent, the Commission's scope of activity is somewhat enlarged. Although technically the

---

[20] 64 *Stat.* 194, 18 *U.S.C.A.* Sec. 1464. For the criteria used in construing the meaning of "indecent, obscene, or profane," see *United States v. Alpers*, 338 U.S. 680, 70 S. Ct. 352, 94 L. Ed. 353 (1949).

Commission's authority over broadcasting lies in its licensing power,[21] most fraudulent advertising practices are resolved before the broadcaster's license comes up for renewal. Where the letter of complaint is a genuine one, and not the malicious effort of a misguided citizen, the station is informed of the complaint. The licensee, upon receipt of the Commission's letter, will usually require the particular advertiser to change his commercial and correct the offensive practices. But when a licensee has ignored the complaint, the Commission retains the complaint in the licensee's file; and when his license comes up for renewal, his past practices are taken into consideration in determining whether he is operating in the public interest, convenience, or necessity.

In terms of the content of commercials, five particular practices have troubled the Commission.

1. *The patriotic appeal in advertising.* A typical example was a 1944 commercial urging the listener to purchase a particular headache powder because an improperly treated headache rendered the listener less able to carry his burden in the war effort. The only effective sanction against the patriotic appeal in advertising is one which prohibits the use of the flag

---

[21] That this power is not ephemeral is best illustrated perhaps by the rapid succession of events in the following account. On February 27, 1952, the Federal Communications Commission disclosed that it was renewing its concern with radio and television stations that emphasize broadcasts of horse race results in the afternoon hours. On February 29, 1952, Mr. F. M. Flynn, president of Television Station WPIX which is owned by the New York Daily News, announced the immediate suspension of broadcasts of racing results, pending consultation with the Federal Communications Commission. While disagreeing with the judgment of the Commission, Mr. Flynn hastened to add:

"Under the circumstances, we are willing to accept the commission's views as to the usefulness of such information to gambling activities and to the public at large. If it is the purpose of the commission to assist Government authorities in their present efforts to wipe out gambling, WPIX is willing to cooperate by ceasing any activities which might reasonably be considered as harmful to such efforts." *New York Times*, February 28, 1952, p. 1, and March 1, 1952, p. 13.

for advertising purposes.[22] The Commission has, however, maintained that an improper appeal to the listener's patriotism in order to sell a commercial product is a violation of the public trust.[23] There is every reason to believe that excessive use of this appeal will remove the licensee from the company of those who are acting in the public interest, convenience, or necessity.

2. *The physiological commercial.* Included under this heading is the myriad of commercials which urge the listener to "be regular," "wake up a sluggish liver," and offer many other panaceas for the strange "American stomach." Lewis Gannett once observed that it was fortunate America was not a sick nation in view of the fact that radio and television devote so much time to commercials for sickness cures. The Commission is concerned about these commercials because patent medicine advertising is taking over a disproportionate share of radio and television time.

3. *Propaganda in commercials.* Radio and television commercials have been used by the public utilities to campaign against government operation of utilities, and by medical groups to resist socialized medicine. The Commission feels that the place of the radio or television commercial in our society is to sell goods and services honestly and not to be used to propagandize one side of a debated issue.

4. *Intermixing programs and advertising.* The profit motive has led the networks and stations into a dangerous situation, adversely affecting the listening public. For example, in some cases the news analyst also delivers the commercial, using the same reportorial style, which leads the listener

---

[22] 61 *Stat.* 641, 4 *U.S.C.* Sec. 3.

[23] Federal Communications Commission, *Public Service Responsibility of Broadcast Licensees* (Washington, D. C.: U. S. Govt. Printing Office, 1946), pp. 45–46.

into believing that he is listening to fact rather than fanciful advertising. Similarly, a character of fiction, enthralling thousands of children with his adventures, urges them to eat a particular food if they would be as strong as their hero. Such an indiscriminate mixing of program content and advertising is an abuse of the public interest. The Association of Radio News Analysts has recognized that the reading of commercials by the news analyst is not in the best interests of broadcasting.

5. *Mail order stations.* Several television and radio stations conduct large-scale mail order advertising without announcing the name of the manufacturer of the product advertised. The listener sends his money to the station, which forwards the order to the manufacturer for delivery. As a result of this sort of operation, the listener receives the impression that the station is in the mail order business. Perhaps in such a situation the Commission may order the station to disclose in the commercial the name of the manufacturer; or perhaps the Commission may act against the station licensee, and the Federal Trade Commission may proceed against the station as though it were the advertiser.

In addition to the nature or quality of radio and television advertising, the Commission is also concerned with the excessive amount of commercialism. The problem lends itself to a sort of syllogistic analysis. The major premise is that the Commission possesses the authority to deny a license where it would not be in the public interest. The minor premise is that at some point, the licensee's programming has become excessively commercial and therefore not in the public interest because it does not cater to the diverse interests of the listeners. The obvious conclusion would be that the Commission may revoke the license of a broadcaster whose programming is excessively commercial. However, the solution is not so simple. The Commission is aware that, on the one hand, advertising revenue is the lifeblood of most broadcasting and telecasting stations. If a station is to broadcast in the public interest, it must be able to continue in business. Advertising permits such continuing existence. On the other hand, the broadcaster is using the air waves that belong to the public and cannot be permitted to use public property for his own personal gain if it is not also in the public interest. The difficult position of the Commission between advertising and public benefit has been defined as follows:

> The Commission must . . . recognize that without advertising, broadcasting would not exist, and *must confine itself to limiting this advertisement in amount and in character,* so as to preserve the largest possible amount of service to the public. Advertising must be accepted for the present as the sole means of support of broadcasting, and *regulation must be relied upon to* prevent the abuse and over-use of the privilege.[24]

With respect to advertising excesses on the radio and television, the Commission has observed in *Public Service Responsibility of Broadcast Licensees* that this problem has usually taken the following forms:

1. *Length of individual commercials.* The individual commercial announcement may run from a 15-second commercial spot announcement to an uninterrupted 5-minute sales talk. The Commission examined the log of Station WCAU, Philadelphia, Pa., for February 12, 1945, and discovered that 70 commercial spot announcements were broadcast during a 15-hour period. Each commercial ranged from 15 seconds to 95 seconds in length, with the majority running about 25 seconds. There was an average of three such commercials per hour. In addition, there were regularly sponsored broadcasts, each with a commercial at the beginning and end of the program, and some with middle commercials.

---

[24] *In re Great Lakes Broadcasting Co.,* Federal Radio Commission, Docket No. 4900 (1927). Italics supplied.

2. *Number of commercials.* The dominance of advertising to the exclusion of noncommercial material is revealed by the fact that Station KMAC, San Antonio, Texas, broadcast 2,215 commercials in 133 hours on the air in one week, for an average of 16.7 commercials each hour. Although this is an extreme case, many stations have been broadcasting in excess of 1,000 commercials each week.

3. *Piling up of commercials.* This problem is reflected by a typical situation. Assuming that a listener desires to hear two consecutive network programs, he must hear the closing commercial of the first program, a "hitchhiker" commercial for another product of the same sponsor, a commercial during the station break, a "cowcatcher" commercial for a minor product of the second sponsor, and the opening commercial of the second program. Thus the listener will be subjected to five commercials in as many minutes.

4. *The middle commercial.* It is conceded that the advertiser who is spending a great deal of money for radio and television time is entitled to have his commercial broadcast. But it is maintained that a commercial at the beginning and end of the program is sufficient, without one in the middle interrupting the content of the program. The Commission and also newspapers have condemned the middle commercial.

5. *Sponsored v. sustaining time.* There can be no doubt that the popularity of radio and television is in a large part based on commercial programs. Such programs are analogous to the staples in one's diet. But sustaining programs also play a part in broadcasting. Sustaining programs may be successfully employed to achieve a balance of public needs in that they may provide programs which cannot be sponsored with propriety, such as, perhaps, sessions of the Congress. In addition, significant minority interests might be catered to through sustaining programs, since a national advertiser cannot wisely

invest his money in a program that will reach only a small segment of the public. Nonprofit organizations, both charitable and educational, and the development of new types of programs could be served by sustaining time. The practical approach to the problem of program-balancing was well stated by a representative of one of the leading networks when testifying before a Congressional hearing:

> One use Columbia makes of sustaining programs is to supplement commercial offerings in such ways as to achieve, as far as possible, a full and balanced network service. For example, if the commercial programs should be preponderantly musical, Columbia endeavors to restore program balance with drama or the like in its sustaining service.[25]

The principal question is whether the stations and networks have tempered the profit motive sufficiently for the public interest. Are sustaining programs given an adequate share of all broadcast time? The answer would seem to be in the negative. In their report, the Commission determined that in January, 1945, the daytime ratio of sustaining programs for all stations was only 46.1 per cent of the time on the air, while during the evening hours, when the listening audience is largest, sustaining programs received only 37.6 per cent of the time on the air. A more recent study of the ratio of sustaining programs for all stations has not been made by the Commission.

Of course, twenty-four hours of sustaining time daily does not necessarily mean that the public interest is being served. It is obvious that a full day devoted to nothing but unsponsored recorded music cannot cater to minority, or educational, or charitable interest. The advocate of sustaining time should realize that the content of the sustaining program must be worthwhile for different groups of listeners; just as the advo-

---

[25] House of Representatives, Committee on Interstate and Foreign Commerce, *Hearings on H.R.* 4597, 77 Cong., 2d Sess. (May 7, 1942), p. 289.

cate who suggests that a program must sell in order to be worth while should realize that:

> The American system of broadcasting—which is a commercial system—is not founded simply to appeal to listeners and sell merchandise. The concept completely brushes aside the valuable, the indispensable role in a station's total programming structure of the program that may appeal only to listeners and of itself may not sell one penny's worth of merchandise. A forum discussion on a million dollar bond issue for a new sewerage plant—an issue which is splitting the town wide open—might not attract a sponsor but it would have almost everyone in town listening in—and would be a major contribution by the radio station. The weekly religious hour presenting various churches, carried by many stations, is usually not sponsored and yet it is considered one of the most appealing programs on the schedule. Do these programs have to sell merchandise to build up radio? Do a President's messages in a national emergency have to sell merchandise to make them good radio? Of course not. They play a stellar role in keeping listeners in the habit of looking to their radio set for the most significant and vital events of the day. Sponsored programs owe as much to them as they owe to sponsored programs. And that points up why a broadcaster cannot serve the public interest unless he has at his command a reasonable amount of sustaining time to allocate to such programs.[26]

When a licensee appears before the Commission for renewal of his broadcast license, the Commission is charged with the duty of determining whether he has been operating his station in the public interest. As an aid to making its determination, the Commission examines the licensee's program log for both the qualitative and quantitative aspects of his programming. Both the Commission and the licensee have a duty to ask this: "Has the licensee's programming served best his community in the light of its particular need and interests?"

---

[26] Wayne Coy, *An Address*, 28th Annual Convention of the National Association of Broadcasters, Chicago, April 18, 1950.

Conclusion

When considering the adequacy of the Federal Trade Commission in the preceding chapter, it was necessary to point out that many of that Commission's failings were due, in a large part, to deficiencies in the legislative act to be administered. The same cannot be said of the Federal Communications Commission. Its basic weakness lies in the field of advertising excesses. Obscene, deceptive, or fraudulent advertising practices are more or less effectively suppressed by the criminal codes and would be virtually stopped by the adoption of some or all of the recommendations made in the chapter on the Federal Trade Commission. The Federal Communications Commission is of the opinion that it need not be overly concerned with advertising practices other than excessive advertising, as indicated by the following statement:

> Since it is not the intention of the Commission to concern itself with advertising excesses other than an excessive ratio of advertising time to program time, no exhaustive study has been undertaken. There is need, however, for a thorough review by the industry itself of current advertising practices, with a view toward the establishment and enforcement of sound standards by the industry itself.[27]

But the excessive advertising problem cannot be dismissed with a suggestion that the industry discipline itself, for it is quite likely that the profit motive would obviate such a procedure. To meet the situation, the Commission has suggested that several changes be introduced into its administrative procedure.

1. In order that a licensee's programming service may be estimated more accurately from an examination of the station's logs, the Commission has proposed the adoption of

---

[27] *Public Service Responsibility of Broadcast Licensees, op. cit.*, p. 47. For the following FCC proposals, see *ibid.*, pp. 56–59.

standard definitions for commercial, sustaining, network, recorded, wire, local-live, public service, and spot programs, so as to eliminate confusion in an already complex field.

2. Because of the fact that various segments of the broadcasting day have different characteristics and require different programming, it has been proposed that the station log be broken down into the various segments so that a standard program analysis of the log will be possible. Thus, for instance, a station that schedules all of its sustaining time between 11 P.M. and 8 A.M. (an extreme example) would not be serving the public as satisfactorily as a station scheduling the same amount of sustaining time between 11 A.M. and 8 P.M.

3. Heretofore, stations were required to submit program reports of the time and type of programs for the entire year. The result was a bookkeeping and accounting burden that was often reflected in careless and inaccurate reports. The Commission has proposed that a station should submit a report each year for seven days only, but that the seven days should be selected by the Commission and they should vary. It is hoped that the new reporting procedure would result in accurate and uniform data.

4. Where a station applies for a new license or the renewal of an old one, representations as to future programming plans must accompany the application. Since the trustworthiness and sincerity of the applicant are an important part of the questionnaire on program plans, the Commission proposes to create a questionnaire that will be flexible enough to induce more truthful representations. These representations will be treated as responsible estimates rather than as binding pledges.

All of these proposed changes are procedural only. Standard definitions, broadcast time segmentation, or less frequent but more accurate station reports, or more flexible and trustworthy representation as to future program plans will only touch the surface. The Commission's basic problem is to wield its licensing power in the cause of the public interest. This power involves a constant process of balancing claims, of choosing recipients for public favor, and of justifying the selection in terms of the statutory standards.

The advent of television has added to the burdens of responsibility of the Federal Communications Commission and at the same time brought into sharper focus its licensing power. The owners of television stations have sensed the trend of public thinking that the channels on the television dial are a national asset and the public is vitally concerned with the management and disposition of these channels. Accordingly, the radio and television broadcasters have drawn up a Television Code which went into effect March 1, 1952. Sections of the code are reprinted in Appendix B.

In the preamble to this code, due recognition is given to the nature of the medium and the responsibility which devolves upon those who control it, in these words:

> Television is seen and heard in every type of American home. These homes include children and adults of all ages, embrace all races and all varieties of religious faith, and reach those of every educational background. It is the responsibility of television to bear constantly in mind that the audience is primarily a home audience, and consequently that television's relationship to the viewers is that between guest and host. . . .
>
> Television, and all who participate in it are jointly accountable to the American public for respect for the special needs of children, for community responsibility, for the advancement of education and culture, for the acceptability of the program materials chosen, for decency and decorum in production, and for propriety in advertising. This responsibility cannot be discharged by any given group of programs, but can be discharged only through the highest standards of respect for the American home, applied to every moment of every program presented by television.

The Television Code differs radically from the Radio Code in that it provides enforcement machinery. All subscribing stations are permitted to display a "seal of good practice." A Review Board has been set up which has the authority to withdraw the seal from an offending station. The Review Board has four major responsibilities:

1) To maintain a continuing review of television programs to insure that they conform to the code.
2) To review complaints which are received about programs.
3) To define and interpret provisions of the code.
4) To develop and maintain liaison with government and responsible civic groups.

Despite the fine sentiments expressed in the preamble to the code and the genuine desire of its membership to adhere to it, recent studies made by the National Association of Educational Broadcasters, financed by the Fund for Adult Education established by the Ford Foundation, showed quite a gap between noble resolutions and performance.

The study showed that in Los Angeles, with eight television stations in the area, 73 per cent of their total time was devoted to drama, variety, popular music, quiz programs, and sports; informational programs took less than 3 per cent of the time, the programs covering public institutions less than 2 per cent and religious programs less than 1 per cent. No program was found to deal with the fine arts and no program was produced in conjunction with an educational institution. Commercials accounted for 18 per cent of the time. According to another study made in New York City in 1952 by the same association, New York's television stations have shown 50 per cent more crime shows than the year before.[28]

That the Federal Communications Commission is aware of this situation can be gleaned from the fact that on January 31, 1952, it granted to twenty-six applicants for an annual renewal of their television licenses, only a three-month renewal

[28] *Variety*, December 19, 1951, p. 30; January 23, 1952, p. 29.

because of dissatisfaction with their programming, i.e., insufficient time was given for religious, educational, or community affairs. The Federal Communications Commission will observe closely the workings of the Television Code, whose subscribers are committed in displaying the seal of good practice to "entertainment, education, culture and information."

The Commission seems to be well aware that the air waves belong to the nation and not to the licensees who are engaged in private enterprise for profit. The public interest, convenience, or necessity is the yardstick; it must apply more firmly to make certain that the caliber of radio and television programs coming into our homes will uplift rather than debase the social and moral standards of the community.

Chapter 7

FALSE, MISLEADING AND OBSCENE ADVERTISING

The Postal Power and Advertising

It is interesting to note that *The Federalist* contains but a single reference to the postage power of Congress. Apparently, it was generally agreed that Congress should possess such power and little opposition was expected. In No. XLII, Madison expressed the opinion:

> The power of establishing postroads must, in every view, be a harmless power, and may, perhaps, by judicious management, become productive of great public conveniency. Nothing which tends to facilitate the intercourse between the states can be deemed unworthy of the public care.

Seventy years after this was written, Joseph Story remarked in his *Commentaries on the Constitution*: "One cannot but feel, at the present time, an inclination to smile at the guarded caution of these expressions, and the hesitating avowal of the importance of the power." It would have been impossible, of course, for the framers of our Constitution to have foreseen the expansion of the postal powers of Congress to the extent we now have them, just as they could not have foreseen the development of the railroad, airplane, radio, or television. With travel as difficult and primitive as it was in their day, who can blame even the authors of *The Federalist* for taking such a narrow and limited view of the possibilities for the future development of the postal power?

The first legislation under the postal power is found in the Act passed by Congress in 1789 which provided for the temporary establishment of a post office. Under this law, the efforts of the Postmaster General as well as of Congress were aimed at establishing post offices as rapidly as possible and to secure speedy and safe transportation of the mail. To insure the safety of the mails, Congress passed the Act in 1792 which provided severe penalties for the obstruction of the passage of the mail. There followed an Act of 1810 by which Congress provided that "no postmaster shall be obliged to receive, to be conveyed by mail, any packet which shall weigh more than three pounds." Congress exercised the right very early to determine what articles were mailable and the conditions upon which they could be carried.

The power of exclusion is particularly important in the consideration of advertising because the postal regulations affecting advertising often relate to what is "nonmailable." In 1845 Congress classified the mail into different categories and for the first time granted the privilege of free mailing to newspapers which were not more than nineteen inches square in size and were distributed within thirty miles of the place of printing. When the post office system became an executive department in 1872, Congress codified the previous laws and organized the post office on its present basis.[1] By the Act of 1872 the use of the mails was denied to obscene matter, cards "upon which scurrilous epithets may have been written or printed, or disloyal devices printed or engraved [and] letters or circulars concerning illegal lotteries." In 1876 letters or circulars concerning all lotteries were prohibited, and in 1890 the law was amended to include lottery advertisements in newspapers and postmasters were permitted to withhold suspected mail. This bill was passed by Congress "on the conceded

[1] *Act of June* 8, 1872, 13 *Stat.* 507; 17 *Stat.* 283.

power of the government to determine what character of matter may be sent through the mails; and its purpose is to protect the general welfare and morality of the people against the pernicious effects of lotteries." [2]

In 1879 the classification now existing was adopted, and newspapers and periodicals were granted second-class mailing privileges, provided they complied with the following four conditions:

> First. It must regularly be issued at stated intervals, as frequently as four times a year, and bear a date of issue and be numbered consecutively.
>
> Second. It must be issued from a known office of publication.
>
> Third. It must be formed of printed paper sheets, without board, cloth, leather, or other substantial binding, such as distinguish printed books for preservation from periodical publications.
>
> Fourth. It must be originated and published for the dissemination of information of a public character, or devoted to literature, the sciences, arts, or some special industry, and having a legitimate list of subscribers; provided, however, that nothing herein contained shall be so construed as to admit to the second-class rate regular publications designed primarily for advertising purposes, or for free circulation, or for circulation at nominal rates.[3]

The exceptional privileges and advantages offered to publishers of newspapers and periodicals through second-class rates are important to advertisers because they share in the pecuniary advantages which result from such low mailing costs. Most publications could not exist without this subsidy from the

---

[2] United States Senate, *Report No.* 1579, 51st Cong., 1st Sess. (1890).
[3] *Act of March* 3, 1879, 20 *Stat.* 359, U.S. Comp. *Stat.* 1901, Chap. 180.

government; and without the subsidy, advertising rates would be prohibitive.[4]

In 1912, Congress enacted a law which constituted a milestone in the development of advertising.[5] In addition to requiring newspaper and periodical publishers to file with the Post Office Department and to publish in the second issue thereafter a sworn statement of average circulation and the names of the editor, publisher, owners, stockholders, principal creditors, etc., it also provided:

> That all editorial or other reading matter published in any such newspaper, magazine, or periodical for the publication of which money or other valuable consideration is paid, accepted, or promised shall be plainly marked advertisement. Any editor or publisher printing editorial or other reading matter for which compensation is paid, accepted, or promised, without so marking the same, shall, upon conviction in any court having jurisdiction, be fined not less than fifty dollars ($50) nor more than five hundred dollars ($500).

This law was held to be constitutional in the case of *Lewis Publishing Co. v. Wyman.*[6] The court held that the question

---

[4] In the case of *Hannegan v. Esquire, Inc.*, 327 U.S. 146, 66 S. Ct. 456, 90 L. Ed. 586 (1946), the Court said "that the second-class privilege is a form of subsidy" and added that "it was found to be worth $500,000 a year to *Esquire* Magazine." "A newspaper editor fears being put out of business by the administrative denial of the second-class mailing privilege much more than the prospect of prison subject to a jury trial!" Chafee, *Freedom of Speech* (1920), p. 199.

[5] 37 *Stat.* 553, Chap. 389.

[6] *Lewis Publishing Co. v. Wyman*, 152 Fed. 787 (1907). See also J. H. Kadin, "Administrative Censorship: A Study of the Mails, Motion Pictures and Radio Broadcasting," *Boston University Law Review* (1939), p. 533 ff., where the statements are made that "the second-class mailing privilege is basic to a free press—the modern newspaper depends to a large extent on the postal service for revenue and circulation. . . . In freedom of circulation lies the key to the free press. Before the motion picture and the radio, the printed word was the only universal medium to reach mass opinion. . . . The only economic carrier was the postal service. . . . Therefore, the laws and regulations of the Post Office Department are definitive of the boundaries of the rights of a free press in the United States."

to be decided related to the enjoyment of a great privilege at public expense and said:

> Under the statute, as we have seen, for a long series of years, a publication primarily devoted to advertisements was not entitled to the benefit of the second-class classification, and by a long administrative construction, embodied in the regulations, the disclosure of the names of the proprietors as well as of the editors of a publication which has sought to be entered as second-class matter, was required. The new conditions imposed are first, that where there is matter the publication of which is paid for, the fact of such payment shall be disclosed by marking the matter as an advertisement; and second, the disclosure as to ownership, etc., previously exacted, is enlarged by making it necessary in the case of a corporation to furnish the names of the stockholders, and also requiring that the names of the principal creditors, etc., be given. As the right to consider the character of the publication as an advertising medium was previously deemed to be incidental to the exercise of the power to classify for the purpose of the second-class mail, it is impossible in reason to perceive why the new condition as to marking matter which is paid for as an advertisement, is not equally incidental to the right to classify.

The court brushed aside the contention that such regulations of newspapers and periodicals were an effort to regulate journalism and to censor the press, and pointed out that:

> The extremely low postage rate accorded to second-class matter gives these publications a circulation and a corresponding influence unequaled in history. It is a common belief that many periodicals are secretly owned or controlled, and that in reading such papers the public is deceived through ignorance of the interests the publication represents. We believe that, since the general public bears a large portion of the expense of distribution of second-class matter, and since these publications wield a large influence because of their special concessions in the mails, it is not only equitable but highly desirable that the public should know the individuals who own or control them.

It is difficult to exaggerate the importance of the second-class mailing privilege to prospective mailers. It has been stated that no publication of the type to which that privilege is granted "could exist for any length of time if required not only to pay the third-class postage, but to prepare it for the mails as such matter. Although there is no express statutory authorization therefor, the second-class mailing privileges may be withheld from publications whose material is obscene, scurrilous, or otherwise offensive. The power to withhold the privilege was implied in the power to grant." [7]

On the other hand, in the previously cited case of *Hannegan v. Esquire* it was held that the power of the Postmaster General to determine whether a periodical contains information of a public character, literature, or art does not include the power to determine whether the contents meet some standard of the public good or welfare. After analyzing the four conditions upon which a publication is admitted to second-class privileges, the Court concluded that the only relevant one for consideration was the fourth. To give the Postmaster General the right to judge whether the contents of

[7] *United States v. Burleson,* 255 U.S. 407, 41 S. Ct. 352, 65 L. Ed. 704 (1921). The Court affirmed an order revoking the second-class mailing privilege of the *Milwaukee Leader.* The Court found that "the order was entered upon the charge that the articles were appearing in relator's paper so violating the provisions of the National Defense Law, approved June 15, 1917, which has come to be popularly known as the Espionage Act of Congress (40 *Stat.* 217), as to render it 'nonmailable' by the express terms of title 12 of that act (Comp. St. 1918, Comp. St. Ann. Supp. 1919, Secs. 10401a–10401d). . . . That the power to suspend or revoke, such second-class privilege was a necessary incident to the power to grant it has long been recognized by statute and by many decisions of this court, 31 *Stat.* 1107; *Smith v. Hitchcock,* 226 U.S. 53, 57, 33 S. Ct. 6, 57 L. Ed. 119; *Houghton v. Payne,* 194 U.S. 88, 24 S. Ct. 590, 48 L. Ed. 888; *Bates & Guild Co. v. Payne,* 194 U.S. 106, 24 S. Ct. 595, 48 L. Ed. 894. Under these statutes and decisions, if the newspaper of the relator had come to be so edited that it contained other than 'mailable matter,' plainly it was the intention of Congress that it should no longer be carried as second-class mail and therefore the order to revoke the permit which had been granted to relator was proper and justified."

a magazine are good or bad would be to grant him the power of censorship. The Court observed:

> We may assume that Congress has a broad power of classification and need not open second-class mail to publications of all types. The categories of publications entitled to that classification have indeed varied through the years. And the Court held in *Ex parte Jackson*, 96 U.S. 727, 24 L. Ed. 877, that Congress could constitutionally make it a crime to send fraudulent or obscene material through the mails. But grave constitutional questions are immediately raised once it is said that the use of the mails is a privilege which may be extended or withheld on any grounds whatsoever. See the dissents of Mr. Justice Brandeis and Mr. Justice Holmes in *United States ex rel. Milwaukee Social Democrat Publishing Co. v. Burleson*, 255 U.S. 407, 421–423, 430–432, 437, 438, 41 S. Ct. 352, 357, 358, 360, 361, 65 L. Ed. 704. Under that view the second-class rate could be granted on condition that certain economic or political ideas not be disseminated. The provisions of the Fourth condition would have to be far more explicit for us to assume that Congress made such a radical departure from our traditions and undertook to clothe the Postmaster General with the power to supervise the tastes of the reading public of the country.

So far as advertising is concerned, the restrictions upon the use of the postal service, rather than the expansion of it, are important. The exclusion from the mail of advertising of lotteries, fraudulent schemes, or obscene matter involves not only the danger to the publication of losing its second-class mailing privilege, but the imposition of criminal penalties and the denial of the mails in the case of fraud orders.

The peculiar nature of the postal service as a federal enterprise intended for the convenience of the public and to produce revenue has made this a fertile field for federal supervision, apparently unencumbered by such constitutional restraints as the guaranties of freedom of speech or of the press. Congress has a proprietary interest in the postal service; the use of the mails, accordingly, is a privilege which can be withheld, and not a constitutional right. Thus it has been said that "the legislative body in establishing a postal service may annex such conditions as it chooses." [8]

As indicated previously, the activity of the postal service with regard to advertising is largely in the fields of lottery, fraud, and obscenity. In preventing the use of the postal service for the accomplishment of these evils, the Post Office Department is provided with two weapons: it may refuse to deliver mails going to and from the guilty party, thus materially curtailing his activities; and it has the power to prosecute him under criminal statute.

Obscenity and the Mails

It is necessary at this point to examine what is meant by "fraud" and "obscene." Lawyers have labeled them "weasel" words, capable of changing meaning to suit any circumstance. This criticism is particularly applicable to the interpretations given the word "obscene." The Postmaster General and the courts have not been able to arrive at a satisfactory definition of what constitutes obscenity within the meaning of the postal laws and so have been forced to consider each case on its peculiarities. In short, cases concerned with the use of the postal service to transmit "obscene" material are almost com-

---

[8] Although freedom is guaranteed by the Constitution to the press, there is not any constitutional guarantee to the press or to anyone else of a free use of the mails; *Gitlow v. Kiely*, 44 F. (2d) 227, 230 (1920); aff'd 49 F. (2d) 1077 (1931). See also *Ex parte Rapier*, 143 U.S. 110, 12 S. Ct. 374, 36 L. Ed. 93 (1892); *Milwaukee Social Democratic Publishing Co. v. Burleson*, 255 U.S. 407, 41 S. Ct. 352, 65 L. Ed. 704 (1921). Compare Robert Cushman, "National Police Power under the Postal Clause of the Constitution," 4 *Minnesota Law Review* (1920), 402, 419 ff.; *Ex parte Jackson*, 96 U.S. 727, 24 L. Ed. 877 (1877); *Missouri Drug Co. v. Wyman*, 129 Fed. 623 (1909); *People's U. S. Bank v. Gilson*, 140 Fed. 1 (1905); *Public Clearing House v. Coyne*, 194 U.S. 497, 506, 24 S. Ct. 789, 45 L. Ed. 1092 (1903). But compare R. L. Hale, "Unconstitutional Conditions and Constitutional Rights," 35 *Columbia Law Review* (1935), p. 321.

pletely devoid of consistent and established legal precedents. Of the many matters excluded from the mails because of alleged obscenity, only a very small portion thereof have been reviewed by the courts. In most situations the alleged offender discontinues the practice complained of without seeking recourse to judicial review.

In the cases involving obscenity that have reached the courts a great variety of practices has been condemned. Equally varied have been the manner and methods employed by the courts in resolving the issues. One of the earliest cases concerning obscenity involved the mailing of a newspaper containing an editorial which reviled a political candidate in almost every conceivable manner with the exception of the charge of sexual immorality.[9] The defendant's contention was that the editorial was not obscene, lewd, or lascivious within the meaning of the statute, because the statute required that the communication or statement be of a debauching or corrupting manner and relate to sexual impurity. By sustaining the defendant's contention, the Supreme Court in effect opened the postal services to the most scurrilous materials, providing there were no sexual references. Fortunately, this permissive doctrine was not allowed to continue very long. By legislation and judicial construction, material of the type in the *Swearingen* case was brought within the scope of the statutes.

The case of *United States v. Limehouse*[10] concerned the mailing of thirty letters containing vilifications of a particular person along with accusations of incest, miscegenation, and general immorality. The Court observed that the applicable statute had been changed since the *Swearingen* case from "obscene, lewd or lascivious" to "obscene, lewd or lascivious, and every filthy" letter, and, therefore the letters in question

---

[9] *Swearingen v. United States,* 161 U.S. 446, 6 S. Ct. 454, 29 L. Ed. 691 (1896).

[10] 285 U.S. 424, 52 S. Ct. 616, 76 L. Ed. 1201 (1932).

were within the purview of the law because they were "filthy." Although presented with what seemed to be a mandate from the legislature to exclude filth from the mails, the Court, when confronted with the government's argument that the statute embraced all filthy materials, expressly declined to consider the question whether filthy materials of a character other than sexual were prohibited. As a result, the Postmaster General did not know whether he had the power to exclude from the mails materials of a vile nature which were not concerned with sex or anatomy.

Assuming then that a letter or pamphlet containing vile language is mailable provided it is not sexual in character, what are the standards employed in determining whether a particular matter transcends the limits of sexual propriety? A test for determining whether material is obscene, lewd, lascivious, or filthy was formulated in a case involving the mailing of a number of spite letters questioning the chastity of a young woman who had jilted the defendant.[11] The defendant took exception to a ruling in a lower court that refused to admit evidence as to the effect of the letters on the minds of the addressees. In ruling that the lower court did not err in denying admission to this evidence, the court held that the actual effect of the allegedly obscene, lewd, lascivious, or filthy material was not important and observed that the mailing of material falls within the statute if the material so mailed has the tendency, no matter how slight, to deprave or corrupt.

As a result of the *Verner* case it may be argued that any material relating to the sex question is unmailable, for in any society there are persons whose psychological structure is such that almost any photograph of a woman or any advertisement relating to marriage, hygiene, underwear, and similar subjects would "tend to deprave or corrupt them." It is obvious that a

---

[11] *Verner v. United States* 183 F. (2d) 184 (C.C.A. 9th, 1950).

doctrine as extreme as this could not persist, because inherent in any test is the implication that the phrase, "tend to deprave or corrupt" has reference to "any reasonable or ordinary man."

A clear and lucid pronouncement of this theory of "reasonableness" is to be found in the case of *Walker v. Popenoe.*[12] In this case the matter alleged by the Postmaster General to be obscene, lewd, lascivious, or filthy was a pamphlet of an educational nature concerned with the physical and emotional aspects of marriage. It contained some scientific comments on birth control, hygiene, and frequency of the marital act. The grounds upon which the prosecution was based were that the subject matter of the pamphlet would tend to stimulate the reader sexually. In rebutting this contention and holding that mere stimulation was not enough to invoke the statute, the court, speaking through Judge Edgerton, observed:

> Despite the purely educational purpose and the uniformly decent language of appellee's pamphlet, it may be that some of its phrases, by reason merely of their subject matter, may stimulate the senses of some persons. But much more than this is necessary to bring a work within the statute. Otherwise, no work on anatomy, and no dictionary, could be sent through the mails and much of our most respected literature would be barred. The effect of the publication on the ordinary reader is what counts.

It is clear from this case that material of an educational nature, although of a content that might stimulate some minds sexually, is permissible within the statute as interpreted. Thus, textual material concerned with methods of birth control if couched in decent terms, illustrations of birth control devices, or statistics on results of the use of various birth control methods are permitted in the mails.[13] But between proper and educational material and boldly lewd and filthy material there

---

[12] 149 F. (2d) 511 (App. D.C., 1945).

[13] *Consumers' Union v. Walker,* 145 F. (2d) 33 (App. D.C., 1944).

is a large, undefined area. It is within this area that the Postmaster General and the courts have had the most difficulty in formulating a fairly precise standard by which the postal officials may be guided. To indicate the problems involved, it is necessary to examine several other cases.

The first case concerned the mailing of advertising to sell books and the books themselves.[14] The materials mailed were of a risqué character, containing short stories of a picaresque and bawdy nature though not flagrantly lewd or obscene. Although the court sustained the Postmaster-General on the ground that his findings were not subject to a *de novo* review if supported by evidence, Judge Frank, in a concurring opinion, observed that the absence of more definite standards compelled him to concur in the opinion of the court. He observed also that he personally saw nothing in the stories more offensive than in Balzac's *Droll Tales*. Judge Frank's comments suggest that a mere difference in time of publication may control the mailability of a book or pamphlet. Assuming that Boccaccio's *Decameron* is mailable because it is a classic, it would seem that stories in a similar vein, if written and published today, would not be mailable. Does it follow, then, that a contemporary painting of a nude is less mailable than one done by Rubens?

With apparently no rationale acceptable for the decision in the *Roth* case, the question remains an open one. Though the issues involved in that case were of no great public concern in that the circulation of the book in question was limited, a similar problem was presented in a previously cited case involving a magazine with a large national circulation. *Esquire* is a popular publication for men, noted for its cartoons and drawings and photographs of alluring women. In addition, the magazine featured clever poems and ditties of a gay and risqué

---

[14] *Roth v. Goldman*, 172 F. (2d) 494 (C.C.A. 2d, 1949).

nature, as well as stories of the sort which made Guy de Maupassant famous. The magazine was primarily a medium for entertainment, subtle enough so that a fair degree of intelligence was necessary for full understanding of the written contents. The Postmaster General, in attempting to revoke the magazine's second-class mailing privilege, agreed that the magazine was not obscene per se but was so close to the borderline that the Postmaster General's findings had to be sustained. The Supreme Court rejected this proposition on the grounds that the Postmaster General's ruling required, in effect, that a publication's duty went beyond merely refraining from obscenity. To permit the Postmaster General to exclude a publication from the mails because some persons might find it morally improper, imposed the requirement that the publication actively contribute to the public good. Mr. Justice Douglas, speaking for the Court, observed that to permit the Postmaster General to evaluate what was or was not for the public good amounted to giving him the power to determine if a particular article, story, poem, or cartoon was good or bad. This is the power of censorship and is contrary to the intent of the Constitution.

When one considers that the *Roth* case excluded from the mails material which the *Esquire* case refused to exclude, it is apparent that there is no clear standard by which to measure obscenity for mailing purposes. In addition to confusion with regard to standards, several other factors exist which serve to complicate matters. One of these is the question of the form which the objectionable matter may take. Granting that the tendency to deprave or corrupt is as acceptable a standard as has been developed, an interesting problem is created in a case concerning film.[15] The defendant was prosecuted for mailing exposed but undeveloped film of a definitely obscene and lewd

[15] *United States v. Peller*, 170 F. (2d) 1006 (C.C.A. 2d, 1948).

nature. The point was raised that inasmuch as the film as mailed revealed nothing, it was harmless; it could not have a corrupting effect until it was developed and printed. When confronted with this issue, the court failed to meet the question as to the form of the lewdness when mailed—the posting itself is the offense according to the statute—and merely affirmed the conviction by declaring that the act complained of was within the evil the statute sought to remedy. Thus, there is the situation where something that is not lewd, as a matter of fact is held to be so as a matter of law.

Conversely, it is possible for something that is lewd as a matter of fact to be held not lewd as a matter of law. This proposition is the inference from a decision in a case involving the mailing of books and advertising brochures which were not phrased in educational terms and which concerned the sexual habits of primitive peoples.[16] In the case of *Verner v. United States* the court had held that the actual effect on the reader was not important. In *United States v. Rebhuhn*, however, the court based its decision on the fact that the books and advertising brochures had been sent to sociologists and anthropologists. The court observed that the sexual habits of primitive people were a subject which addressees studied, and therefore the books and brochures could have no tendency to deprave or corrupt their minds. Hence, the *effect* was made the fulcrum upon which the decision turned.

With regard to the postal laws on obscenity, one has no choice but to observe that unless the practices complained of are of one extreme or another, predictability is virtually impossible. Until now the statute barring obscene matter from the mails has not raised a serious problem for the advertiser. But it could provide problems were it extended to such matters as soap and lingerie advertisements.

---

[16] *United States v. Rebhuhn*, 109 F. (2d) 512 (C.C.A. 2d, 1940).

Mail Fraud

Postal regulations concerning the use of the mails for fraudulent purposes are far more important to the business of advertising. This is so because advertising methods such as the free offer, money-back guaranty, unconditional representation, and the like are as old as advertising itself. Each of these advertising schemes, if improperly employed, can lend itself to fraudulent use.

Countless devices have been employed to lure the addressee's dollars through the mails. Some have been astoundingly clever and others so blatantly obvious that only the most gullible might succumb. Typical of the great range of artifices used have been schemes that: solicited funds in the guise of puzzle contests; offered the addressee greater power through a "cosmic generator"; promised fabulous results from equally fabulous reducing plans; sold an inhaling compound certain to cure almost every disease known to mankind; advertised a preparation that would effect an immediate cure for trench mouth, pyorrhea, or syphilis; illustrated rings that actually contained rough-cut industrial diamonds to look as though they contained the finest cut diamonds; recruited members for a plan similar to the "pyramid" club; floated a fraudulent municipal bond issue; advertised an ineffective pill as a means of restoring lost youth and virility; advertised a special blend of incense, the burning of which would change the user's luck from bad to good, overcome poverty, impotence, and old age.[17]

---

[17] All these schemes were respectively exposed in the following cases: *Donaldson v. Read Magazine*, 333 U.S. 178, 68 S. Ct. 591, 92 L. Ed. 628 (1947); *Neher v. Marwood*, 128 F. (2d) 846 (C.C.A. 9th, 1942); *Fanning v. Williams*, 173 F. (2d) 95 (C.C.A. 9th, 1949) and *Reilly v. Pinkus*, 338 U.S. 269, 70 S. Ct. 110, 94 L. Ed. 63 (1949); *Jarvis v. Shackelton*, 136 F. (2d) 23 (C.C.A. 6th, 1945); *Cable v. Walker*, 152 F. (2d) 23 (App. D.C., 1945); *Bersoff v. Donaldson*, 174 F. (2d) 494 (App. D.C., 1949); *Public Clearing House v. Coyne*, 194 U.S. 497, 24 S. Ct. 789, 45 L. Ed. 1092 (1903); *Durland v. United States*, 161 U.S. 306, 16 S. Ct. 508, 40 L. Ed. 709 (1896);

And there are other frauds almost as numerous as the stars.[18]

In considering the efficacy of the postal laws with regard to advertising and mail fraud, it is important to keep in mind the fact that the fraud order, which denies the right of the offending party to receive mail or money orders, is not designated as a means of punishment. The fraud order, having been clearly held to be an instrument for protecting the public, may at any time be modified at the discretion of the Postmaster General.[19] This power of the Postmaster General to modify fraud orders serves some practical purposes. The first is that it precludes any arguments that question the power of the Congress to attach such conditions to the use of the postal service as it may prescribe. The second is that the modification of the order, not requiring court sanction, often offers sufficient inducement to the defrauder to desist from his scheme without challenging the Postmaster General's order.

Leach v. Carlile, 258 U.S. 138, 42 S. Ct. 227 (1922); and *Cates v. Haderlein*, 189 F. (2d) 369 (C.C.A. 7th, 1951).

[18] *Zimmerman v. United States*, 179 F. (2d) 790 (C.C.A. 5th, 1949) [fraudulently advertising notes for sale as being secured by mortgages]; *Estep v. United States*, 140 F. (2d) 40 (C.C.A. 6th, 1949) [intercorporate transaction schemes to milk minority stockholders]; *Baker v. United States*, 115 F. (2d) 533, cert. denied 312 U.S. 692, rehearing denied 312 U.S. 715, rehearing denied 325 U.S. 894 (C.C.A. 10th, 1945) [fraudulent and ineffective cancer cure]; *Holdsworth v. United States*, 179 F. (2d) 933 (C.C.A. 1st, 1950) [fraudulent bills of lading, invoices, and confirmations]; *United States v. Crummer*, 151 F. (2d) 958 (C.C.A. 10th, 1945) [fraudulent scheme for the redemption of securities]; *Deaver v. United States*, 155 F. (2d) 740 (App. D.C., 1946) [fraudulent and misrepresentation in the sale of family burial plots]; *Glover v. United States*, 125 F. (2d) 291 (C.C.A. 5th, 1942) [illegally and fraudulently employing prisoner labor for personal gain]; *Crooker v. United States*, 161 F. (2d) 944 (C.C.A. 1st, 1947) [using the mails to transmit unregistered statements to foster the sale of securities]; *Bradford v. United States*, 129 F. (2d) 274 (C.C.A. 5th, 1942) [selling overpriced buses to a municipality with "kickbacks" for municipal purchasing agents]; *Ballard v. United States*, 138 F. (2d) 540 (C.C.A. 9th, 1944) [establishment of an "I Am" movement promising self-immortality to those who, through contribution, would be permitted to communicate with the "ascended masters"].

[19] *Donaldson v. Read*, 333 U.S. 178, 68 S. Ct. 591, 92 L. Ed. 628 (1947).

The question naturally arises as to the scope of the powers possessed by the Postmaster General with respect to mail fraud and the legal checks which have been imposed. Although the question is incapable of a definite reply, it can in part be answered by an examination and analysis of a series of cases which reviewed orders issued by the Postmaster General. To determine with reasonable precision the qualitative content of a mail fraud is a difficult problem. Contributing to this difficulty are matters to be considered presently, which include a consideration of the overt acts necessary to constitute a mail fraud, the conclusiveness of the Postmaster General's findings in fraud cases, the relative strength or weakness of the mail fraud statute, the relation of the effects of the fraudulent scheme, and the peculiarities involved in fraud cases where medical science is a factor.

In a common law action for fraud the plaintiff is generally required to prove the making of the misrepresentation, defrauder's knowledge of the falsity and intention to deceive, and plaintiff's reliance upon the misrepresentation and damages. The postal laws on mail fraud do not make the same requirements. In a case involving a scheme which promised interest to depositors at the rate of 10 per cent each month provided certain conditions occurred, which conditions the defendant knew could never occur, the question of the requisite act or elements of mail fraud was considered.[20] The defendant's principal contention was that the scheme and the letters mailed in furtherance of the scheme were not calculated to be effective in perpetrating the fraud. The defendant, in essence, suggested that since the recipients did not rely upon the misrepresentations in the letters, mail fraud was not committed. The Court, through Judge Brewer, took note of this contention as follows:

---

[20] *Durland v. United States,* 161 U.S. 306, 16 S. Ct. 508, 40 L. Ed. 709 (1896).

> We do not wish to be understood as intimating that in order to constitute the offenses it must be shown that the letters so mailed were of a nature calculated to be effective in carrying out the fraudulent scheme. It is enough if, having devised a scheme to defraud, the defendant, with a view of executing it deposits in the Post Office letters, which he thinks may assist in carrying it into effect, although in the judgment of the jury they may be absolutely ineffective therefor.

It appears that with regard to mail fraud statutes, unlike the common law, reliance is of no importance. By the doctrines advanced in other cases, the requirements for a mail fraud order or for a prosecution have been made much less strict than common law requirements. In three separate cases, the principal argument employed by each of the defendants was the same, namely, that in the absence of actual damage to the addressees there could not, as a matter of law, be a finding of fraud. The first case concerned a group of men who set up two hospitals for the cure of cancer and many other diseases.[21] To advertise and attract patrons they mailed pictures of the hospitals and of satisfied or cured patients, copies of testimonials, and pseudoscientific pamphlets. Their defense was based on the failure of the government to establish a prima facie case in that no evidence was introduced to show that persons receiving the advertisements were damaged thereby. Although the case is important principally because of the problems presented in connection with medical opinions, the Court did rule, as a subsidiary holding, that the element of damage was unnecessary to sustain the conviction for fraud.

The second case, which concerned damages as a secondary problem, also delimits the elements of mail fraud. The acts complained of consisted of mailing circulars to advertise and sell cemetery burial plots. The scheme was to induce the pur-

---

[21] *Baker v. United States*, 115 F. (2d) 533, cert. denied 312 U.S. 692, rehearing denied 312 U.S. 715, rehearing denied 325 U.S. 894 (1945).

chase of burial plots in a new cemetery, which could subsequently be sold at an enormous profit. The inducement was achieved through misrepresentations as to the resale possibilities and the completion of work on the cemetery.[22] In meeting the same contention that no damages were incurred, the court again rejected the contention and held that conviction is proper if the scheme is designed or contrived to defraud, regardless of actual injury to the addressee.

The last case in point concerned the use of prisoner labor by a prison warden for his own gain and profit.[23] The problem here, as related to damages, was unique in that only the municipality and not any member of the general public could be defrauded. It may be argued that the *Deaver* and *Baker* cases merely held that proof of damage to the public was not a necessary element of mail fraud, but that from the scheme itself it must appear more probable than not that the public would be damaged before a conviction can be sustained. The instant case immediately dispels that argument. Since it is evident that no member of the public was damaged as such, there can be little doubt that the element of damage required in common law fraud is dispensed with entirely in mail fraud.

As a result of the foregoing cases, the law of mail fraud as applied to the qualitative elements necessary to invoke the statute differs from common law fraud in two respects. The first is that reliance upon the fraud is not necessary in mail fraud, and the second is that damage to the addressee is not required to be proved or inferred. The only remaining elements are the making of the misrepresentation, knowledge of the falsity, and the intention to defraud. Briefly, then, a mail fraud is committeed when a scheme to defraud is contrived and the mails are used in its furtherance.

---

[22] *Deaver v. United States,* 155 F. (2d) 740 (App. D.C., 1946).
[23] *Glover v. United States,* 125 F. (2d) 291 (C.C.A. 5th, 1942).

Two questions arise in connection with the law of mail fraud. Are the elements of misrepresentation, knowledge, and intention always necessary? What constitutes using the mails in furtherance of the fraud? The first question may be answered in the affirmative, with but one exception. This occurs in the case when the mails are used in connection with a stock or security promotion not wholly complying with the regulations of the Securities and Exchange Commission. A case in point [24] involved a mail fraud conviction for the mailing of a statement to sell securities, the statement being unregistered in violation of the Securities and Exchange Commission regulations. It is interesting to note that the court affirmed the conviction despite the absence of any allegations or proof of fraud. In fact, although the statement was unregistered, it was completely factual and in no other way illegal. This case has been mentioned to indicate the possibility that the mail fraud statutes may, without constitutional objections, be extended to include the mailing per se of any statement or document which may contravene a federal statute.

It is quite clear from the cases discussed previously that the mailing of a fraudulent advertisement or prospectus invokes the statute. This is so because the mailing of the advertisement or prospectus is, without doubt, in furtherance of the scheme. But it is obvious that in the course of committing a fraud other items may be mailed which will not, in and by themselves, be fraudulent or misleading. This problem arose in an appeal from a conviction for mailing a check representing profits from a fraudulent scheme,[25] which consisted of the sale of buses to the city of Alexandria, Louisiana, at greatly inflated prices. The municipality's purchasing agent, who had made the sale possible, was to receive a "kickback." It appeared that all communications in furtherance of the scheme were done in per-

[24] *Crooker v. United States,* 161 F. (2d) 944 (C.C.A. 1st, 1947).
[25] *Bradford v. United States,* 129 F. (2d) 274 (C.C.A. 5th, 1942).

son or by telephone. The mails were only used by the municipality to send a check for the buses, and by the seller to send the "kickback" check to the agent. It was on this latter case of the mails that the indictment, prosecution, and conviction were based. The defendant on appeal did not deny the fraud but based his defense on the theory that the sending of the "kickback" check was not in furtherance of the fraud, since the check was not deceiving or misleading but was merely a draft on a bank. The court, in sustaining the conviction, observed that the payment to the agent was a vital part of the scheme. It is quite evident that the use of the mails in furtherance of fraudulent schemes will be interpreted quite broadly.

With the observation that a fraudulent scheme need only be devised and the mails used in furtherance thereof to bring it within the statute, it is important to understand the powers of the Postmaster General and the limits, if any, imposed upon him. Since the Postmaster General may issue a fraud order or revoke a second-class license without the necessity of a formal hearing to provide the "defendant" with his day in court,[26] what becomes of the concept of due process of law?

The answer is that the "defendant" has the right to challenge the Postmaster General in the courts through the injunction process. However, upon review of the Postmaster General's findings by the court, the appellate review is not *de novo*. This question was considered by the Supreme Court in *Donaldson v. Read*,[27] and the Court, through Justice Black, observed:

> But they [truthful sentences] did not stand alone. They were but small and inconspicuous portions of lengthy descriptions used by respondents to present their contest to the public in their advertisements and letters. In reviewing fraud findings of the Postmaster General, neither this Court nor any other is

---

[26] *Bersoff v. Donaldson*, 174 F. (2d) 494 (App. D.C., 1949).
[27] 333 U.S. at 186, 68 S. Ct. at 599, 92 L. Ed. at 636.

> authorized to pick out parts of the advertisements on which respondents particularly rely, decide that these excerpts would have supported different findings, and set aside his order for that reason. We consider all the contents of the advertisements and letters, and all the evidence, not to resolve contradictory inferences but only to determine if there was evidence to support the Postmaster General's findings of fraud.

The same theories had been advanced by the Court much earlier in *Leach v. Carlile* [28] and *United States v. Burleson*.[29] In the latter case, the court indicated that its lack of power to review *de novo* extended to all executive departments by observing:

> There remains the question whether substantial evidence to support his order may be found in the facts stated in the Postmaster General's answer, which are admitted by the demurrer, for the law is, that the conclusion of the head of an executive department of the government, in such a question, when within his jurisdiction, will not be disturbed by the Courts unless they are clearly of the opinion that it is wrong.

Even though the Postmaster General's powers with regard to findings of fact are broad, he has encountered considerable difficulties in fraud cases where medical and other scientific questions have been raised. Unlike cases of financial manipulation or misrepresentation of a mechanical device, medical science is a comparatively indefinite field, with any question susceptible to medical testimony both pro and con. As will be shown later, the problem of proving fraud in cases involving medical preparations or treatments is peculiar only to the Post Office Department. To elaborate on the problem we need only contrast two cases. The first case concerned a fraud order directed at the advertising of a reducing plan.[30] Both the gov-

---

[28] 258 U.S. 138, 42 S. Ct. 227 (1922).
[29] 255 U.S. 407, 41 S. Ct. 352, 65 L. Ed. 704 (1920).
[30] *Fanning v. Williams*, 173 F. (2d) 95 (C.C.A. 9th, 1949).

ernment and the respondent introduced expert medical testimony. The respondent's doctors asserted the plan was safe and effective; government witness asserted exactly the contrary. In essence, the testimony was balanced. The court sustained the Postmaster General. The fraud order in the second case went against the advertising of an inhaling compound asserted to be effective in the cure of colds, hay fever, sinus trouble, asthma, and almost every other ailment of the respiratory tract.[31] Once again both sides introduced conflicting medical testimony as to safety, effectiveness, and germicidal effect of the preparation. This time, however, the court found against the Postmaster General. The only difference between the two cases was that in the latter the company did 95 per cent of its business by mail order, had conducted its business for 50 years without aid of advertising, had a bona fide money-back guaranty, and presented apparently unsolicited testimonials. The argument that the weight of the evidence was in favor of the respondent is quite true; but the difficulty is created when one attempts to reconcile this argument with the theory, demonstrated previously, that if the Postmaster General's findings are supported by evidence (no quantitative requirements are prescribed),[32] his findings will not be questioned by the courts. If the Postmaster General believes there is evidence to indicate fraud, it seems unreasonable to suggest that the evil will be cured by the fact that it has existed for many years.

The present status of the law on mail fraud was best summed up in a recent case before the Supreme Court.[33] The facts in the case were substantially as follows. The defendant had made expansive claims in advertising a fat-reducing plan

---

[31] *Jarvis v. Shackelton*, 136 F. (2d) 116 (C.C.A. 6th, 1943).

[32] In *Leach v. Carlile*, 258 U.S. 138, 42 S. Ct. 227 (1922), the Court sustained the Postmaster General's findings in a medical case on the grounds that there was "some" evidence to support the findings.

[33] *Reilly v. Pinkus*, 338 U.S. 269, 70 S. Ct. 127, 94 L. Ed. 79 (1949).

which consisted of taking quantities of granulated kelp containing iodine. The advertisements asserted that the kelp and the reducing plan were effective and perfectly safe for all people of all ages. In addition, the plan was alleged to be such that the user need not refrain from eating candy, ice cream, or similar foods. The Court acknowledged that there can be no exact standard of absolute truth with regard to any matter susceptible to differing opinions or interpretations. Although there was some evidence supporting the Postmaster General's findings, the Court observed that since the condemned practices were in a field where knowledge was undeveloped, the Court must consider the situation more carefully. The Court pointed out that the crime of mail fraud consisted of fraudulent purpose, not merely of a mistake in a field where there was much room for doubt. The Court, speaking through Mr. Justice Black, observed:

> Proof of fraudulent purpose is essential . . . an "actual intent to deceive." See *Seven Cases v. United States,* 239 U.S. 510, 517. Consequently, fraud under the mail statutes is not established merely by proving that an incorrect statement was made. An intent to deceive might be inferred from the universality of scientific belief that advertising representations are wholly unsupportable: conversely, the likelihood of such an inference might be lessened should cross-examination cause a witness to admit that the scientific belief was less universal than he had first testified.

Although the *Reilly* case resulted in a ruling against the Postmaster General, the Court was actually limiting its doctrine to the medical cases. But the case is important because it demonstrates that in mail fraud cases the fraudulent intent must be shown. This is different from the powers of the Federal Trade Commission in that the latter may assail any erroneous or false statements with regard to drug advertising. However, the difference is based not on the weakness of the postal laws but rather on their strength. The postal laws with regard to fraud orders and criminal prosecutions are far more severe than the injunctive relief afforded the Federal Trade Commission. To prevent the abusive use of a powerful weapon, the Court has been more strict in its supervisory capacity.

The present trend in the mail fraud law is to assure greater protection for the gullible members of the public. As a key to the approach taken by the Postmaster General and the courts, the following quotation from a recent case is offered:

> The buying public does not ordinarily carefully study or weigh each word in an advertisement and the ultimate impression upon the mind of the reader arises not only from what is said but also all of that which is reasonably implied. . . . The important criterion is the net impression which the advertisement is likely to make upon the purchasers to whom the advertisement is directed. It has been held that even if an advertisement is so worded as not to make any express misrepresentations, nevertheless, if it is artfully designed to mislead those responding to it, the mail fraud statutes are applicable.[34]

It may be observed that the fraud-order power of the Post Office Department is concurrent in some respects, with the jurisdiction of another federal administrative agency. The relation of the fraud statutes administered by the Department to the statutes administered by the Federal Trade Commission gives rise to the query whether, in the interest of unified and economical action, the fraud powers—including the power to return all mail marked "Fraudulent"—should not rest in the hands of one agency. The Federal Trade Commission, of course, strikes down only the fraudulent representations and other deceptive features of an enterprise. Its cease and desist orders are directed only toward correction. As already noted, however, the Post Office Department, although dealing

---

[34] *Cates v. Haderlein*, 189 F. (2d) 369, 373 (C.C.A. 7th, 1951).

with the same question of fraud, at least has the power to destroy the entire business in so far as it is dependent on the use of the mails.[35]

Yet, with respect to all respondents in interstate commerce who use the mails, the jurisdiction of the two agencies and the subject matter with which they deal are identical; the methods of enforcement, however, are different. Even more striking is their identity of power since the recent addition of Section 12(a) to the Federal Trade Commission Act, which makes it unlawful to disseminate, or cause to be disseminated, either by United States mail or by any means, any false advertisement for the purpose of inducing, or which is likely to induce, directly or indirectly, the purchase of foods, drugs, devices, or cosmetics.

The phenomenon of two agencies exercising concurrent jurisdiction over the same matter may be justified on the ground that, while the Federal Trade Commission's interest is centered solely upon the bad practice to be remedied, the Post Office Department is concerned not only in the elimination of the evil, but also in protecting itself from providing the means, through its own services, of bilking the public. Thus it may be argued that the Post Office Department is engaged in a business; therefore, it is the proper agency to determine with whom to do business and under what circumstances. This contention has only surface plausibility. Aside from the fact that it is uneconomical to have two groups partly engaged in precisely the same activities, there is another objection to the existing set-up for controlling advertising. It is at least possible that a person may be called to account simultaneously by the Federal Trade Commission, the Post Office Depart-

[35] Attorney General's Committee on Administrative Procedure, *Administrative Procedure in Government Agencies*, Part XII (Washington, D. C.: U. S. Govt. Printing Office, 1940), p. 37.

ment, and even the Food and Drug Administration for the same act or acts.

Doubtless the time is not ripe for merging control over all fraud cases, including the denial of mail privileges, in the Federal Trade Commission, particularly since fraud cases handled by the Department require expeditious treatment, while the Commission's cases often continue for a long time. But some sort of integration, whether by statute or by voluntary action, would be desirable. Especially is this so in view of the contrasting sanctions of the two agencies. As a matter of economy of effort and to prevent harassment of respondents, steps toward coordination of policy between the agencies seem desirable. A general program could well be devised that assigns inherently fraudulent schemes where the use of the mails is an important factor to the Post Office Department and cases involving fraudulent execution of certain phases of business to the Federal Trade Commission.

One other feature of the Post Office Department's concern with advertising should be noted, namely, its advisory service. Until recently, advertisers, their agencies, and publishers submitted proposed advertisements to the Office of the Solicitor in the Department in order to discover whether the materials were mailable or whether they fell under the proscription against lotteries. If the advance ruling was adverse the inquirer generally did not mail the matter so as not to risk seizure of an issue or, possibly, criminal penalties. But for reasons of economy and an overload of work, the Department no longer gives advance opinions on proposed advertisements. In exceptional cases the Solicitor will give opinions to publications and private persons who submit questions respecting the use of the mails where violations of the statutes may be involved. Generally, though, it is the Department's practice to issue a "no opinion" letter which simply sets out relevant portions of the statute.

The Department's officials do not consider that such advance opinions are in the nature of final judgments. Nor are they considered binding upon the Department in the event that action becomes necessary under the postal laws and regulations. Thus, even if the advance opinion is favorable and there is no claim that the operation of the enterprise was different from that originally described, subsequent action is not precluded. For example, in a case arising a few years ago the sponsors of a proposed contest submitted full details of their plans, their operations, and their advertisement to the Solicitor who ruled that the contest did not offend the lottery statute. Although it was not claimed that the sponsors deviated in any way from the plans proposed or that the contest was other than described, the Department issued a letter of citation and ultimately a fraud order against the persons conducting the contest.

Advertisers fully realize the power inherent in these fraud orders. Publishers are aware not only of the criminal liability for violating the postal laws, but also of the threat to their very existence in the "nonmailability" of an issue, or the suspension of the second-class privilege. Perhaps the success of the regulations of advertising under the postal laws is to be found in the attitude of the Supreme Court when reviewing the orders of the Postmaster General. The Court's comment on this point in the *Donaldson v. Read Magazine* is apropos and can bear repetition:

> In reviewing the fraud findings of the Postmaster General, neither this Court nor any other is authorized to pick out parts of the advertisements on which respondents particularly rely, decide that these excerpts would have supported different findings, and set aside his order for that reason. We consider all the contents of the advertisements and letters, and all of the evidence, not to resolve contradictory inferences, but only to determine if there was evidence to support the Postmaster General's finding of fraud.

The Federal Alcohol Tax Unit

In planning an advertising campaign, the problems confronting the distiller, bottler, or retailer of alcoholic beverages are more complex than those affecting the producer and distributor of any other commodity. The long-standing opposition to alcohlic beverages by various temperance and religious groups is common knowledge. Although tremendous sums of money are spent for liquor, the opposition forces have enjoyed a measure of success. In addition to their own reserved powers, the states have been given by federal statute enacted under the Twenty-first Amendment the power and authority to control the traffic in alcoholic beverages within their own borders, regardless of the effect that such control might have on interstate commerce.[36] That the states have responded to the demands of the temperance groups and have taken advantage of the permission given by the federal government is demonstrated by the fact that every state has enacted laws relating to the advertising of alcoholic beverages. In some situations, state and federal law may conflict, but inasmuch as this book is concerned only with federal regulations, a discussion of state laws is inappropriate.

Although the federal government was concerned with alcoholic beverages as early as 1919 when the Eighteenth Amendment to the Constitution prohibited traffic in liquor, it was not until 1933 after the Twenty-first Amendment repealed prohibition that regulating authority over the liquor industry came to be exercised. The first federal agency to regulate the liquor industry was the Federal Alcohol Control Administration, which was created as a phase of the New Deal's recovery program to negotiate successful industry codes for the amelioration of mass unemployment and depression. Thus, as in

---

[36] The *Webb-Kenyon Act of 1933*, 37 *Stat.* 699, 27 *U.S.C.* 122.

the case of other agencies concerned with advertising, the Federal Alcohol Control Administration was created originally for the solution of economic difficulties. To maintain free trade and fair and active competition, it was deemed necessary to formulate rules and regulations for the prevention of practices inimical to fair standards of competition. Included among such practices are those which divert trade from competitors by means other than superior production at lower prices. Thus, false and fraudulent advertising may induce the consumer to buy the product so advertised rather than a product which is advertised honestly. The manner in which the protection of competitors has been extended to many deceptive alcoholic beverage advertisements will be discussed in subsequent pages.

With the demise of the National Recovery Administration all its lesser administrative units went out of existence, including the Federal Alcohol Control Administration. In 1935, a Federal Alcohol Administration was created as a division of the Treasury Department for the control of the advertising of alcoholic beverages and other practices in the liquor industry;[37] in 1940 this control became vested in the Federal Alcohol Tax Unit, a part of the Bureau of Internal Revenue. It was created to:

> . . . protect the revenue derived from distilled spirits, wine and malt beverages, to regulate interstate and foreign commerce and enforce the postal laws with respect thereto, to enforce the twenty-first amendment, and for other purposes.

To accomplish the above purposes, the Unit requires that members of the liquor industry, with the exception of brewers, retailers, and state monopolies, secure special permits. The duration of the permit depends upon compliance with the provisions of the Act and all other federal laws relating to alcoholic beverages. The Unit's authority extends to many other phases

---

[37] 49 *Stat.* 977, 27 U.S.C.A. Sec. 201 *et seq.*

of the liquor industry in addition to advertising,[38] but it is only the advertising provisions which are germane to this discussion. To understand better the adequacy of the controls imposed upon the advertising of liquor, it is necessary to be aware of the controls themselves and the manner in which they have been established.

Unlike other regulatory bodies, the Federal Alchohol Tax Unit's rule-making power permits it to promulgate categorical prohibitions with respect to liquor advertising. All these prohibitions of certain undesirable advertising practices are grouped under Part V, Article VI, Title 27 of the *United States Code,* and a general summary of the important provisions follows:

Sec. 60. The Unit can act against any advertisement appearing in any media or disseminated in any manner whatsoever, which does not conform to the advertising regulations.[39]

Sec. 61. (1) The advertising regulations do not extend to labels, bottle containers, or cartons.[40] (2) The advertising regulations do not extend to editorials and other published matter for which no consideration has been paid.

Sec. 62. (1)(a) The regulations require that the advertisement must state the name of the advertiser and such identification must be so conspicuous as to be readily legible. (b) The advertisement must state the class, type or nature

---

[38] The Unit also controls and supervises outlet agreements, "gifts" to retailers, credit transactions, bulk sales, and labeling.

[39] The Unit may proceed only against the advertiser. This means that a newspaper or magazine publisher, or a radio or television station licensee does not come under the Administration's jurisdiction because a violative advertisement appeared in the particular medium. The same exemption applies to advertising agencies.

[40] However, the exclusion of labeling does not mean that a liquor manufacturer may label falsely with impunity. Labeling is regulated effectively by Sec. 5(e) of the Act.

of the product.[41] (c) The advertisment, if of whiskey, must state the alcoholic content in terms of proof, or if of cordial or other "specialty," must state the content in terms of volume. (d) In the event the liquor contains neutral spirits, the percentage thereof must also be stated in the advertisement.

Sec. 63. All the necessary information shall be lettered in a manner that renders it conspicuous and easy to read. There cannot be, of course, any hard and fast rules as to letter size, for the requirements are met or neglected on the basis of each particular advertisement, and on the basis of the size of the lettering of the required information as compared to that of nonrequired information.

Sec. 64. The advertiser of alcoholic beverages shall not do the following: [42]

1) Make false and misleading statements generally. This category includes the making of extravagant claims and the use of superlatives which, though literally true, may have a misleading effect.[43] Examples are "original and only extra dry rum," or "the rum of His Majesty's Navy," or "John Doe was one of the seven distillers permitted by the government to make medicinal whiskey throughout prohibition."

---

[41] An advertisement of "Scotch" instead of "Scotch-type," or "whiskey" instead of "blended whiskey," or "dry gin" instead of "distilled dry gin" does not meet the requirements of the regulation.

[42] The Unit has not specifically prohibited what might be termed "socially objectionable advertising." This broad term probably includes pictures of women, children, or domestic scenes. But, on the basis of advice by the Unit and of public opinion, most liquor advertisers have refrained from using such advertising.

[43] A condemned practice that belongs properly in this category is the advertising of an alcoholic beverage as having a cooling or refreshing effect. Such advertisements, which may be best presented in the form of an athlete enjoying a drink after a strenuous game or match, are permissible as to mixed drinks but not as to the distilled product used in mixing the drink.

2) Disparage or belittle a competitor's product, expressly or by implication.[44]
3) Use obscene statements, designs, devices, or representations. The tests of profanity or obscenity which are applied to other advertising is applied also to the advertising of alcoholic beverages.
4) Make misleading statements relating to analyses, tests, or standards, even though they may be literally true.[45]
5) Make money-back guaranties which do not clearly state the terms. These are prohibited even if the manner in which they are stated is merely misleading and not actually false.
6) Make statements as to governmental authorization for distilling and bottling.[46]
7) Make claims that the product is "bonded," "bottled in bond," or "aged in bond" unless the entire contents of the bottle are so manufactured or bottled.
8) Feature the word "pure" in connection with the quality or brand-name of the product unless the word "pure" appears in the advertiser's corporate name.
9) Make claims of "double" or "triple" distillation even if the product is actually "double" or "triple" distilled. The reason for this is that the number of times of distillation makes no difference in the quality of the product, and

---

[44] Statements like "contains no neutral spirits or alcohol" or "our product does not contain chemical ingredients" are believed by the Unit to lead the consumer into inferring that other liquors of the same type and grade contain neutral spirits, alcohol, or chemical ingredients. Since the Administration requires uniformity in the content of all products of one type or grade, the inference could be false.

[45] Typical of the practices condemned are advertisements featuring taste or blindfold tests. The prohibition extends also to situations where favorable analyses results are reported only. For comparison, see the discussion in Chap. V of *P. Lorillard Co. v. Federal Trade Commission*, 186 F. (2d) 52 (1950).

[46] All distillers and bottlers of alcoholic beverages must secure permits from some division of government, i.e., federal, state, municipal. Therefore authorization is no index of a superior product and the Unit restricts the advertisement so that it may contain only the permit numbers.

therefore the inference that a "double" or "triple" distilled liquor is superior is erroneous.

10) Make any statement in an advertisement that is inconsistent with a statement on a label.[47]

11) Make, in connection with the regulation immediately preceding, any statements in an advertisement pertaining to the age of the whiskey that does not appear on the label. This prohibition includes statements like "fine old whiskey," "natured," or "aged."

12) Make false and misleading claims as to the product's curative or therapeutic effects.[48]

13) Make false statements as to the character of the distiller or place of distillation. Thus, a statement that the distiller has had 50 years of experience or was official distiller to the King of Siam violates the regulation. In addition, a claim that the whiskey was distilled in the heart of Kentucky's bourbon country, when it was distilled in Indiana, is unlawful.

14) Advertise simultaneously more than one brand in a confusing manner.[49]

15) Use in an advertisement of any flag, seal, coat of arms, crest, or insignia. This practice is condemned because the use of such symbols in an advertisement conveys the false impression that the product has been endorsed.

---

[47] The reasons underlying this prohibition are obvious. Regulations requiring truthful labeling on liquor bottles would be rendered nugatory if advertising were permitted to depart from the same standards. The consumer's first introduction to the product is through advertising and advertising can do more to sell a product than a label.

[48] Statements that are considered questionable or doubtful are those alleging that the product leaves no after effects (hangover), relaxes the nerves, improves the appetite or digestion, or develops athletic powers. Even the more subtle statements, like "Treats you kindly" or "Be seeing you bright and early," are prohibited. Expenditures by leading distillers amounting to hundreds of thousands of dollars were wasted when campaigns like "Clear Heads Call for Blank" or "Be Bright! Go Right! Go Blank!" were abandoned because of this regulation.

[49] This regulation prohibits the practice of advertising two different liquors of the same distiller in the same or adjoining advertisement, when the total impression received is that a claim, true of one liquor, is advertised in such a manner as to lead the reader to believe that it is true of the other.

Thus, the Unit has promulgated specific rules for specific advertising practices, and in the event a new or different deceptive practice is developed, the Unit can act immediately and formulate a new regulation. To enforce the prohibitions of the Act the Unit may apply to a district court for an injunction to restrain the unlawful practice. But even more effective than an injunction and contempt citation for violation thereof is the provision of the Act which makes a violation thereof a misdemeanor punishable by a maximum fine of $1,000. The effectiveness of the sanctions embodied in the laws relating to the control of the alcoholic beverage industry is demonstrated, in so far as liquor advertising is concerned, by the fact that a majority of bad liquor advertisements have been stopped quickly by a letter from the Unit to the advertiser. Unlike the other federal regulatory bodies discussed previously, the Federal Alcohol Tax Unit has not had to seek the aid of the courts beyond the injunctive procedure, in order to control the advertising of alcoholic beverages.

To understand how the Unit goes about its task of regulating liquor advertising, an examination of its various activities for the fiscal year ending June 30, 1950, will be helpful.[50] Unlawful liquor advertisements come to the Unit's attention in two ways, one of which is by way of letters of complaint from individual members of the public, competing distillers or bottlers, and many religious, educational, and temperance organizations. From July 1, 1949, to June 30, 1950, the Unit received approximately 2,600 complaints, queries regarding interpretation of advertisements and regulations, comments on proposed advertisements and other miscellaneous questions and comments. The second way in which unlawful hard liquor advertising is unearthed is by means of a continuing

---

[50] At the request of the author, the Research Department of the Alcohol Tax Unit supplied the data for the fiscal year ending June 30, 1950, as well as the information on its procedure.

review conducted by the Unit. During the period here discussed, the Unit examined 29,448 issues of various newspapers and periodicals. The number of alcoholic beverage advertisements reviewed in these publications totaled 143,996. In addition, 8,900 beer and wine commercials on the radio and television were examined. The Unit's review of liquor advertising has not been restricted to those advertisements appearing in publications or on the air waves, but includes also point-of-sale pieces, of which it made 3,728 examinations in the above-mentioned period.[51]

The manner in which the Unit acts against unlawful liquor advertising is best demonstrated by an examination of the procedure followed in a hypothetical case. The Blank Distillery, Inc., advertised that its whiskey will relax the nerves and improve digestive processes. This advertisement, which contravened the regulation prohibiting the advertising of curative or therapeutic effects, was discovered as a result of the Unit's survey. The Unit, after considering the seriousness of the violation and the past advertising history of the company, determined the amount of penalty or fine that fitted the seriousness of the offense. The charge against the company and the penalty assessment were forwarded to the field office in the area where the company's principal offices were located. The field office contacted the company and invited it to submit an offer in compromise, which consisted of an agreement to pay the fine and was accompanied by representations to the effect that the advertising in question would not be resumed. This was accepted.

Several interesting observations may be made with respect to the offer in compromise. As indicated previously, the

[51] Point-of-sale includes alcoholic beverage advertising displays in the windows and on the counters of various retail liquor stores. Since the point-of-sale advertising is prepared and distributed by the advertiser, the Unit is not required to go into every retail store. The Unit requests and receives the advertising samples from the distiller or bottler.

liquor industry depends upon a license for its existence. In the event that the company will not submit an offer in compromise, the Unit orders the company to show cause why its license should not be suspended or revoked. In addition, the minutes of the hearing and any order resulting from the hearing are matters of public record. It is obvious that by refusing to compromise, the company runs the risk of being put out of business or suspended and of being subjected to bad publicity. The fact that only a foolhardy corporation would run this risk rather than pay a comparatively small fine is quite apparent. Therefore, almost all unlawful practice cases are disposed of by offers in compromise.

It is because of the Unit's authority to put a distiller either temporarily or permanently out of business and to subject a distiller to harmful publicity that the Unit's authority to control the advertising of acoholic beverages has never been questioned in the courts. The advertising of alcoholic beverages is under strict control. Unlike problems confronting the Federal Trade Commission, the Alcohol Tax Unit has enjoyed a large measure of success without being hampered by limiting appropriations, restrictive legislation, or judicial review. The reasons for the Unit's success may be summed up as follows:

1. As indicated, the inclusion of specific prohibitions in the regulations, supported by the threat of criminal sanctions, has deterred a great many members of the industry from using false or deceptive advertising.

2. Because of an advisory service that this Unit makes available, the distillers and bottlers need not run the risk of criminal penalties for bad advertising. Proposed advertisements may be submitted to the Unit for approval, disapproval, or pertinent suggestions. Although approval of an advertisement by the Unit does not preclude the taking of regulatory action, as a matter of policy the Unit has never proceeded against an ad-

vertiser for an advertisement that had been approved previously. The value of the advisory service, which passed on 872 advertisements submitted by mail from July 1, 1949, to June 30, 1950, lies in the fact that its success is based on cooperation between the Unit and the members of the industry. Thus, when an advertisement is not approved, the advertiser generally will not use it. As a result, the number of violations is lessened substantially.

3. In addition to strict legal regulations and the cooperation fostered by the advisory service, there is another factor responsible for the fact that liquor advertising has been, on the whole, amenable to control. Unlike manufacturers and producers generally, the distiller, bottler, or retailer of alcoholic beverages must have the special permission of the government, both national and state, to go into business and may remain in business only so long as the government permits him to retain his license. Moreover, because of the very nature of the liquor business, an unfavorable public reaction can affect the government's attitude toward the liquor industry.

The distillers and bottlers are well aware that public sentiment may result in prohibition. The members of the industry are, therefore, careful to avoid arousing public antipathy. In addition, advertising agencies and media, particularly radio and television, are anxious to retain the advertising revenue they receive at present from the alcoholic beverage industry. Consequently, the industry, the agency, and the media tread warily. Typical of the opposition groups who seek to eliminate the liquor industry is the National Temperance and Prohibition Council, which has directed much criticism at liquor advertising. Their platform is based on the logical arguments that advertising induces people to "drink," and the majority of accidents on the highways and crimes are caused by persons under the influence of alcohol. They have argued that the use of alcoholic beverages can never be effectively controlled until advertising, "powerful, fraudulent sales talk for a commodity which scientific surveys show to be one which creates widespread poverty and moral degradation," is eliminated.[52]

That the liquor industry, the advertising agencies, and media are aware of the trouble that lies ahead if they do not respect public opinion is demonstrated by the fact that some of the leading advertising men in the country are recommending that the liquor industry drop promotional advertising in favor of institutional and educational copy.[53]

In order to temper public reaction and avert censorship by law several self-disciplinary measures have been taken. Although there is no law prohibiting the advertising of liquor on the radio and television, station licensees have resisted strongly any attempts by distillers to buy radio time for alcoholic beverages other than beer and wine. In 1948 one of the leading distillers announced its intention to commence advertising on television and completed negotiations for time with a leading network. Thousands of letters were sent to the distiller, the television and radio network, and to governmental bodies, all protesting the proposed advertising. The distiller and the network were forced to submit to public opinion, and shortly thereafter the network announced that it would not accept programs advertising hard liquor. It is interesting to note that the network maintained it had the same right to accept all

---

[52] "Hint New Dry Tactics Against Liquor Ads," 14 *Spirits*, May, 1947, pp. 1, 12–14. Note also, "Can there be a valid argument advanced by any detached person why all liquor advertising in all media, magazines, newspapers, and radio shall not be banned by Federal action? It may be fairly argued that the liquor industry has been licensed to meet an admitted demand for drink. But it has not been licensed in order to increase that demand. . . . To ban liquor advertising would be a good place to begin to check, to some degree, the crime now getting worse than under Repeal." Roscoe Drummond, "Bootlegging Menace Spreads," *Christian Science Monitor*, February 4, 1949, p. 1.

[53] "Our Advertising Critics Speak," 16 *Spirits*, March, 1949, pp. 13–15, 38–39. For the effect that the "drys" have had on Congress and antiliquor advertising legislation see "Ads and the Big Club," 16 *Spirits*, March, 1949, pp. 18–19, 51–53.

liquor advertising as newspapers or magazines; but the network's decision to refuse hard liquor advertising was explained as follows:

> We have had discussions on accepting programs sponsored by a liquor company, but have decided against their acceptance at the present time because of a variety of factors. There is at the present a divided feeling on the part of the liquor industry itself; various important organizations and significant segments of public opinion throughout the country have evidenced their strong disapproval of such sponsored programs; and there have been certain indications that, if liquor advertising over the radio were accepted now, a campaign to prohibit the advertising of wine and beer on the radio would be undertaken, both nationally and on a state level.[54]

Thus, both the network and the distiller yielded to public opinion. Their acquiescence was not based on the desire to conform to standards believed best for the nation, but was based rather on the desire to avoid the imposition of additional restrictions on the liquor industry. Apart from the pros and cons, however, there is one bright note: it is heartening to observe that at times public opinion can be marshalled to correct or prevent advertising abuses.

---

[54] Robert E. Kintner, *American Broadcasting News* (Fort Worth, Tex.: American Broadcasting Co., 1948), pp. 1–2.

Chapter 8

OBSERVATIONS AND CONCLUSIONS

Stages in the Law of Advertising

The first stage in the American jurisprudence affecting advertising was the so-called "laissez faire" era, a "free-booting" period epitomized by the slogan of *caveat emptor*. In selling an article, it made no difference how one described it, provided the purchaser had an opportunity of inspecting it. Abuses in business relations and particularly in advertising were many. With the bulk of advertising expenditures concentrated on quack cures, patent medicines, and promotion schemes of every type, the newspapers, periodicals, and the mails were filled with false and flamboyant claims. Under the legal maxim of "let the buyer beware" many unfair trade practices were taken for granted and, in fact, became the unofficial standard of doing business: "Those were the good old days, that is to say, they were good for the Jay Goulds, the Jim Fiskes and the Commodore Vanderbilts of yesteryear when the public could be damned." [1]

The second stage in the development of the law of advertising was the legislative stage. Simultaneously with the emergence of an organized business of national advertising, reformers and public-spirited citizens appeared on the scene to urge upon Congress the concepts that the seller should also beware and that the public had a right to be protected against

---

[1] Isaac W. Digges, "Courts Adopting Less Tolerant Attitude Toward Advertising," *Printers' Ink*, March 30, 1951, p. 33.

the fraudulent and even the over-enthusiastic claims of advertising men. With the tremendous increase in mass production and distribution at the turn of the century, it was impossible for the consumer to maintain personal relationships with the producers of thousands of products. The consumer was often deprived of a chance to inspect the product and had to rely upon the label or package. As the national Better Business Bureau expressed it:

> There was too much "risk" for the consumer in buying. This "risk" had to be eliminated if the system was to have a healthy growth. For the mutual benefit of a business and the public, two things must be done. The public must be protected from frauds. Legitimate business must develop and use high standards of advertising and selling. Above all, business must earn and justify the confidence of the public.[2]

Consideration of the consumer's interest played a leading role in the growth and development of the regulations which were enacted. The periodic waves of popular indignation against unfair practices, adulteration of foods, and other misrepresentation finally brought about a small measure of special governmental protection for the consumer. State and local provisions against the more glaring instances of adulteration or fraud proved to be inadequate because the proportion of interstate to intrastate commerce increased, and federal supplementation of state protection became essential. Interstate competition prevented any single state from setting up a standard very far out of line with the standard of other states. The struggle for a federal pure food and drug law began about 1880, but it required more than a quarter of a century to secure the enactment of such a law.

It was soon found that in addition to affording the consumer protection against fraud in the food and drug fields, it

---

[2] *Facts You Should Know About Your Better Business Bureau* (New York: Better Business Bureau, 1950), p. 4.

was necessary for the nation to fix a basic plane of legitimate business activity that would also be applicable to advertising, forbidding or eliminating practices deemed "cutthroat," "ruinous," or "unfair." The familiar regulatory machinery of statutory prohibition which the consumer could enforce through a lawsuit, or even through criminal prosecution, was found to be inadequate in this era of complicated production and distribution.[3]

The newer governmental techniques which had resulted from the enactment of the Interstate Commerce Act could and did provide a pattern for the regulatory machinery to be invoked. The Federal Trade Commission, a bipartisan, permanent, specialized administrative tribunal, was created to prevent the free enterprise system from being stifled or fettered by monopoly or corrupted by unfair or deceptive trade practices.[4]

---

[3] "The doctrine of 'breach of warranty' affords remedies for misrepresentation which can be extended beyond the retailer as far back as the manufacturer. Fraud lays the seller open to criminal as well as civil action. Damages may be collected for injury or death consequent upon a seller's negligence. Except for his rare purchase of expensive, durable consumer's goods, such as houses or automobiles, however, or cases of serious injury with heavy damage claims in the balance, such legal protection without administrative enforcement is of no avail to the ultimate consumer. A multitude of fraudulent misrepresentations will bilk the entire consuming public of many fortunes without costing any single individual enough to repay a lawsuit." Fainsod and Gordan, *Government and the American Economy* (New York: W. W. Norton & Co., Inc., 1941), p. 199.

[4] The statutes which express this basic purpose are the Federal Trade Commission Act and the Clayton Antitrust Act. The Federal Trade Commission Act makes unlawful the use in commerce of "unfair methods of competition" and "unfair or deceptive acts or practices." The Clayton Act prohibits specific monopolistic practices. Under both statutes, the Commission seeks to stop in their early stages practices which are unfair, promotive of monopoly, or tending substantially to lessen competition . . .

"Other statutes administered by the Commission are the Export Trade Act, the Wool Products Labeling Act, and certain sections of the Lanham Trade-Mark Act. And shortly after the close of the fiscal year, the Commission was given the duty of enforcing the newly enacted Fur Products Labeling Act. The statute, which becomes effective August 7, 1952, expands and strengthens the Commission's jurisdiction over the misbranding and false advertising of

In so far as they are directly applicable to advertising, the Commission's principal functions under the statutes which it administers are to promote free and fair competition in interstate commerce in the interest of the public through prevention of unfair methods of competition and unfair or deceptive acts or practices, and to protect the public interest by preventing the dissemination of false or deceptive advertisements of food, drugs, cosmetics, and therapeutic devices.

The early attitude of the judiciary toward the Commission's jurisdiction and functions was most discouragng. It took many years of patient pioneering and plodding, in the face of this opposition, to hammer out standards of regulation and control and proper techniques of procedure and administration.

Not until 1934 did the Supreme Court hold in the *Algoma* case [5] that the crucial test in cases of misbranding was not whether dealers were deceived, but whether such misrepresentation of product confused ultimate buyers, tending to make some accept what they did not want. The Supreme Court's admonition to the lower court to do more than give "lip service" to the findings of the Commission ushered in a new era in the judicial attitude toward the Commission; and the Wheeler-Lea Act of 1938 further broadened the scope of the Commission's activities to include the prohibition of "unfair and deceptive practices in commerce."

Thus we find that since 1938 the Commission has encountered a more sympathetic judicial attitude toward its campaign to raise the ethical standards of business by eliminating false and misleading advertising. The Commission's findings of fact are now given "full faith and credit" by the courts. A

---

furs and fur products." *Annual Report of the Federal Trade Commission,* 1951, pp. 1–2.

[5] *Federal Trade Commission v. Algoma Lumber Co.,* 291 U.S. 67 (1934).

new day has dawned for the Commission and the consumer.[6] This marks the third stage in the development of advertising. Buttressed by such decisions as the *Ford, Old Gold,* and *Progress Tailoring* cases,[7] the Federal Trade Commission can

[6] The attitude of the Supreme Court, since 1937, has indicated a deliberate retreat from the "legislative" functions of the judicial power. The disinclination of the Court to examine the social and economic purposes behind federal legislation has made for a more liberal interpretation of the powers of Congress under the Constitution. The Court seems to be willing to accept the fact that its function is to pass upon the powers of Congress and the observance of constitutional requirements, but not upon the social or economic acceptability of the law. "At any rate, the suggestions imply that the court may and ought to refuse the enforcement of the provisions of the act if, in its judgment, Congress was not wise in prescribing as a rule by which the conduct of interstate and international commerce is to be governed, that every combination, whatever its form, in restraint of such commerce and the monopolizing or attempting to monopolize such commerce, shall be illegal. These, plainly, are questions as to the policy of legislation which belong to another department, and this court has no function to supervise such legislation from the standpoint of wisdom or policy." *United States v. South-Eastern Underwriters Association,* 322 U.S. 533, 549, 64 S. Ct. 1162, 88 L. Ed. 1440 (1944).

[7] *Ford Motor Company v. Federal Trade Commission,* 120 F. (2d) 175 (1941); *P. Lorillard Co. v. Federal Trade Commission,* 186 F. (2d) 52 (1950); and *Progress Tailoring Co. v. Federal Trade Commission,* 153 F. (2d) 103 (1946). In this case the Court disposed of the petitioner's contention that because there was no evidence that any salesman was ever deceived, or that the ultimate purchaser was in any way affected by the advertisement, or that a competitor was injured, the proceeding was not in the "public interest." In holding that none of these requirements were needed to halt false and misleading representations of the petitioner, the Court said:

"The Commission may require advertisements to be so carefully worded as to protect the most ignorant and unsuspecting purchaser, *Charles of the Ritz Distributors Corp. v. Federal Trade Commission,* 143 F. (2d) 676, 679; and a statement in an advertisement which is false cannot be qualified or modified. *H. N. Hauser and Son v. Federal Trade Commission,* 106 F. (2d) 596. . . . To be sure, the purpose of the Act is to protect the public and a substantial public interest must appear, but since the amendment of par. 5 of the Act, 1938, 52 *Stat.* 111, 15 *U.S.C.A.* par. 45, the Commission has had jurisdiction of all cases in commerce affecting the public interest whether or not competition is involved; hence it is no longer necessary to show competition, if there is an act or practice in commerce inimical to the public interest. *Wolf v. Federal Trade Commission,* 135 F. (2d) 564, 567. As to the argument that no salesman was ever deceived we need only to say that it is sufficient to show that the advertisements have a tendency or capacity to deceive, *Federal Trade*

now assume a positive attitude toward advertising which fails to comply with the spirit as well as the letter of the law.

Advertising and Its Regulation Today

An examination of the orders issued by the Commission in 1951 against deceptive practices shows that they were directed as much against leading advertisers as against the typical "small fry" patent medicine and mail order advertisers. Included in the corporations against whom orders were issued to refrain from deceptive practices were such major advertisers as Sterling Drug, Bristol-Myers, Emerson Drug, P. Lorillard Company, Reynolds Tobacco Company, Miles Laboratories, American Tobacco Company, and many others.

Sterling Drug was cited in connection with the sale of Bayer Aspirin, Phillips' Milk of Magnesia Cleansing Cream, and Phillips' Milk of Magnesia Skin Cream; the Commission found, among other things, that formerly Sterling falsely represented the "druggists of America" as sponsors of a radio program promoting the sale of Bayer Aspirin; the order also restricted advertising claims as to the results stemming from the use of the Phillips' cosmetic preparations.

By agreement with the Federal Trade Commission, advertisements for Hick's Liquid Capudine, Bromo-Seltzer, Dr. Miles Nervine, Dr. Miles Nervine Tablets, and Dr. Miles Anti-Pain Pills must reveal that users should follow the label and avoid excessive use. Five cases involving antihistamine prep-

---

Commission v. Algoma Lumber Co., 291 U.S. 67, 81; *D.D.D. Corporation v. Federal Trade Commision*, 125 F. (2d) 679, 682. The purpose of the Act is 'to prevent potential injury by stopping unfair methods of competition in their incipiency.' *Federal Trade Commission v. Raladam Company*, 316 U.S. 149, 152, and actual deception of purchasers need not be shown. *Koolish v. Federal Trade Commission*, 129 F. (2d) 64, 65; *Charles of the Ritz Distributors Corp. v. Federal Trade Commission*, 143 F. (2d) 676, 680; *Parloff v. Federal Trade Commission*, 150 F. (2d) 757, 759; and *Keller v. Federal Trade Commission*, 132 F. (2d) 59, 61. 153 F. (2d) at 104."

arations were also formally disposed of by stipulation agreements; complaints issued in 1950, challenging as false the advertising representations made for Resistab, Anahist, Kriptin, Inhiston, and Antamine, were dismissed when their sellers agreed to discontinue unjustified claims for their effectiveness in the treatment of colds.

In the food field, the makers of Nu-Maid Margarine were ordered to stop claiming that their product, because of its Vitamin A content, provides the user with increased pep, energy, vitality, vigor, strength, or endurance, or that it has any therapeutic value in the treatment of digestive troubles.

The Commission issued a sweeping order against the maker of Lucky Strikes: the order prohibited claims that Luckies—or the smoke from them—contain less nicotine or less acid than other leading brands; that they are easy on the throat; or that they provide protection against throat irritation or coughing. The Commission's findings in this case paralleled those made earlier in cases involving Old Gold and Camel cigarettes; the Commission held that there is no significant difference in the amount of nicotine, acid, and throat irritants contained in the leading brands of cigarettes.

Federal court cases involving antideceptive proceedings of the Commission were featured by a successful suit for a preliminary injunction against Rhodes Pharmacal Co. to stop allegedly false advertising of the medicinal preparation Imdrin. The Commission's orders were affirmed without change against Bristol-Myers Co. for false and misleading advertising of Ipana toothpaste; against P. Lorillard Co. for false advertising of Old Gold cigarettes and other tobacco products; against Steelco Stainless Steel, Inc., for misrepresentation in the sale of cooking utensils and unfair disparagement of competitive products.[8]

---

[8] *Annual Report of the Federal Trade Commission*, 1951, pp. 50–52, 62–63.

We must also consider in this connection that the important advertising accounts are placed through the most responsible and respectable advertising agencies; that, because of the limited resources available to the Commission, only a fraction of the offenses are detected, and of those many are settled informally or by stipulation; that the Federal Trade Commission can only stop companies from doing what they have done in the past but cannot issue a general injunction;[9] and finally that the Commission has no jurisdiction over advertising which may be in the worst possible taste from the public viewpoint and yet is not legally fraudulent.[10]

These facts and the mounting criticism of advertising from responsible sources are giving serious concern to all who believe in the vital part which advertising plays in our economic system. Firmly convinced that this serious problem requires an immediate solution from within the industry and not from more government regulation, the publisher of *Printers' Ink*, in an article intriguingly captioned "Thunder on the

---

[9] Joseph S. Wright, assistant FTC general counsel in charge of compliance, said that FTC's cigarette cases bog down because the commission can only stop companies from doing what they have done in the past, and cannot issue a general injunction.

"In the Reynolds case," he said, "they had used hundreds of different types of testimonials that had these false types of statements and our order literally required them in using testimonials to tell the truth.

"The court modified our order and said we did not have the power to go that far. We can only stop them from doing what they have done in the past. We cannot issue a general injunction forbidding any false statement." *Advertising Age*, March 10, 1952, p. 77.

[10] C. B. Larrabee, publisher of *Printers' Ink*, in an editorial expressed himself as having a "slight feeling of nausea" at some current advertising methods. Speaking of a television commercial he asked:

"When will they come out of this Cloud Cuckoo-Land of business as usual and who cares anyway so long as we make a dollar or two? When will they realize that advertising written for half-wits and dimbrains may get by in normal times, but in times like these can only lead to nausea and disgust on the part of people who really count? When will they realize that quietness, dignity, decency and good sense are still commodities that have precious values beyond anything that Starch or Hooper or Nielsen or Gallup can uncover?" *Printers' Ink*, February 14, 1951, p. 4.

Right" in the March 7, 1952, issue, boldly challenges "advertising" to put its house in order before it is compelled to do so because of public clamor and indignation.

After summarizing the opinions of educators, labor leaders, government officials, writers, and consumers, Mr. Larrabee attempts to catalog the current objections to advertising as follows:

> What are the things objected to? For one thing, the public doesn't like many of the exaggerations of advertising. It not only resents the exaggerations themselves, but it resents the fact that advertisers seem to think the public is stupid enough to believe the exaggerations.
>
> The public doesn't like a lot of senseless repetition, particularly when it is done by voice on the air. Somehow it resents being urged vocally to do something again and again more than it resents being urged to do it by the printed word.
>
> The public doesn't like some of the evidences of bad taste. It seems to distinguish fairly well between excusable frankness and out-and-out vulgarity. Here the resentment comes more from parents than from any other group of the public. People just don't like to have youngsters bombarded with vulgarity, particularly when it gets over on the side of sex.
>
> The more thoughtful sections of the public resent some of the more blatant snob appeals. When it comes to the advertising of specific products, here again the area of resentment is comparatively limited. Cigarette advertising has been under attack for years. Perhaps the most spectacular attack, or rather series of attacks, were those delivered by the *Reader's Digest* ten years ago. But cigarette advertising has been building resentment against itself for years.
>
> A lot of cosmetic advertising is resented because of its vulgarity, its snob appeal and its overt use of sex appeals.
>
> Liquor advertising, of course, has been under continual attack from the drys since repeal. It is so badly hamstrung by state legislation that in many states the advertiser can do little beyond announcing his brand name. Because of the wet-dry controversy, liquor advertising is particularly vulnerable to attack, and by the same token, with one or two exceptions, it probably is the cleanest advertising copy today.

Proprietaries and dentifrices are attacked more frequently in professional journals than elsewhere. But they, too, arouse resentments.

Taking note of the fact that the advertising apologists seem unconcerned with the storm of criticism because they are convinced a great segment of the public does believe that advertising is valuable and helpful, Mr. Larrabee points out that the apologists overlook several important facts. He puts it in this manner:

First, when you mention the advertisers in the field of cosmetics, proprietaries and dentifrices, liquor and cigarettes, you are talking of some of the heaviest advertising spenders. Although the number of advertisers under attack is comparatively few, the volume of advertising they do is out of proportion to their numbers.

To talk about the small number of things objected to by the public as though that is an ameliorating circumstance overlooks the fact that the small number of things bulk comparatively large in the amount of times they are used. And, even if this was not true, a consumer who resents one or two campaigns out of the many he listens to can make his resentment cover a far wider area.

When opinion leaders in business, education, labor and Government are attacking certain phases of advertising and attacking them vigorously, then people in advertising should look out. When leaders of the right, friends of the American system of free enterprise, express their discontent with certain phases of advertising, that is far more important than the nagging attacks from the people on the left. Advertising always has its enemies. When it begins to wear thin the patience of its friends, then advertisers should stop and take a good long look.[11]

If any corroboration were needed for these observations it can be found in a decision delivered by the Federal Trade

[11] *Printers' Ink,* March 7, 1952, pp. 86, 87.

Commission in the case of *In re Carter Products, Inc.*[12] The decision of the Federal Trade Commission, and the accompanying statement of Commissioner Carson, represent a landmark in the development of federal practices and regulations regarding advertising. An analysis of the case, the ruling, and the comments of the Commission is in order.

The findings in this case, as set forth by Commissioner Carson, are substantially as follows: the advertising claims that Carter's Little Liver Pills were not harmful, would give the consumer "bounce and pep," and would "relieve his blues" were untrue.

As a matter of fact the findings of the Commission showed that Carter's Pills were nothing more than an irritative laxative compound, having no effect whatsoever on the liver or on the bile. Commenting upon the advertising claims, Commissioner Carson said:

> This case parades before us the questionable flights of fancy of an advertising agency. Carter Products, Inc., through employing the agency and thus approving and condoning its work, cannot escape from its responsibility. The case is illustrative of scores of cases which flow across this bench, week in and week out. This Commission has encouraged and will encourage lawful business activity to the extent of its authority, that of Carter Products, Inc., as well as that of other corporations. But it is obligated to outlaw such conduct as is in evidence here.

He made it quite clear that neither the Commission nor any of its employees were opposed to advertising, nor were they opposed to the manufacture and distribution of medical preparations as long as the consumer was protected against fraudulent claims or representation. The comments of the Commissioner on this point were as follows:

---

[12] Federal Trade Commission, *Docket No.* 4970, March 28, 1951, pp. 1–14.

> The advertising profession is an honorable profession. It has contributed, tremendously, to the sale and distribution of the products of business and thus has served the public interest.
>
> Likewise, the manufacture and distribution of medical preparations is an honorable business. It has every right to the respect had for the profession of medicine and many will agree that the medical profession is generally and should always be the most honorable of professions. But the time is here, in fact it has long passed, when those engaged in associated advertising businesses must take steps again, as they did some years ago, to rid the house of those who have less regard for the truth of their representations to the public.

Commissioner Carson also served notice upon the advertising agencies that they too would be held responsible for false or misleading advertisements which they placed.

> The Commission was asked to include in its order to cease and desist, not only Carter Products, Inc., but the advertising agency, Street and Finney. The evidence seems to indicate that Street and Finney were equally culpable of the unlawful practices involved. The Commission has included advertising agencies in orders on some occasion and on others it has not done so. The Commission will be asked to instruct its staff that hereafter advertising agencies will be cited in every case when the facts warrant such action.

Despite the ruling of the Commission that the Carter advertisements cease claiming that the pills benefit the liver, both periodical and radio advertisements continue blithely to disregard this injunction. The theory back of the advertiser's reasoning is the fact that an appeal is pending in the Courts.

Why should periodicals and radio stations, however, continue to accept such advertising claims in the face of a decision by a duly constituted federal regulatory body that such claims were false and misleading? This very question raises the point as to what responsibility rests on the advertising media to help curb objectionable and misleading advertising.

To begin with, it must be understood that the various media reserve to themselves the broadest latitude to reject at their sole discretion any and all advertising which they deem objectionable.[13]

It would seem logical to assume that where the Federal Trade Commission after prolonged hearings determines that an advertisement is misleading and deceptive, such findings should serve as a guide to these media to reject such advertisements, since they have the power under their contracts to do so. With respect to such advertising, these media are in a different position from the advertiser or even the advertising agency. These media, although engaged in business for profit solely, are the beneficiaries of a public bounty. The periodicals which qualify enjoy the privileges of second-class mailing rates; the radio and television stations are granted a license to use the national resource of radio and television channels. Unlike the advertiser and the advertising agency, they cannot be concerned with advertising revenue solely without regard to the public welfare.

The television networks and independent station owners have made a move in the right direction by establishing on March 1, 1952, a television code with means of enforcement to it. Every station which adheres to the code is permitted to display a symbol of its membership and one can see the symbol displayed by the networks and stations with the appropriate announcement that the particular station is "proud to display the symbol." The interesting feature of this code

---

[13] "All copy, text and illustrations are subject to the publisher's approval before execution of the order; and the right is reserved to reject or exclude copy which is unethical, misleading, extravagant, challenging, questionable in character, in bad taste, detrimental to public health or interest, otherwise inappropriate or incompatible with the character of the publication, or that does not meet with the approval of the Federal Trade Commission; whether or not the same has already been accepted and/or published." Standard Rate and Data Service, "Contract and Copy Regulations," *Consumer Magazine*, January, 1952, p. 2.

is that it carries with it a penalty for violation resulting in the loss of the right to use the symbol. This may be a pattern for the periodicals to use, and if they adopt it it may mean that advertising will succeed in putting a quietus on a great deal of the criticism against advertising as well as eliminating the need for further government regulation. The adoption of a code with a symbol and with the penalty provision of the loss of such a symbol for violation of the code would also mean that the periodicals observing the code would not be at a disadvantage in losing advertising revenue to the unscrupulous newspaper or magazine which evades the code.

Assuming that the various advertising media are too dollar-hungry not to recognize their obligations to society and to the advertising business itself, are there any means at hand to bring about the desired result? The answer would seem to be in the affirmative. At present when an advertiser uses false and misleading advertising, not only the advertiser, but also the advertising agency, will be cited and included in the complaint. Inquiries at the Federal Trade Commission have disclosed that as a matter of "policy" the periodicals are not included in the complaints, although the advertisements can only see the light of day via the periodicals. One cannot avoid the suspicion that the failure to include the periodicals in the proceedings because of policy is due more to a fear of the power of the Fourth Estate than to any lack of power to do so.

Newspapers and magazines should definitely be made respondents in proceedings against false and deceptive advertising. Since they have the unquestioned right under their contracts with the advertiser to reject such copy, they need have no difficulty in adhering to standards of decency and propriety. What has been said about periodicals applies equally to making radio and television stations respondents.

The advisability of including these media as respondents lies in the fact that in case of repeated violations, the periodicals would not only be subject to the penalties under the Federal Trade Commission Act, but would run the risk of the loss of the second-class mailing privilege without which they could not exist; and the radio and television stations would run the risk of being put out of existence because the renewal of their licenses could be denied.

Just how effective this power could be has been indicated in a previous chapter where it was shown that the merest intimation by the Federal Communications Commission that it might question the renewal of licenses for television stations carrying horse-racing results brought immediate elimination of such a practice by as prominent a television station as WPIX, owned by the *New York Daily News.*

In addition to the Federal Trade Commission, other administrative bureaus and departments such as the Federal Alcohol Tax Unit, the Federal Communications Commission, the Post Office Department, the Food and Drug Administration, and several others,[14] are, as we have seen, primarily concerned with the regulation and control of the advertiser in the remedial sense. It is the aim and the purpose of such regulation to prevent the advertiser, through the means of false and deceptive practices, to mislead the consumer, to injure a competitor, or to injure the public interest.

---

[14] Securities and Exchange Commission (stocks and securities), Interstate Commerce Commission (railroads), Civil Aeronautics Authority (airlines), United States Public Health Service (medicinal preparations), Commodities and Exchange Authority (exchanges, e.g., New York's Stock Exchange), National Bureau of Standards (standards of performance), Housing and Home Finance Agency (building and loan associations), Federal Power Commission (public utilities), Bureau of Animal Husbandry (meat inspection and packing). These and many other federal regulatory bodies exercise an indirect control on advertising through licensing requirements imposed by them. For example, the Bureau of Animal Husbandry determines what sort of beef may be called "U.S. Grade A-1." Thus, the meat packer cannot advertise beef as "U.S. Grade A–1" unless it has been so certified by the Bureau.

Control of Advertising as an Economic Force

The impact of an advertising expenditure of over $6.5 billion a year on our economy and well-being is a phenomenon of such recent occurrence that its effect has hardly been perceived or evaluated. The time has come, however, to recognize the fact that our national policy, which is aimed at preventing a disastrous inflationary economy, can be negated and thwarted by permitting the unrestrained expenditure of billions of dollars for advertising at the very time when the government—proclaiming a national emergency—has sought to restrain increased consumption. It is difficult to comprehend how, in the face of efforts by the nation to control credits, installment buying, stock and commodity margins, prices, and consumption, advertisers can be permitted to urge the American people to spend more and buy more without regard to any limits. The torrent of sales messages directed at the consumer, urging, pleading, cajoling him to hurry and "buy" and "buy," are financed by advertising dollars which the government permits the advertiser to deduct as normal operating expenses.[15]

---

[15] "You are entitled to deduct the ordinary and necessary costs of running your business. What does that mean? It covers any costs that are: usual, or common, or appropriate, even if they are not essential; even unusual or non-recurring if their purpose is really to secure income now or in the future; normal to protect your business or to defend it or to increase it! Our expenses, says the law, must be ordinary and necessary. It does not say they must be reasonable, average, comparable to other years, commonplace or anything else that might limit ordinary and necessary costs. So we had plenty of instances in the last war in which we were asked about tax deductions for: expenses for advertising which were many times what they were in pre-war years; costs that boosted normal advertising outlay way up, even without increased space or time; people with nothing to sell who wanted to maintain their position with large gobs of institutional copy; war babies who wanted to plug their products in the hope of getting post-war sales—sometimes that was new stuff developed while working 100 per cent under government contracts; war plants which started out on brand new lines never before manufactured by them in the pre-war period; brand new companies that started up and wanted to push their

Is the government seriously concerned about inflation? An examination of the report by the Joint Committee on the Economic Report will quickly dispose of the query.

> The continuation of inflation represents a multiple threat to productive efficiency. . . . By encouraging the hoarding of materials and of labor, inflation disorganizes the flow of production and makes a shambles of allocation orders and procedures. Price rises inevitably lead to wage increases which if unsatisfactory are bound to bring strikes. Inflation frustrates the thrifty, especially those who patriotically buy Government bonds or life insurance, rewards individuals who scoff at the public interest, and brings bitterness and disillusionment to those seeking to cooperate with the defense effort. By inflation they suffer partial repudiation in the buying of their bonds, something which, insofar as it is controlled by Government, comes close to being governmental breach of faith. Inflation gives its biggest rewards to the parasites and speculators whose spending and manipulative activities provide a sardonic contrast to the sacrifices of the savers and of the fixed income groups and their sons on the battlefield.[16]

The report suggests the following methods to be employed to curb inflation: (1) increased production; (2) rigid limitation of government expense; (3) preventing past savings from being spent and rigidly limiting newly created credit; (4) increased thrift; (5) preventing incomes from rising through price and wage controls; (6) increased taxation. After a careful analysis of these methods keeping in mind the difficulty of holding down consumption, particularly of the high-income

---

war-developed lines. With all that, I insist, I have not yet heard of one single instance in which there has been a denial of a tax deduction." J. K. Lasser, "Is Advertising a Tax Deduction in a War Period?" *Printers' Ink*, September 8, 1950, pp. 8–9.

[16] *Joint Economic Report* (Washington, D. C.: U.S. Govt. Printing Office, 1951), pp. 30–31.

consumer,[17] the report concludes that taxation can eliminate the difficulties because:

> Taxation has the great advantage of finality. It leaves no overhang of assets to create inflationary danger for the future. By the same token it holds out no promise that those who forego consumption now will be repaid in the future. If the military program is very big, and lasts for a long period of time, the main reliance for restraining consumption must fall on those whose incomes afford more than efficiency levels of consumption.[18]

Along with this recommendation came a suggestion that advertising itself be taxed.

The recommendation of the Joint Committee to tax advertising has brought a flood of discussion both in the press and in Congress. Much of the opposition is due to the fact that, except for a few brief years during the Civil War period, the United States has never had a tax on advertising.[19] Some of it stems from the failure to evaluate the significance of advertising as an economic force and its effect on inflation. The major opposition to such a tax comes from the well-organized and ably led group of advertising federations and organizations.

What are the proposals of the *Joint Economic Report* on an advertising tax? To begin with, the reason for the need of such a tax is given:

---

[17] "But the problem of holding down the consumption of the high-income consumer is difficult because the high-income consumer is well organized and represented by intelligent and sophisticated leaders. This means that the consumption of high-income consumers cannot be held down in any way that is not acceptable to them. The problem, then, is to find a way of holding down their consumption that is not only effective but acceptable without too many undesirable side effects and after effects." *Ibid.*, p. 58. [18] *Ibid.*, p. 60.

[19] Section 88 of the Act of July 1, 1862, provided that all periodicals pay a duty of 3 per cent on all receipts from advertisements or paid matter. The taxpayer was required to file quarterly returns with payment for the full amount of the tax. Advertising receipts that amounted to less than $1,000 were exempt, as were newspapers whose circulation did not exceed 2,000 copies. In 1867, the tax was repealed.

From a general economic point of view, one of the most desirable excise taxes that could be levied would be a tax on advertising, especially on that urging consumers to buy consumer goods. This is obviously not the time to whip up inflation further by stimulating consumer buying, nor is it a time for making still worse the already grave shortage of so vital and critical a material as newsprint or woodpulp. Yet, notwithstanding this, an increased volume of advertising continues to spur the consumers on to additional spending.[20]

After a review of the expenditures for advertising in 1949 and 1950, the *Report* continues:

A heavy tax currently imposed may have a variety of results. The advertisement of some types of products may be discontinued for the duration. Others may reduce the amount of their advertising. In some cases advertising media would reduce their rates of advertising and absorb part of the tax. In others, advertisers may shift to direct advertising by mail or by handbill in case the tax could not be made to apply to these types of advertising. If the heavy tax had no effect on the volume of advertising or the prices charged, the yield from a 20 to 25 per cent tax would be well over one billion. If the heavy tax discouraged the volume of advertising, the result would be a lowering of the estimated tax revenue, a reduction in demand for goods and materials going into advertising, and also a reduction in the stimulus by advertising to cause people to buy. To the extent advertising media reduced their rates and absorbed part of the excise tax, their net income would also be reduced and hence the revenue from the income tax would be reduced.

On the other hand, to the extent reduced volume of advertising resulted in reduced sales, the profits of advertisers would be reduced and the revenue from the income tax would be reduced. Should people buy less because of a reduced volume of advertising, inflationary pressures might be reduced and consumer saving increased. It is even conceivable that the yield from other taxes might also be increased, especially if the tax on advertising resulted in reduced expenditures for

---

[20] *Ibid.*, p. 73.

"good will" advertising more or less deliberately engaged in to avoid excess profits and corporation income taxes.[21]

Is a tax on advertising the only method of regulating, harnessing, and integrating this giant force with the national purpose and welfare? The very reasons given by the sponsors of the suggestion suggest the economic dislocation which would result from such a tax, and on this ground alone such a tax is undesirable.

Great Britain faced this question squarely in 1948 and decided against it. Faced with a proposal by the Chancellor of the Exchequer in the 1947 budget to tax advertising, the British advertisers and agents devised a voluntary scheme for the limitation of advertising as a substitute for the tax.[22] Under the plan of action adopted, advertisers who endorsed the plan agreed to limit their expenditures and:

> . . . to use their best endeavours to conduct their advertising and to arrange the tone of their "copy" in accordance with the spirit of this voluntary scheme, which is to refrain from increasing inflationary pressure of demand for scarce or rationed goods and services, and where possible to encourage attainment of the country's export and production objectives.[23]

The plan received wide support and has been continued during the succeeding years with the modification of the financial limitation. The British plan is important, not because it necessarily applies to American advertising, but rather because it involves a mature recognition by a government of the extent to which unregulated advertising can stimulate inflation and jeopardize governmental purposes.

In addition to the method of voluntary control as adopted by British advertisers and agencies, there is still another

---

[21] *Ibid.*, pp. 73, 75.

[22] The Federation of British Industries, *The Voluntary Limitation of Advertising* (London: Times Publishing Co., 1948). See Appendix D.

[23] *Ibid.*, p. 4.

method available of regulating the expenditure of billions for advertising so as to coordinate it with the national purpose.

Without accepting at full value the prognostication of government economists that the present tension and consequent defense expenditures may last ten to twenty years, there can be little doubt that it will be with us for some time. All seem to agree that inflation can be prevented if, along with other restraints, the great consumer demand can be restrained.

It is recommended that to ease the tension of the increasing demand for more consumer goods—which threatens the national effort to curb inflation—the Congress, under its broad constitutional powers of taxation and commerce, limit the amount advertisers be permitted to expend for advertising. This can be accomplished by a change in the construction of the present law [24] which permits an advertiser to deduct from his taxable income all the millions he spends as "ordinary and necessary costs" of running his business.

There is no logic or reason to a policy of the government which, on the one hand, proclaims a national emergency and embarks upon a program of wage and price controls to ward off inflation, and which, on the other hand, makes available to advertisers by a tax deduction billions of dollars that largely stimulate greater consumer demand and hence defeat the national economic policy.[25]

---

[24] *Internal Revenue Code,* Sec. 23(a).

[25] Even more reprehensible is the expenditure of millions of dollars in advertising by companies which have nothing to sell to the consumer, but make these expenditures because they are tax deductible. This point is well summed up in an editorial in *Printers' Ink,* February 29, 1952, p. 94, under the caption "Advertising Can Grow Without Tax Dollars":

"Mr. Doan is the head of a company that will pay about $90,000,000 in federal taxes this year. Dow Chemical, he says, has expanded its plant considerably—but it has not expanded its advertising beyond its logical productive level.

"Instead of going on a spending spree (a policy that some companies and business advisors seem to favor), Dow is going to pay its taxes and at the same time economize in every way possible. A policy of this kind, he

There is no question about the power of Congress to correct the evil. A government which can curtail production of automobiles, refrigerators, television sets, and all other civilian products, can freeze wages, regulate prices, and allocate materials surely has the power to limit expenditures for advertising which have a tendency to thwart the effort of the nation to curb inflation. This is particularly so when we consider that such expenditures are sanctioned as being tax deductible under Section 23(a) of the Internal Revenue Code.

It is proposed that Congress, basing its judgment on a careful study, determine that only a specified portion of the advertising budget be expended for advertising, the balance either to be taxed or to be set aside tax-free under such conditions as Congress may provide. The moneys to be set aside are to be made available for expenditure at a time when Congress shall declare it to be necessary to aid the national purpose in a fight against deflation, by stimulating more employment, more sales, and more production.

Along with the problem of regulating advertising expenditures in an inflationary period, consideration should be given in this congressional study to a more liberal tax deduction for advertising during a deflationary period with a view of achiev-

---

believes, will help to avoid still higher taxes and will give corporations the right to demand that the federal government spend its revenues wisely and with equal economy.

"Mr. O'Connor argues that there is no room today for waste in corporate spending: no reason to throw away 80 cents of an advertising dollar to get 20 cents' worth of results. But there is nothing wrong with expanding your advertising, he says, when a definite increase in sales can be expected. This would mean, of course, expanding it to its logical productive level, as Dow Chemical has done.

"Any company that spends money on advertising merely to cheat the government is really cheating itself, its neighbors, its employees, its stockholders and other companies that will have to pay higher taxes."

ing greater employment, production, and consumption. In other words, the aim must be, at all times, to integrate the advertising expenditure with the national welfare.[26]

The discussion in this book leads to an inevitable conclusion: advertising today is truly "big business." The expenditure of over $6.5 billion is equal to the total agricultural economy in this country in 1932, which rated a Department of Agriculture and a cabinet member. Advertising, on the other hand, having grown helter-skelter and having suddenly and imperceptibly become an important economic and social force, has been distributed for its supervision, regulation, and control among a large number of unrelated governmental bureaus, each concerned with some particular phase of advertising regulation. There is undoubtedly a measure of cooperation among these agencies, but even with the best of intentions

---

[26] Under the caption, "Are You Taking Advantage of the New Excess Profit Tax?" the *Joint Economic Report* points out the ways in which firms subject to excess profit taxes can obtain the maximum exemption so that research projects and repairs will be paid for by the government. The suggestions made point the way to the possible use of advertising moneys for similar purposes and hence are deemed sufficiently important to warrant enumeration:

"Some worth-while expenditures will actually reduce a firm's excess tax liability . . .

"Recommended: Expended spending for research, particularly on long-term projects that will pay off at a much later date, is advantageous under high corporate taxation. For firms subject to excess profit taxes the Government will be footing from 62 to 77 per cent of the cost. Small quantities of materials that may be needed for such research projects should not be too hard to obtain, and will generally not be restricted by NPA limitation orders . . .

"Recommended: Maximum spending for maintenance and repairs is generally indicated. New construction for unessential uses will become increasingly more difficult, price trends are firm and rising, so the prospect of having the Government foot the bill for most of your repair costs should certainly be inviting . . .

"Recommended: Pension and profit-sharing plans can be initiated or expanded at comparatively low cost. Dollars deposited in approved pension or profit-sharing plans are entirely exempt from corporate income and excess profit taxes. Thus the Government pays from 62 to 77 per cent of the cost for firms liable to excess profit taxes." *Ibid.*, p. 72.

it cannot be expected that with so many other problems confronting them they can cope adequately with the problem of regulating and supervising a force as gigantic as advertising is today. And the social and economic impact of advertising on our very existence is undeniable.

The new medium of television has accentuated the influence of advertising on our homes, on young and old alike. Questions have arisen as to how to curb advertising that is in bad taste and obnoxious as well as deceptive and misleading; the problem of taxing advertising is coupled with curbing the needless expenditure of tax dollars; the responsibility of the advertiser, the agency, and the media is a problem that requires a great deal of attention. All this leads to the recommendation that Congress entrust to one administrative bureau the regulation, supervision, and control of advertising in all of its phases. The Federal Trade Commission is perhaps ideally suited for this purpose. It has the nucleus of the structure; all that it requires is the needed manpower and financial support as well as the statutory enactments to clothe it with the necessary jurisdiction. Since the Federal Trade Commission has been in the forefront of the fight against abuses in advertising it is more cognizant of the problems confronting advertising than any other federal administrative body. While it will not condone deceptive practices, it is not opposed to "advertising" but on the contrary it recognizes that "the advertising profession is an honorable profession. It has contributed, tremendously, to the sale and distribution of the products of business and thus has served the public interest." Reputable advertisers, agencies, and owners of advertising media should welcome the recommendation to entrust the Federal Trade Commission with such powers, for this Commission has demonstrated as well as declared publicly that it "is ready and anxious to cooperate in every way and at all times with everyone interested in protecting these honorable professions and businesses from the unlawful practices of the few." [27] The wise advertiser or agent will not balk at any measure which will make advertising a constructive part of the economic structure of the nation.

We all have had to adjust our habits, thoughts, and methods to the requirements of the age in which we are living. Advertising too, must adjust itself to the tempo of the era. It is by now too fine a profession and too great an economic force in our existence to permit the disreputable few to bring discredit on all. The voluntary cooperation in this direction of the advertiser, the agency and, above all, the media will in the long run help advertising to prosper and to grow; it will likewise obviate the necessity for any stringent or drastic federal regulations.

---

[27] *In Re Carter Products, Inc.*, Federal Trade Commission, *Docket No.* 4970, March 28, 1951, p. 2.

APPENDIX

APPENDIX A

TYPICAL STIPULATION—FEDERAL TRADE COMMISSION

United States of America
Before Federal Trade Commission

In the Matter of Elroy Naval Stores Company, a corporation, Vidalia, Georgia.	File No. 1-21353

Stipulation as to the Facts and Agreement to Cease and Desist

Pursuant to the provisions of the Federal Trade Commission Act (38 Stat. 717; as amended 52 Stat. 111; 15 U.S.C.A., Sec. 41), the Federal Trade Commission caused an investigation to be made of the acts and practices used by Elroy Naval Stores Company, a corporation, in commerce as defined by the Act, and based on such investigation believes that the aforesaid corporation has been or is using in commerce certain acts and practices, herein specified, which are violative of the provisions of said Act.

It now appearing that Elroy Naval Stores Company is willing to stipulate as to the facts and to enter into an agreement to cease and desist from the use of the acts and practices as hereinafter set forth in such agreement; and it appearing that settlement by stipulation of the matters here involved would not violate the Commission's stated policy of encouraging law observance through cooperation in certain types of cases where there has been no intent to defraud or mislead; and that the Federal Trade Commission may be willing to accept such stipulation and agreement to cease and desist without prejudice to its right to issue a complaint and institute formal proceedings against Elroy Naval Stores Company if at any time the Commission shall deem that such action is warranted;

It Is Hereby Stipulated by and between the Federal Trade Commission and Elroy Naval Stores Company that the following is a true statement of the facts:

Elroy Naval Stores Company is a corporation organized and existing under the laws of the State of Georgia with its principal office and place of business located in Vidalia, Georgia. It is now and has been for more than one year last past engaged in offering for sale and selling, in commerce as defined by said Act, a paint thinner designated "Lone Pine Paint Thinner" and causing the same, when sold, to be shipped from its place of business in the State of Georgia into and through various other States of the United States to purchasers located in said other states and in the District of Columbia.

In the course and conduct of its business as hereinbefore described, Elroy Naval Stores Company has made, published, and caused to be published certain advertising matter, including the following statements, claims, and representations for the purpose of inducing and which is likely to induce the purchase of said product:

> "Lone Pine Paint Thinner (depictions of pine cones and pine trees)"
>
> "* * Based On Gum From The Living Pine * *"
>
> "* * Lone Pine has been * * redistilled, making it a genuine distilled paint thinner * *"
>
> "Blended Pine Products"

By disseminating and causing to be disseminated the foregoing advertising matter, statements, claims, and representations, Elroy Naval Stores Company has directly and impliedly represented through use of the statement "Blended Pine Products," through depictions of pine trees and pine cones, and through use of the word "pine" in the brand name, and otherwise, that the product is composed primarily or solely of blended pine products, and that it contains such products in a significant amount; that the product is a distilled or a redistilled product and that it is based on gum derived from pine; whereas the product is neither distilled nor redistilled, nor is it composed primarily or solely of blended pine products, nor does it contain such products in a significant amount, nor is it based on gum derived from pine.

It Is Hereby Agreed by Elroy Naval Stores Company, that in connection with the offering for sale, sale, and distribution of the product now designated "Lone Pine Paint Thinner" in commerce as defined by said Act, it will forthwith cease and desist from:

(a) Representing in any manner that the product is a distilled or redistilled product or that it is other than a blend of the ingredients of which it is composed;
(b) Representing through the use of such statements as "Blended Pine Products," through the use of depictions of pine trees and pine cones and through the use of the word "pine" in the brand name, or otherwise, that the product is composed solely or primarily of blended pine products or that it contains such products in a significant amount; provided, however, that this shall not be construed as an agreement not to use the word "pine" as a part of the trade name for the product if, in connection with the trade name "Lone Pine Paint Thinner," or any similar name, the respondent clearly and accurately states the percentage of blended pine products contained in said product;
(c) Representing in any manner that the product is based on gum derived from pine.

* * *

APPENDIX B

EXCERPTS FROM THE TELEVISION CODE OF THE NATIONAL ASSOCIATION OF RADIO AND TELEVISION BROADCASTERS [1]

Acceptability of Program Material

Program materials should enlarge the horizons of the viewer, provide him with wholesome entertainment, afford helpful stimulation, and remind him of the responsibilities which the citizen has towards his society. Furthermore:

a) (i) Profanity, obscenity, smut and vulgarity are forbidden, even when likely to be understood only by part of the audience. From time to time, words which have been acceptable, acquire undesirable meanings, and telecasters should be alert to eliminate such words.

(ii) The Television Code Review Board shall maintain and issue to subscribers, from time to time, a continuing list of specific words and phrases which should not be used in keeping with this subsection. This list, however, shall not be considered as all-inclusive.

b) (i) Attacks on religion and religious faiths are not allowed.

(ii) Reverence is to mark any mention of the name of God, His attributes and powers.

(iii) When religious rites are included in other religious programs, the rites are accurately presented, and the ministers, priests and rabbis portrayed in their callings are vested with the dignity of their office and under no circumstances are to be held up to ridicule.

c) (i) Contests may not constitute a lottery.

---

[1] *The Television Code of the National Association of Radio and Television Broadcasters* (Washington, D.C., 1952).

(ii) Any telecasting designed to "buy" the television audience by requiring it to listen and/or view in hope of reward, rather than for the quality of the program, should be avoided. (*See Contests.*)

d) Respect is maintained for the sanctity of marriage and the value of the home. Divorce is not treated casually nor justified as a solution for marital problems.

e) Illicit sex relations are not treated as commendable.

f) Sex crimes and abnormalities are generally unacceptable as program material.

g) Drunkenness and narcotic addiction are never presented as desirable or prevalent.

h) The administration of illegal drugs will not be displayed.

i) The use of liquor in program content shall be de-emphasized. The consumption of liquor in American life, when not required by the plot or for proper characterization, shall not be shown.

j) The use of gambling devices or scenes necessary to the development of plot or as appropriate background is acceptable only when presented with discretion and in moderation, and in a manner which would not excite interest in, or foster, betting nor be instructional in nature. Telecasts of actual sport programs at which on-the-scene betting is permitted by law should be presented in a manner in keeping with Federal, state and local laws, and should concentrate on the subject as a public sporting event.

k) In reference to physical or mental afflictions and deformities, special precautions must be taken to avoid ridiculing sufferers from similar ailments and offending them or members of their families.

l) Exhibitions of fortune-telling, astrology, phrenology, palm-reading, and numerology are acceptable only when required by a plot or the theme of a program, and then the presentation should be developed in a manner designed not to foster superstition or excite interest or belief in these subjects.

m) Televised drama shall not simulate news or special events in such way as to mislead or alarm.

n) Legal, medical and other professional advice, diagnosis and treatment will be permitted only in conformity with law and recognized ethical and professional standards.

o) The presentation of cruelty, greed and selfishness as worthy motivations is to be avoided.

p) Unfair exploitation of others for personal gain shall not be presented as praiseworthy.

q) Criminality shall be presented as undesirable and unsympathetic. The condoning of crime and the treatment of the commission of crime in a frivolous, cynical or callous manner is unacceptable.

r) The presentation of techniques of crime in such detail as to invite imitation shall be avoided.

s) The use of horror for its own sake will be eliminated; the use of visual or aural effects which would shock or alarm the viewer, and the detailed presentation of brutality or physical agony by sight or by sound are not permissible.

t) Law enforcement shall be upheld, and the officers of the law are to be portrayed with respect and dignity.

u) The presentation of murder or revenge as a motive for murder shall not be presented as justifiable.

v) Suicide as an acceptable solution for human problems is prohibited.

w) The exposition of sex crimes will be avoided.

x) The appearances or dramatization of persons featured in actual crime news will be permitted only in such light as to aid law enforcement or to report the news event.

Responsibility Toward Children

1. The education of children involves giving them a sense of the world at large. Crime, violence and sex are a part of the world they will be called upon to meet, and a certain amount of proper presentation of such is helpful in orienting the child to his social surroundings. However, violence and illicit sex shall not be presented in an attractive manner, nor to an extent such as will lead a child to believe that they play a greater part in life than they do. They should not be presented without indications of the resultant retribution and punishment.

2. It is not enough that only those programs which are intended for viewing by children shall be suitable to the young and immature. Television is responsible for insuring that programs of all sorts which occur during the times of day when children may normally be expected to have the opportunity of viewing television shall exercise care in the following regards:

a) In affording opportunities for cultural growth as well as for wholesome entertainment.
b) In developing programs to foster and promote the commonly accepted moral, social and ethical ideals characteristic of American life.
c) In reflecting respect for parents, for honorable behavior, and for the constituted authorities of the American community.
d) In eliminating reference to kidnapping of children or threats of kidnapping.
e) In avoiding material which is excessively violent or would create morbid suspense, or other undesirable reactions in children.
f) In exercising particular restraint and care in crime or mystery episodes involving children or minors.

Decency and Decorum in Production

1. The costuming of all performers shall be within the bounds of propriety, and shall avoid such exposure or such emphasis on anatomical detail as would embarrass or offend home viewers.

2. The movements of dancers, actors, or other performers shall be kept within the bounds of decency, and lewdness and impropriety shall not be suggested in the positions assumed by performers.

3. Camera angles shall avoid such views of performers as to emphasize anatomical details indecently.

4. Racial or nationality types shall not be shown on television in such a manner as to ridicule the race or nationality.

5. The use of locations closely associated with sexual life or with sexual sin must be governed by good taste and delicacy.

Presentation of Advertising

1. Ever mindful of the role of television as a guest in the home, a television broadcaster should exercise unceasing care to supervise the form in which advertising material is presented over his facilities. Since television is a developing medium, involving methods and techniques distinct from those of radio, it may be desirable from time to time to review and revise the presently suggested practices:

a) Advertising messages should be presented with courtesy and good taste; disturbing or annoying material should be avoided; every effort should be made to keep the advertising message in harmony with the content and general tone of the program in which it appears.

b) A sponsor's advertising messages should be confined within the framework of the sponsor's program structure. A television broadcaster should seek to avoid the use of commercial announcements which are divorced from the program either by preceding the introduction of the program (as in the case of so-called "cow-catcher" announcements) or by following the apparent sign-off of the program (as in the case of so-called "trailer" announcements). To this end, the program itself should be announced and clearly identified before the sponsor's advertising material is first used, and should be signed off after the sponsor's advertising material is last used.

c) Advertising copy should contain no claims intended to disparage competitors, competing products, or other industries, professions or institutions.

d) Since advertising by television is a dynamic technique, a television broadcaster should keep under surveillance new advertising devices so that the spirit and purpose of these standards are fulfilled.

e) Television broadcasters should exercise the utmost care and discrimination with regard to advertising material, including content, placement and presentation, near or adjacent to programs designed for children. No considerations of expediency should be permitted to impinge upon the vital responsibility towards children and adolescents, which is inherent in television, and which must be recognized and accepted by all advertisers employing television.

f) Television advertisers should be encouraged to devote portions of their allotted advertising messages and program time to the support of worthy causes in the public interest in keeping with the highest ideals of the free competitive system.

g) A charge for television time to churches and religious bodies is not recommended.

Acceptability of Advertisers and Products—General

1. A commercial television broadcaster makes his facilities available for the advertising of products and services and accepts commercial presentations for such advertising. However, a television broadcaster should, in recognition of his responsibility to the

public, refuse the facilities of his station to an advertiser where he has good reason to doubt the integrity of the advertiser, the truth of the advertising representations, or the compliance of the advertiser with the spirit and purpose of all applicable legal requirements. Moreover, in consideration of the laws and customs of the communities served, each television broadcaster should refuse his facilities to the advertisement of products and services, or the use of advertising scripts, which the station has good reason to believe would be objectionable to a substantial and responsible segment of the community. The foregoing principles should be applied with judgment and flexibility, taking into consideration the characteristics of the medium and the form and content of the particular presentation. In general, because television broadcast is designed for the home and the family, including children, the following principles should govern the business classifications listed below:

a) The advertising of hard liquor should not be accepted.
b) The advertising of beer and wines is acceptable only when presented in the best of good taste and discretion, and is acceptable subject to Federal and local laws.
c) Advertising by institutions or enterprises which in their offers of instruction imply promises of employment or make exaggerated claims for the opportunities awaiting those who enroll for courses is generally unacceptable.
d) The advertising of firearms and fireworks is acceptable only subject to Federal and local laws.
e) The advertising of fortune-telling, occultism, spiritualism, astrology, phrenology, palm-reading, numerology, mind-reading or character-reading is not acceptable.
f) Because all products of a personal nature create special problems, such products, when accepted, should be treated with especial emphasis on ethics and the canons of good taste; however, the advertising of intimately personal products which are generally regarded as unsuitable conversational topics in mixed social groups is not acceptable.
g) The advertising of tip sheets, race track publications, or organizations seeking to advertise for the purpose of giving odds or promoting betting or lotteries is unacceptable.

2. Diligence should be exercised to the end that advertising copy accepted for telecasting complies with pertinent Federal, state and local laws.

3. An advertiser who markets more than one product should not be permitted to use advertising copy devoted to an acceptable product for purposes of publicizing the brand name or other identification of a product which is not acceptable.

Advertising of Medical Products

1. The advertising of medical products presents considerations of intimate and far-reaching importance to the consumer, and the following principles and procedures should apply in the advertising thereof:

a) A television broadcaster should not accept advertising material which in his opinion offensively describes or dramatizes distress or morbid situations involving ailments, by spoken word, sound or visual effects.

b) Because of the personal nature of the advertising of medical products, claims that a product will effect a cure and the indiscriminate use of such words as "safe," "without risk," "harmless," or terms of similar meaning should not be accepted in the advertising of medical products on television stations.

Contests

1. Contests should offer the opportunity to all contestants to win on the basis of ability and skill rather than chance.

2. All contest details, including rules, eligibility requirements, opening and termination dates should be clearly and completely announced and/or shown, or easily accessible to the viewing public, and the winners' names should be be released and prizes awarded as soon as possible after the close of the contest.

3. When advertising is accepted which requests contestants to submit items of product identification or other evidence of purchase of product, reasonable facsimiles thereof should be made acceptable.

4. All copy pertaining to any contest (except that which is required by law) associated with the exploitation or sale of the

sponsor's product or service, and all references to prizes or gifts offered in such connection should be considered a part of and included in the total time allowances as herein provided.

Premiums and Offers

1. Full details of proposed offers should be required by the television broadcaster for investigation and approval before the first announcement of the offer is made to the public.

2. A final date for the termination of an offer should be announced as far in advance as possible.

3. Before accepting for telecast offers involving a monetary consideration, a television broadcaster should satisfy himself as to the integrity of the advertiser and the advertiser's willingness to honor complaints indicating dissatisfaction with the premium by returning the monetary consideration.

4. There should be no misleading descriptions or visual representations of any premiums or gifts which would distort or enlarge their value in the minds of the listeners.

5. Assurances should be obtained from the advertiser that premiums offered are not harmful to person or property.

6. Premiums should not be approved which appeal to superstition on the basis of "luck-bearing" powers or otherwise.

Time Standards for Advertising Copy

1. As a guide to the determination of good telecast advertising practice, the time standards for advertising copy, presently suggested, are as follows:

	Length of Advertising Message (minutes and seconds)		
Length of Program	News Programs	All Other Programs	
(minutes)	Day and Night	Class "A" Time	All Other Hrs.
5	1:00	1:00	1:15
10	1:45	2:00	2:10
15	2:15	2:30	3:00
25		2:50	4:00
30		3:00	4:15
45		4:30	5:45
60		6:00	7:00

2. The time standards set forth above do not affect the estab-

lished practice of reserving for station use the last 30 seconds of each program for station break and spot announcements.

3. Announcement programs are designed to accommodate a designated number of individual live or recorded announcements, generally one minute in length, which are carried within the body of the program and are available for sale to individual advertisers. Normally not more than 3 one-minute announcements (which should not exceed approximately 125 words if presented live) should be scheduled within a 15-minute period and not more than six such announcements should be scheduled within a 30-minute period in local announcement programs; however, fewer announcements of greater individual length may be scheduled, provided that the aggregate length of the announcements approximates three minutes in a 15-minute program or six minutes in a 30-minute program. In announcement programs other than 15 minutes or 30 minutes in length, the proportion of one minute of announcement within every five minutes of programming is normally applied. The announcements must be presented within the framework of the program period designated for their use and kept in harmony with the content of the program in which they are placed.

4. Programs presenting women's services, features, shopping guides, market information, and similar material, provide a special service to the listening and viewing public in which advertising material is an informative and integral part of the program content. Because of these special characteristics the time standards set forth above may be waived to a reasonable extent. In the present state of experimentation in programming and advertising techniques in television programs of this type no definite limitations to these exceptions are set forth at this time.

5. Any casual reference in a program to another's product or service under any trade name or language sufficiently descriptive to identify it should, except for normal guest identifications, be condemned and discouraged.

6. Stationary backdrops or properties in television presentations showing the sponsor's name or product, the name of his product, his trade mark or slogan may be used only incidentally. They should not obtrude on program interest or entertainment. "On

Camera" shots of such materials should be fleeting, not too frequent, and mindful of the need of maintaining a proper program balance.

Dramatized Appeals and Advertising

Appeals to help fictitious characters in television programs by purchasing the advertiser's product or service or sending for a premium should not be permitted, and such fictitious characters should not be introduced into the advertising message for such purposes. When dramatized advertising material involves statements by doctors, dentists, nurses or other professional people, the material should be presented by members of such profession reciting actual experience or it should be made apparent from the presentation itself that the portrayal is dramatized.

Regulations and Procedures

The following Regulations and Procedures shall obtain as an integral part of the Television Code of the National Association of Radio and Television Broadcasters:

Subscribers

Section 2. Certification of Subscription. Upon subscribing to the Code, subject to the approval of the Television Board of Directors, there shall be granted forthwith to each such subscribing station authority to use the "NARTB Television Seal of Good Practice," a copyrighted and registered seal to be provided in the form of a certificate, a slide and/or a film, signifying that the recipient thereof is a subscriber in good standing to the Television Code of the NARTB. The seal and its significance shall be appropriately publicized by the NARTB.

Section 4. Suspension of Subscription. Any subscription, and/or the authority to utilize and show the above-noted seal, may be voided, revoked or temporarily suspended for television programming, including commercial copy, which, by theme, treatment or incident, in the judgment of the Television Board constitutes a continuing, willful or gross violation of any of the provisions of the Television Code, by an affirmative two-thirds vote of the Television Board of Directors at a regular or special meeting.

V

The Television Code Review Board

Section 1. Composition. The Television Board of Directors shall establish a continuing committee entitled The Television Code Review Board, upon the promulgation of the Television Code. The Review Board shall be composed of five members, all of whom shall be from the Television membership of NARTB. Members of the Television Board of Directors shall not be eligible to serve on the above specified Review Board. Members of the Review Board shall be appointed by the President of the NARTB, subject to confirmation by the Television Board of Directors. Due consideration shall be given, in making such appointments, to factors of diversification of geographical location, company representation and network affiliation. Those members appointed, following promulgation of the Code, shall serve until immediately following the annual NARTB Convention of 1952. Thereafter a term shall be for one year.

Section 3. Authority and Responsibilities. The Television Code Review Board is authorized and directed:

(1) To maintain a continuing review of all television programming, especially that of subscribers to the Television Code of the NARTB; (2) to receive, screen and clear complaints concerning television programming; (3) to define and interpret words and phrases in the Television Code; (4) to develop and maintain appropriate liaison with governmental agencies and with responsible and accountable organizations and institutions; (5) to inform, expeditiously and properly, a subscriber to the Television Code of complaints or commendations, as well as to advise all subscribers concerning the attitude and desires programwise of accountable organizations and institutions, and of the American public in general; (6) to review and monitor, if necessary, any

certain series of programs, daily programming or any other program presentations of a subscriber, as well as to request recordings, aural or kinescope, or script and copy, with regard to any certain program presented by a subscriber; (7) to reach conclusions, and to make recommendations or prefer charges to the Television Board of Directors concerning violations and breaches of the Television Code by a subscriber; (8) to recommend to the Television Board of Directors, amendments to the Television Code.

APPENDIX C

OFFER IN COMPROMISE

Of liability incurred under

Federal Alcohol Administration Act, as amended

(To be filed in duplicate with District Supervisor, Alcohol Tax Unit)

. . . . (Date) . . . .
(Name)

. . . .
(Address)

DEPUTY COMMISSIONER OF INTERNAL REVENUE,
ALCOHOL TAX UNIT

SIR:

The following offer in compromise is submitted to you by the undersigned:

Charges of violation of the Federal Alcohol Administration Act, as amended, have been made against the proponent as follows . . . .

. . . .
(State specifically the pending charge)

Date and place of alleged violation . . . .

The alleged violation is due to the following cause or causes:

. . . .
(State in detail)

. . . .

. . . .

To secure the release of the proponent from the liability resulting from the violation or failure above specified, the sum of $ . . . . is hereby tendered voluntarily with request that it be accepted in compromise of the said liability, to wit: . . . .

. . . .

The following facts and reasons are submitted as grounds for acceptance of this offer: . . . .

. . . .
(If space provided is insufficient, attach supplemental affidavit and supporting evidence)

It is understood that this offer does not afford relief from the liability sought to be compromised, unless and until it is actually accepted by the Deputy Commissioner of Internal Revenue in charge of the Alcohol Tax Unit.

In making this offer the proponent expressly understands and agrees that the acceptance of the offer will not in any way affect any liability, civil, forfeiture, or criminal, which he may have incurred by reason of violation of the internal revenue laws or regulations issued pursuant thereto, or of the Liquor Enforcement Act of 1936, whether or not connected with the violation herein sought to be compromised.

....

(If offer is made by agent, the reason therefor must be stated on this line)

Sworn to and subscribed before me

this.......day of.............,194..

....

(Signature of proponent or agent)

....

(Signature of officer administering oath)

....

(Address of agent)

APPENDIX D

THE VOLUNTARY LIMITATION OF ADVERTISING[1]

Definition of Terms and Plan of Action

This document is published on behalf of the Working Committee (representing Advertisers, Agents, and Media Owners) set up to devise a voluntary scheme for the limitation of advertising as a substitute for the tax proposals made by the Chancellor of the Exchequer in the Autumn Budget, 1947.

All recipients are earnestly requested to study and endorse the Plan, and, without delay, to sign and return the appropriate undertaking on page five or six. A copy of this undertaking is provided for record purposes.

The Working Committee consisted of representatives of the following organisations:—The Advertising Association; The Association of British Chambers of Commerce; The Association of Specialised Film Producers Ltd.; The British Poster Advertising Association; The Federation of British Industries; The Incorporated Society of British Advertisers Ltd.; The Institute of Incorporated Practitioners in Advertising; The London Poster Advertising Association Ltd.; The National Chamber of Trade; The National Union of Manufacturers; The Newspaper Proprietors' Association Ltd.; The Newspaper Society; The Periodical, Trade Press & Weekly Newspaper Proprietors' Association Ltd.; The Retail Distributors Association, Inc.; The Solus Outdoor Advertising Association Ltd.

DEFINITION OF TERMS

"Advertiser" means any firm or undertaking which incurs costs on advertising in the U.K. in any of the following forms:—

Press — including books containing advertising	except publications intended purely for circulation overseas.
Outdoor Advertising	except on the advertiser's own premises and vehicles.
Cinematograph Films and Slides	except those primarily of an instructional or documentary character or designed for trade or technical audiences.

[1] The Federation of British Industries, *The Voluntary Limitation of Advertising* (London: The Times Publishing Co., Ltd., 1948).

Point of Sales Displays	except the costs of packets and packaging, and the costs of displays on the advertiser's own premises.
Direct mail to the consumer public	
Exhibitions and Trade Fairs	except those supported by the Board of Trade as being of importance to export sales.

NOTE I.—It is fully appreciated that a proportion of the costs incurred on advertising in the U.K. produces overseas trade, and is in effect export advertising. Such advertising is greatly to be encouraged. But as there is no general rule by which this can be measured, it has been impossible to propose a division of expenditure. The point has been taken specially into account in arriving at the percentage reduction below.

NOTE II.—Press advertising is taken to include both display and classified advertising, but to exclude Companies' compulsory advertising, and Companies' Annual Reports.

NOTE III.—While there is a case for excluding the Technical and Trade Press from this definition, there is no line of demarcation that enables this to be done. Moreover, the whole of this plan is based upon the principle of leaving the advertiser free to make his own decisions about choice of advertising media. The exclusion by definition of any important U.K. media would seriously conflict with this principle. Therefore, all sections of the Press are included in the definition.

NOTE IV.—Any extensive use of "Advertising Gifts and Novelties" is, of course, at present impossible because of material shortages. They are excluded from the definition partly on these grounds, but also because they are mostly utilitarian.

NOTE V.—Direct Mail is, of course, also subject to very severe restrictions because of material shortages. It has, however, been included because, in spite of these restrictions, it remains one of the principal advertising media.

NOTE VI.—Other forms of advertising have been excluded as being of insignificant relative importance, and because some of them involve impossible distinctions between advertising and sales promotion costs.

"REFERENCE PERIOD" means the last completed financial year of twelve months in the advertiser's account up to and including February 29th, 1948.

NOTE.—The overriding consideration in arriving at this definition was the fact that the Chancellor's request for a reduction was made late in the year 1947, and was presumably made in terms of the scale of advertising then existing.

"OPERATIVE PERIOD" means a period of twelve calendar months from the 1st of March, 1948.

NOTE.—In suggesting an Operative Period of 12 months, it is to be understood that a complete review towards the end of this period will be absolutely necessary. At this stage no observations can be made about the case that may then exist for continuance or abandonment of some measure of restraint.

"ADVERTISING EXPENDITURE" means all costs of advertising (as defined under "Advertiser") within the U.K. during the Reference Period or the Operative Period as the case may be, except the advertiser's Advertising Department expenses. In calculating Advertising Expenditure for the Operative Period, the advertiser should use the same rates and prices as he was paying at the beginning of that period.

NOTE.—It is intended that this definition shall exclude costs of material sent overseas.

"DESIGNATED GOODS" means: Consumer and household goods covered by ration books, coupons or dockets.
Liquid or solid fuels.
Alcoholic drinks and tobacco goods.
Goods subject to purchase tax of 66⅔ per cent. and over.

NOTE I.—This definition is based primarily upon the Government's request for reductions in advertising of luxury goods and goods in short supply.

NOTE II.—Considerable thought was given to the advertising of "Services," e.g., travel, sport, entertainment, &c. Much of such advertising is informative in character and necessary. It is by no means clear that the public interest is at stake, except possibly in a moral sense, but this is a matter outside our responsibilities. There are, however, certain aspects of the advertising of services that would appear to be out of line with the Government's objectives, and we are relying upon Clause 2 of the Voluntary Plan of Action to deal with this.

NOTE III.—The problem of defining the meaning of "goods in short supply" involves matters of opinion rather than of fact, and an impossible comparison between the availabilities of innumerable commodities, or even types of makes within a single category. Our definition may therefore unavoidably omit items that might be judged to be in short supply in a particular district at a particular moment, but here, too, we are relying upon Clause 2 of the Voluntary Plan of Action, and upon the good offices of Trade Associations to guide their members towards a common interpretation.

THE PLAN OF ACTION

1. Advertisers who endorse this plan agree, in accordance with the spirit of this voluntary scheme, to comply with the following rules:—

(*a*) Any advertiser whose advertising expenditure within the U.K. during the Reference Period on designated goods exceeded £2,500 will reduce his corresponding expenditure during the Operative Period at the rate of 15 per cent, provided that such reduction shall not bring his expenditure below £2,500 per annum.

(*b*) Any advertiser whose advertising expenditure within the U.K. during the Reference Period on designated goods was below £2,500 will not exceed £2,500 during the Operative Period.

(*c*) New Advertisers wishing to commence advertising of designated goods during the Operative Period will limit their expenditure to the maximum rate of £2,500 per annum, except with the agreement of the Standing Advisory Committee referred to in Clause 4, which will consult with the Trade Association concerned.

(*d*) Advertisers who have been prevented by concentration, requisition or other wartime arrangements, from marketing their brands during the Reference Period are excepted from the limit of £2,500 subject to their consulting with the Standing Advisory Committee with the object of agreeing a standard of advertising expenditure for the Operative Period.

(*e*) Existing advertisers of designated products wishing to advertise new brands or products falling within the designated list shall find the costs of so doing from within the reduced advertising expenditure for the Operative Period as set out in Clause 1 (*a*).

(*f*) If any advertiser has selected, or now wishes to select, some national purpose known to have the support of the Government (e.g., Road Safety, Recruitment to Undermanned Industries, National Savings, Fuel Economy, &c.), and provides for that purpose, without visual acknowledgment, the use of media, sites or facilities, he may count the costs involved in the Reference Peroid as advertising expenditure. He may count the costs involved in the Operative Period as a contribution towards his obligations under this Plan.

2. All advertisers who endorse the Plan, whether concerned with goods or services falling within or outside the designated list, will undertake to use their best endeavours to conduct their advertising and to arrange the tone of their "copy" in accordance with the spirit of this voluntary scheme, which is to refrain from increasing inflationary pressure of demand for scarce or rationed goods and services, and where possible to encourage the attainment of the country's export and production objectives.

3. Media owners and Advertising Agents who endorse this plan agree to use their best endeavours to operate in the spirit of this voluntary scheme when considering new business or the renewal of existing contracts.

4. All who endorse this plan agree to collaborate with a small Standing Advisory Committee representative of Advertisers, Agents and Media Owners, to be appointed by the Working Committee with the following terms of reference:—

(*a*) to be readily available for advice on the interpretation of this plan.

(*b*) to maintain a general oversight of the operation of the plan in terms of the undertakings given.

THE VOLUNTARY LIMITATION OF ADVERTISING

This form should be returned without delay to:—

The Advertising Secretary,
FEDERATION OF BRITISH INDUSTRIES,

(*a*) Form of reply for Representative Organisations and Trade Associations.

Dear Sir,

I am authorised by the Governing Body of this organisation to inform you that we endorse in its entirety the Plan for the Voluntary Limitation of Advertising submitted to us by the F.B.I. Working Committee, and that we shall advise all our members affected by the Plan to give it their full endorsement.

Yours faithfully,

(Signed) ....

Name of Organisation ....

(*b*) Form of reply for Individual Advertisers.

Dear Sir,

I am authorised by my Directors/Principals to inform you that we endorse the Plan for the Voluntary Limitation of Advertising submitted to us by the F.B.I. Working Committee and

*that we will undertake to make at least the quantitative reductions therein specified in so far as they affect us.

*that we are not affected by the quantitative requirements.

We will use our best endeavours to comply with the spirit of this Plan to which special reference is made under "The Plan of Action, Clause 2."

Yours faithfully,

(Signed) ....

Name of Company ....

*strike out whichever does not apply.

(*c*) Form of reply for Advertising Agents and Media Owners.

Dear Sir,

I am authorised by my Directors/Principals to inform you that we endorse the Plan for the Voluntary Limitation of Advertising submitted to us by the F.B.I. Working Committee, and accept the obligations set out in Clause 3.

Yours faithfully,

(Signed) ....

Name of Advertising Agent or Media Owner ....

BIBLIOGRAPHY

BOOKS

ABBOT, W. *Handbook of Broadcasting*, 3d ed. New York: McGraw, 1950.

ABRAMS, E. R. *Power in Transition*. New York: Scribner, 1940.

AGNEW, HUGH E. *Outdoor Advertising*, 1st ed. New York: McGraw, 1938.

ARCHER, G. *Big Business and Radio*. New York: American Historical Society, 1938.

———. *History of Radio to 1926*. New York: American Historical Society, 1938.

ALANNE, V. S. *Fundamentals of Consumer Cooperation*. Wis.: Cooperative Pub. Assn. Superior, 1948.

ALCOHOLIC BEVERAGE INDUSTRIES. *1947 Red Book*. New York: Liquor Publications, Inc., 1947.

AMDUR, L. H. *Trade-Mark Law and Practice: Lanham Act Edition*. New York: Clark Boardman, 1948.

AMERICAN ASSOCIATION OF ADVERTISING AGENCIES. *Standards of Practice*. New York, 1951.

AMERICAN ASSOCIATION OF ADVERTISING AGENCIES and ASSOCIATION OF NATIONAL ADVERTISERS. *Self-Regulation of Advertising*. New York, 1950.

APPEL, J. H. *Growing Up With Advertising*. New York: Business Bourse, 1940.

AYER, N. W. & SON. *Directory of Newspapers and Periodicals*. New York: 1951.

BACKMAN, A. E. *Do's and Don'ts in Advertising Copy*. New York: Better Business Bur., 1949.

BALDWIN, W. E. *Digest, Patent, Copyright, Trade-Mark Cases, Including Unfair Competition; Covering Volumes 1–297, U.S. Supreme Court Reports*. Cleveland: Banks-Baldwin, 1936.

BALL, H. C. *Law of Copyrights and Literary Property*. New York: Bender, 1944.

BALLIETT, C. J., and KLEPPNER, O. *Advertising Fields and Agencies*. Scranton, Pa.: International Textbook, 1945.

BARNHART, T. F. *Newspaper Sales Promotion*. Minneapolis: Burgess, 1950.

BARTON, R. *Advertising Handbook*. New York: Prentice-Hall, 1950.

BASTER, A. S. J. *Advertising Reconsidered*. London: 1935.

BAUM, M. *Readings in Business Ethics*. Dubuque, Iowa: W. C. Brown, 1950.

BAUS, H. M. *Public Relations at Work*. New York: Harper, 1948.

BEDELL, C. *How to Write Advertising that Sells*. New York: McGraw, 1950.

BENNETT, C. *Influencing the Buyer's Mind*. St. Louis: Am. Efficiency Bur., 1936.

BETTER BUSINESS BUREAU. *Facts You Should Know About Your Better Business Bureau*. New York: 1950.

BEVILLE, H. M., JR. *Social Stratification of the Radio Audience.* New York: Columbia Univ. Bur. of Applied Social Research, 1939.
BIRD, HARRY L. *This Fascinating Advertising Business.* Indianapolis: Bobbs, 1947.
BISHOP, F. *Economics of Advertising.* Forest Hills, N. Y.: Transatlantic, 1945.
———. *The Ethics of Advertising.* London: Robert Hale, Ltd., 1949.
BLACKLY, F. F. and OATMAN, M. E. *Federal Regulatory Action and Control.* Washington: Brookings, 1940.
BORDEN, N. H. *Advertising in Our Economy.* Chicago: Irwin, 1945.
———. *Advertising: Text and Cases.* Chicago: Irwin, 1950.
———. *The Economic Effects of Advertising.* Chicago: Irwin, 1947.
———. *Problems in Advertising.* New York: McGraw, 1950.
BORDEN, N. H., TAYLOR, M., and HOVDE, H. T. *National Advertising in Newspapers.* Cambridge, Mass.: Harvard Univ. Press, 1946.
BOYLE, J. N., and LIFFINGWELL, W. H. *Advertising Law and Management.* Scranton, Pa.: International Textbook, 1936.
BRAINERD, J. G. *Consumer's Cooperation.* Philadelphia: Academy of Pol. and Soc. Sciences, 1937.
BRANDEIS, L. D. *Other People's Money.* New York: Stokes, 1914.
BRIDGE, D. *Men and Methods of Newspaper Advertising.* New York: Arco, 1948.
BRIDGE, H. P. *Practical Advertising.* New York: Rinehart, 1949.
BRITT, S. H. *Social Psychology of Modern Life.* New York: Rinehart, 1949.
BURNETT, VERNE E. *You and Your Public.* New York: Harper, 1947.
BURNS, A. R. *The Decline of Competition.* New York: McGraw, 1936.
BURTT, H. E. *Psychology of Advertising.* Boston: Houghton, 1938.
CALKINS, E. L. *And Hearing Not; Annals of an Ad Man.* New York: Scribner, 1946.
CALLMAN, R. *The Law of Unfair Competition and Trade-Marks.* Chicago: Callaghan, 1950.
CAMPBELL, P. *Consumer Representation in the New Deal.* New York: Columbia Univ. Press, 1940.
CAPLES, J. *Tested Advertising Methods.* New York: Harper, 1947.
CLARK, J. D. *Federal Trust Policy.* Baltimore: Johns Hopkins Press, 1931.
COLES, J. V. *Standards and Labels for Consumers' Goods.* New York: Ronald, 1949.
COLUMBIA BROADCASTING SYSTEM. *Television Today.* New York, 1950.
COMMITTEE FOR ECONOMIC DEVELOPMENT, RESEARCH AND POLICY COMMITTEE. *Paying for Defense.* New York, 1950.
CORWIN, E. S. *The Commerce Power versus States' Rights.* Princeton: Princeton Univ. Press, 1936.
———. *The Twilight of the Supreme Court.* New Haven: Yale Univ. Press, 1934.
CURTIS PUBLISHING CO. *A Short History of the Saturday Evening Post.* Philadelphia: 1949.
———. *National Magazines As Advertising Media.* Philadelphia: 1950.
DAY, E. *Radio Broadcasting for Retailers.* New York: Fairchild, 1948.
DE FORREST, L. *Television: Today and Tomorrow.* New York: Dial, 1942.
DEMING, W. E. *Some Theories of Sampling.* New York: Wiley, 1950.
DIGGES, I. W. *The Modern Law of Advertising and Marketing.* New York: Funk, 1948.

DIRECT MAIL ADVERTISING ASSOCIATION. *The Story of Direct Advertising.* New York: 1950.

DODD, WALTER F. *Cases and Materials on Constitutional Law.* St. Paul, Minn.: West Pub. Co., 1950.

DOREMUS, W. L. *Advertising for Profit.* New York: Pitman, 1947.

DUFFY, B. *Advertising Media and Markets.* New York: Prentice-Hall, 1950.

DUNLAP, ORRIN E., JR. *Dunlap's Radio & Television Almanac.* New York: Harper, 1951.

———. *The Future of Television.* New York: Harper, 1947.

DUNN, C. W. *Federal Food, Drug, and Cosmetic Act.* New York: Stechert-Hafner, 1938.

DYGERT, W. B. *Advertising Principles and Practice.* Paterson, N. J.: Littlefield, 1949.

———. *Radio as an Advertising Medium.* New York: McGraw, 1939.

ELLIOT, W. Y. *The Need for Constitutional Reform.* New York: McGraw, 1935.

EMMETT, B., and JEUCK, J. E. *Catalogues and Counters: A History of Sears, Roebuck & Co.* Chicago: Univ. of Chicago Press, 1950.

FAINSOD, M., and GORDON, L. *Government and the American Economy.* New York: Norton, 1941.

FALTZ, E. *The Slogan in Modern Advertising.* New York: Assoc. of Nat. Advertisers, 1949.

FEDERATION OF BRITISH INDUSTRIES. *The Voluntary Limitation of Advertising.* London: Times Pub. Co., 1948.

FELDMAN, G. J., and ZORN, B. A. *Advertising and Promotional Allowances.* Washington, D. C.: Bur. of Nat. Affairs, 1948.

FRANKFURTER, F. *The Commerce Clause under Marshall, Tuney and Waite.* Chapel Hill: Univ. of North Carolina Press, 1937.

FREER, R. E. *Robinson-Patman Act Symposium: The Federal Law Against Price and Other Discrimination.* Chicago: Commerce Clearing House, 1946.

FREY, A. W. *Advertising.* New York: Ronald, 1947.

FRIEDRICH, C. J., and SAYRE, J. *The Development of the Control of Advertising on the Air.* Cambridge: Harvard Univ. Press, 1940.

FROST, S. E. *Is American Radio Democratic?* Chicago: Univ. of Chicago Press, 1937.

GARVER, R. I. *Successful Radio Advertising with Sponsor Participation Programs.* New York: Prentice-Hall, 1949.

GASKILL, N. B. *The Regulation of Competition.* New York: Harper, 1936.

GLIM, AESOP. *How Advertising Is Written and Why.* New York: McGraw, 1945.

GOLDMAN, E. F. *Two Way Street—The Emergency of PR Counsel.* Boston: Bellman, 1947.

GOODE, K. M., and KAUFMAN, M. Z. *Showmanship in Business.* New York: Harper, 1948.

HANDLER, M. *Cases and Materials on Trade Regulation.* Brooklyn: Foundation Press, 1937.

HARPER, M. J. *Getting Results from Advertising.* New York: Funk & Wagnalls, 1949.

HARRAL, S. *Patterns of Publicity Copy.* Norman: Univ. of Oklahoma Press, 1950.

HATTWICK, M. S. *How to Use Psychology for Better Advertising.* New York: Prentice-Hall, 1950.

HENDERSON, G. C. *Federal Trade Commission.* New Haven: Yale Univ. Press, 1924.

HERRICK, A. D. *Drug Products: Labelling, Packaging, Regulation.* New York: Revere, 1948.

———. *Food Regulation and Compliance, 1944–1947.* New York: Revere, 1948.

HERRING, J. M., and GROSS, G. C. *Telecommunications.* New York: McGraw, 1936.

HESS, H. W. *Advertising—Its Economics, Philosophy and Technique.* Philadelphia: Lippincott, 1931.

HOKE, H. *Direct Mail Advertising.* Boston: Bellman, 1946.

HOLCOMBE, A. N. *Government in a Planned Democracy.* New York: Norton, 1935.

HOPKINS, C. C. *My Life in Advertising.* New York: Harper, 1936.

HOTCHKISS, G. B. *Advertising Copy.* New York: Harper, 1949.

———. *An Outline of Advertising—Its Philosophy, Science, Art and Strategy,* 3d ed. New York: Macmillan, 1950.

———. *Milestones in Marketing.* New York: Macmillan, 1938.

HOVDE, H. T. *Marketing in Our American Economy.* Philadelphia: Academy of Pol. and Soc. Sciences, 1940.

HOWELL, H. *The Copyright Law.* Washington, D. C.: Bur. of Nat. Affairs 1947.

HOWENSTINE, E. J. *Post-War Markets.* Washington, D. C.: Public Affairs Press, 1945.

HOWER, RALPH. *The History of an Advertising Agency.* Cambridge: Harvard Univ. Press, 1949.

ICKES, H. L. *Freedom of the Press Today.* New York: Vanguard, 1941.

IRION, F. C. *Public Opinion and Propaganda.* New York: Crowell, 1950.

JENKINS, J. G. *Psychology in Business and Industry.* New York: Wiley, 1935.

JOHNSEN, J. E. *Interstate Trade Barriers.* New York: Wilson, 1940.

JONES, R. W. *Copyrights and Trade Marks.* Seattle: Univ. of Washington Bookstore, 1949.

KALLET, A., and SCHLINK, F. J. *100,000,000 Guinea Pigs.* New York: Vanguard, 1933.

KEMPER, S. *Television Encyclopedia.* New York: Fairchild, 1948.

KENNEDY, A., and VAUGHN, C. *Consumer Economics.* Peoria, Ill.: Bennett, 1947.

KENNER, H. J. *The Fight for Truth in Advertising.* New York: Round Table Press, 1936.

KLEINFELD, V. A., and DUNN, C. W. *Federal Food, Drug and Cosmetic Act—Judicial and Administrative Record, 1938–1949.* Chicago: Commerce Clearing House, 1949.

KONEFSKY, S. J. *Chief Justice Stone and the Supreme Court.* New York: Macmillan, 1945.

KUZNETS, S. *National Income and Its Composition, 1919–1938.* New York: Nat. Bur. of Economic Research, 1941.

LAZARSFELD, P. F., and KENDALL, P. L. *Radio Listening in America.* New York: Prentice-Hall, 1948.

LAZARSFELD, P. F., and STANTON, F. N. *Communications Research, 1948–49.* New York: Harper, 1949.
LEE, ALFRED MCCLUNG. *Daily Newspaper in America.* New York: Macmillan, 1937.
LESLY, P. *Public Relations Handbook.* New York: Prentice-Hall, 1950.
LEVER, E. A. *Advertising and Economic Theory.* New York: Oxford, 1947.
LINDQUEST, C. *How to Tell If Your Ads Will Sell.* Omaha: Helpful Press, 1950.
LUMLEY, F. H. *Measurement in Radio.* Columbus: Ohio State Univ. Press, 1934.
LUND, JOHN V. *Newspaper Advertising.* New York: Prentice-Hall, 1947.
LYON, L. S., AND ASSOCIATES. *Government and Economic Life.* Washington, D.C.: Brookings, 1939.
MCCLURE, L. W. *Newspaper Advertising and Promotion.* New York: Macmillan, 1950.
MCCORMICK, C. D., EVEREST, P. J., and BARTLETT, K. G. *Transit and Radio Advertising.* Scranton, Pa.: International Textbook, 1946.
MAGAZINE ADVERTISING BUREAU. *The National Magazine and American Life.* New York, 1950.
MAYTHAM, T. E. *Introduction to Advertising Principles and Practice.* New York: Harper, 1948.
MERCER, F. A., and ROSNER, C. *Modern Publicity, 1950.* New York: Crowell, 1950.
MILLER, C. R. *The Process of Persuasion.* New York: Crown, 1946.
MILLER, J. P. *Unfair Competition—A Study in Criteria for the Control of Trade Practices.* Cambridge: Harvard Univ. Press, 1941.
MOTT, FRANK LUTHER. *American Journalism.* New York: Macmillan, 1950.
MULLEN, W. H. *The Absolutes of Magazine Advertising.* New York: Magazine Advertising Bureau Inc., 1950.
NATIONAL ASSOCIATION OF RADIO AND TELEVISION BROADCASTERS. *The Television Code.* Washington 6, D. C., 1952.
NATIONAL BROADCASTING COMPANY. *Behind Your Radio Dial.* New York, 1947.
NIELSEN, A. C. 1950 *Radio-TV Audience Analyses.* Broadcasting-Telecasting 1951 Yearbook. Washington, D. C.: Broadcasting Pubs. Inc., 1951.
NORRIS, R. T. *The Theory of Consumer's Demand.* New Haven: Yale Univ. Press, 1941.
OPPENHEIM, S. C. *Cases on Federal Anti-Trust Laws.* St. Paul: West, 1948.
PATMAN, W. *The Robinson-Patman Act.* New York: Ronald, 1938.
POLITZ, ALFRED, RESEARCH, INC. *A Study of the Accumulated Audience of Life—The Life Market.* New York, 1951.
POOLE, L. *Science via Television.* Baltimore: Johns Hopkins Press, 1950.
PRESBREY, FRANK. *The History and Development of Advertising.* Garden City, N. Y.: Doubleday Doran, 1929.
PURDY, F. *Mass Consumption.* New York: Talisman, 1936.
REICH, E., and SIGLER, C. J. *Consumer Goods.* New York: American Book, 1947.
REID, M. G. *Consumers and the Market,* 3d ed. New York: Appleton-Century-Crofts, 1942.

ROBERT, D. *The New Trade-Mark Manual.* Washington, D. C.: Bur. of Nat. Affairs, 1948.

ROGERS, L. *The Postal Power of Congress.* Baltimore: Johns Hopkins Press, 1916.

ROYAL, J. F. *Television Production Problems.* New York: McGraw, 1948.

RUDOLPH, H. J. *Attention and Interest Factors in Advertising.* New York: Funk & Wagnalls and Printers' Ink, 1948.

SAMPSON, HENRY. *A History of Advertising From The Earliest Times.* New York: Chatto and Windus, 1874.

SANDAGE, C. H. *Advertising: Theory and Practice.* Chicago: Irwin, 1948.

———. *Radio Advertising for Retailers.* Cambridge: Harvard Univ. Press, 1945.

SCHECHTER, F. L. *The Historical Foundation of the Law Relating to Trade-Marks.* New York: Columbia Univ. Press, 1925.

SHARPE, L. *Artist in Commerce.* New York: Macmillan, 1936.

SHIELDS, H. G., and WILSON, W. H. *Consumer-Economic Problems.* Cincinnati: South-Western, 1945.

SIEPMANN, C. A. *Radio, Television, and Society.* New York: Oxford, 1950.

SILL, J. *The Radio Station.* New York: Stewart, 1946.

SOCOLOW, A. W. *The Law of Radio Broadcasting.* New York: Baker, Voorhis, 1939.

STOCKING, GEORGE W., and WATKINS, MYRON W. *Monopoly and Free Enterprise.* New York: Twentieth Century Fund, 1951.

SUNNERS, W. *American Slogans.* New York: Paebar, 1949.

SWAN, C. J. *Which Ad Pulled Best?* New York: Funk & Wagnalls & Printers' Ink, 1950.

SWENSON, RINEHART JOHN. *The National Government and Business.* New York: Century, 1924.

THAYER, F. *Legal Control of the Press.* Brooklyn: Foundation, 1950.

TOULMIN, A. H., JR. *The Anti-Trust Laws of the United States.* Cincinnati: Anderson, 1950.

———. *The Law of Foods, Drugs, and Cosmetics.* Cincinnati: Anderson, 1942.

———. *Trade-Mark Act of 1946: Analyzed, Annotated and Explained.* Cincinnati: Anderson, 1946.

WAITE, W. C., and CASSADY, R., JR. *The Consumer and the Economic Order.* New York: McGraw, 1949.

WALDROP, F. C., and BORKIN, J. *Televising; A Struggle for Power.* New York: Morrow, 1938.

WALLER, J. D. *Radio, The Fifth Estate.* Boston: Houghton, 1946.

WARBASSE, J. P. *Cooperative Democracy.* New York: Harper, 1947.

WARNER, H. P. *Radio and Television Law.* New York: Bender, 1948.

WASHBURN, C. *Press Agentry.* New York: Nat. Library Press, 1937.

WATKINS, J. L. *The 100 Greatest Advertisements.* New York: Moore, 1950.

WATKINS, MYRON W., *et al. Public Regulation of Competitive Practices in Business Enterprise,* 3d ed. New York: Nat. Industrial Conference Board, 1940.

WEBSTER, R. *Advertising Appropriations.* New York: Assoc. of Nat. Advertisers, 1949.

WHITE, P. *Advertising Research.* New York: Appleton Century, 1927.

WILLIAMS, A. N. *Listening.* Denver: Univ. of Denver Press, 1948.
WILLOUGHBY, WESTEL W. *Principles of the Constitutional Law of the United States,* 2d ed. New York: Baker, Voorhis, 1935.
WISEMAN, M. *The Anatomy of Advertising.* Vol II. New York: Harper, 1942.
WITTENBERG, P. *Dangerous Words.* New York: Columbia Univ. Press, 1948.
WOLFE, C. H. *Modern Radio Advertising.* New York: Funk & Wagnalls, 1949.
WOODS, H. F., JR. *How to Become Well Known.* New York: Duell, 1947.
WOOLF, J. D. *Advertising to the Mass Market.* New York: Ronald, 1946.
WYLIE, M. *Radio and Television Writing.* New York: Rinehart, 1950.
YOUNG, J. O. *Adventures in Advertising.* New York: Harper, 1949.
YOUNG, JAMES W. *Advertising Agency Compensation in Relation to the Total Cost of Advertising.* Chicago: Univ. of Chicago Press, 1933.
ZUTAVERN, A. B., and BULLOCK, A. E. *The Consumer Investigates.* Baltimore: Rowe, 1938.

PERIODICALS

"A Symposium on the Law of Unfair Competition," 21 *Iowa Law Review* (January, 1936).
"Ads and the Big Club," *Spirits,* Vol. XVI (March, 1949), pp. 18–19, 51–53.
CALDWELL, O. H. *Retail Radio Sales in the United States,* 1922–1950. Broadcasting-Telecasting 1951 Yearbook. Washington, D. C.: Broadcasting Pubs. Inc., 1951.
"Creeping Paralysis," *New York Times,* February 7, 1951, p. 28.
CRICHTON, JOHN. "50 over $10,000,000 Agencies Billed $1,567,000,000 in 1951." *Advertising Age,* Vol. XXIII, No. 8 (February 25, 1952), pp. 1 ff.
CUSHMAN, R. "National Police Power under the Postal Clause of the Constitution," 4 *Minnesota Law Review* (1920), pp. 402, 419.
DAVIS, JAMES J. "How Modern Selling and Advertising Can Check Unemployment," *Printers' Ink,* Vol. CXXXVIII, No. 12 (March 24, 1927), pp. 3 ff.
"December Box Score," *Broadcasting Magazine,* January 8, 1951, p. 79.
DIGGES, ISAAC W. "Courts Adopting Less Tolerant Attitude Toward Advertising," *Printers' Ink,* Vol. CCXXXIV, No. 13 (March 30, 1951), p. 33.
DONOVAN, WILLIAM J. "Origin and Development of Radio Law," 2 *Air Law Review* (Brattleboro, Vermont) (1931), pp. 107–129, 349–370, 468–477.
DRUMMOND, ROSCOE. "Bootlegging Menace Spreads," *Christian Science Monitor,* February 4, 1949, p. 1.
DUFFY, BEN. "Profitable Advertising," *Broadcasting Magazine,* February 5, 1951, p. 58.
EDITORIAL. *Barron's Weekly,* January 8, 1945, p. 1.
"FTC Drives Against Cigaret Ad Claims Don't Do Much Good, Congressmen Say," *Advertising Age,* Vol. XXIII, No. 10 (March 10, 1952), p. 2.
Federal Trade Commission Silver Anniversary Commemorative Issue. *George Washington Law Review* (January–February, 1940).
GILLESPIE, HARRIS. "Magazine Mortality," *Magazine World,* Vol. 1, No. 11 (October, 1945), pp. 26–30.
HALE, ROBERT L. "Unconstitutional Conditions and Constitutional Rights," 35 *Columbia Law Review* (1935), p. 321.

HEWETT, LIST. Proceedings of the American Antiquarian Society (October, 1934).

"Hint New Dry Tactics Against Liquor Ads," *Spirits*, Vol. XIV (May, 1947), pp. 1, 12, 14.

JAMES, EDWIN H. "Hadacol," *Broadcasting Magazine*, March 5, 1951, pp. 26–27.

Journal of the American Medical Association, Vol. LXXVII, No. 5 (February 3, 1945).

KADIN, J. H. "Administrative Censorship: A Study of the Mails, Motion Pictures and Radio Broadcasting," *Boston University Law Review* (1939), pp. 533 ff.

KINTER, R. E. "American Broadcasting News" (American Broadcasting Co., Fort Worth, Texas, 1948), pp. 1–2.

KLEPPNER, OTTO. "Is There Too Much Advertising?" *Harper's Magazine*, Vol. CCII, No. 1209 (February, 1951), pp. 85–91.

LARRABEE, C. B. Editorial, *Printers' Ink*, Vol. CCXXXIV, No. 7 (February 14, 1951), p. 4; Editorial, Vol. CCXXXVIII, No. 9 (February 29, 1952), p. 94; "Thunder on the Right," Vol. CCXXXVIII, No. 10 (March 7, 1952), p. 39.

LASSER, J. K. "Is Advertising a Tax Deduction in a War Period?" *Printer's Ink*, Vol. CCXXXII, No. 10 (September 8, 1950), pp. 8–9.

MONTAGUE, G. H. "Unfair Methods of Competition," 25 *Yale Law Journal* (1915), pp. 29 ff.

New York Times, October 14, 1852; September 14, 1926, p. 27; January 28, 1951, Sec. IV, p. 1; February 12, 1951, p. 16; February 15, 1952, p. 28; February 28, 1952, p. 1; March 1, 1952, p. 13.

"Our Advertising Critics Speak," *Spirits*, Vol. XVI (March, 1949), pp. 13–15, 38–39.

"*Printers' Ink* Presents Revised Model Statute," *Printers' Ink*, Vol. CCX, No. 10 (March 9, 1945), pp. 17–18.

REGNIER, C. C. "The Struggle for Federal Food and Drug Regulation," 1 *Law and Contemporary Problems* (November, 1933), p. 3.

"Review of Treasury Policy on Advertising from the Tax Standpoint," *Advertising Age*, Vol. XXII, No. 9 (February 26, 1951), pp. 25–30.

ROWELL, GEORGE P. "The Principles of Advertising," *American Newspaper Reporter* (November 20, 1871).

St. Louis Post-Dispatch, February 5, 1945; April 20, 1945.

SCHWAB, VICTOR. "Ten Copy Appeals," *Printers' Ink*, Vol. CCV, No. 12 (December 17, 1943), pp. 17–19.

"Tell and Sell," *Spirits*, Vol. XV (March, 1948), p. 22.

"The J. Walter Thompson Company," *Fortune Magazine*, Vol. XXXVI, No. 5 (November, 1947), pp. 93, 233 ff.

"The New Food, Drug, and Cosmetic Legislation," 6 *Law and Contemporary Problems* (January, 1939).

"The Sherman Antitrust Act and Its Enforcement," 7 *Law and Contemporary Problems* (January, 1940).

THOMPSON, HUSTON. "Highlights in the Evolution of the Federal Trade Commission," 3 *George Washington Law Review* (January–February, 1940), pp. 257–59.

"U.S. Advertising Volume Passes Five Billion, Hits New High," *Printers' Ink*, Vol. CCXXXI, No. 11 (June 16, 1950), pp. 28–30; "U.S. Advertising Volume Passes 6.5 Billions," Vol. CCXXXVIII, No. 2 (January 11, 1952), p. 36.

Consumer Magazine Advertising Rates and Data. Vol. XXXIV, No. 1 (January 11, 1952), pp. 2, 16–19.

Variety (November 14, 1951), pp. 24–27; (December 19, 1951), p. 30; (January 23, 1952), p. 29; (February 13, 1952), p. 29.

WATKINS, MYRON W. "An Appraisal of the Work of the Federal Trade Commission," 32 *Columbia Law Review* (February, 1932), pp. 272–89.

WELD, L. D. H. "Annual Estimate of Advertising Volume by Media," *Printers' Ink*, Vol. CXCV, No. 1 (April 4, 1941), p. 15; Vol. CXCVIII, No. 13 (March 27, 1942), p. 19; Vol. CCII, No. 13 (March 26, 1943), p. 18; Vol. CCVI, No. 12 (March 24, 1944), p. 17.

ZEISEL, HANS. "Annual Estimate of Advertising Volume by Media," *Printers' Ink*, Vol. CCXVIII, No. 13 (March 28, 1947), p. 34; Vol. CCXXIII, No. 5 (April 30, 1948), p. 28; Vol. CCXXVII, No. 12 (June 17, 1949), p. 27; Vol. CCXXXI, No. 11 (June 16, 1950), p. 28.

OFFICIAL REPORTS

BENNETT, PHILIP A. *Television as an Advertising Medium.* United States Department of Commerce. Government Printing Office. Washington, D. C., 1949.

Congressional Record. 63rd Cong., 2d Sess. 1913–1914. Vol. 51. Government Printing Office. Washington, D. C.

———. 74th Cong., 2d Sess. May 4, 1936.

———. 76th Cong., 1st Sess. January 12, 1938.

Federal Communications Commission. Commission Order in Docket No. 5060. Washington, D. C., 1941.

———. Order of February 28, 1940.

———. Order of May 2, 1941.

———. Order of June 29, 1949.

———. Public Service Responsibility of Broadcast Licensees. Government Printing Office. Washington, D. C., 1946.

———. Report on Chain Broadcasting, 1941.

———. Supplemental Report. October 11, 1941.

Federal Trade Commission. Annual Report. 1929, 1949, 1951. Government Printing Office. Washington, D. C.

———. Report on Distribution Methods and Costs. Part V. Advertising as a Factor in Distribution. 1944.

Joint Committee on the Economic Report. The Economic Report No. 210. 82nd Cong., 1st Sess., April 2, 1951. Government Printing Office. Washington, D. C., 1951.

Temporary National Economic Committee. Hearings on Investigation of Concentration of Economic Power. 75th Cong., 3d Sess., Part I. Economic Prologue. Government Printing Office. Washington, D. C., 1939.

The Economic Report of the President. Harry S. Truman. Transmitted to the Congress. January 12, 1951. Government Printing Office. Washington, D. C., 1951.

United States Attorney General's Committee on Administrative Procedure. Administrative Procedure in Government Agencies. Part XII. Government Printing Office. Washington, D. C., 1940.

United States Bureau of the Census. Biennial Census of Manufacturers. Government Printing Office. Washington, D. C., 1924.

———. Census for 1910 Manufacturers, Principal Industries. 1913.

United States Department of Commerce. Advertising and Its Role in War and Peace. Industrial Series No. 5. Government Printing Office. Washington, D. C., 1942.

———. Bureau of the Census. Release Series BC–2–5–7. 1948.

———. Establishing and Operating a Mail-Order Business. 1947.

———. Market Research Sources. 1950.

United States Department of Labor. Bulletin No. 475. Government Printing Office. Washington, D. C. 1929.

United States House of Representatives. Bill No. 3143. 75th Cong., 1st Sess. January 18, 1937. Washington, D. C.

———. Bill No. 5854. March 23, 1937.

———. Document No. 483. 69th Cong., 2d Sess. 1926.

———. Hearings on House Resolution No. 3143. Interstate and Foreign Commerce Committee. 75th Cong., 1st Sess. 1937.

———. Hearings on House Resolution No. 4597. Committee on Interstate and Foreign Commerce. 77th Cong., 2d Sess. May 7, 1942.

———. Hearings on Interstate Trade Commission. Committee on Interstate and Foreign Commerce. 63rd Cong., 2d Sess. January 20 to February 16, 1914.

———. Report No. 597. Committee on Interstate and Foreign Commerce. 63rd Cong., 2d Sess. June 13, 1914.

———. Report No. 1174. 76th Cong., 1st Sess. February 8, 1938.

———. Report No. 1613. 76th Cong., 1st Sess. January 12, 1938.

———. Report No. 2844. 51st Cong., 1st Sess. 1890.

United States Senate. Bill No. 1077. 75th Cong., 1st Sess. January 22, 1937. Washington, D. C.

———. Bill No. 3744. 74th Cong., 2d Sess. May 4, 1936.

———. Hearings on Bills Relating to Trust Legislation. Committee on Interstate Commerce. 2 Vols. 63rd Cong., 2d Sess. Government Printing Office. Washington, D. C. 1914.

———. Hearings on Senate Bill No. 3744. Committee on Interstate Commerce. 74th Cong., 2d Sess. March 18, 1936. Washington, D. C.

United States Senate. Report No. 597. Committee on Interstate Commerce. 63d Cong., 2d Sess. 1914.

———. Report No. 1326. 62d Cong., 3d Sess. 1914.

———. Report No. 1579. 51st Cong., 1st Sess. 1890.

STATUTES

Act of February 14, 1903, 32 Stat. 825.
Bituminous Coal Act of 1937, 50 Stat. 727.
Child Labor Act of 1916, 39 Stat. 675, Chap. 432.
Child Labor Act of 1919, 40 Stat. 1057, 1138.
Classification Act of 1879, 29 Stat. 358, 43 Stat. 928, 39 U.S.C. Sec. 14, 226, 39 U.S.C.A. Sec. 226.
Clayton Act, 38 Stat. 730, 15 U.S.C. Sec. 13 (1914).
Export Trade Act, 40 Stat. 516, 15 U.S.C. Secs. 61–65.
Federal Alcohol Tax Unit Act, 49 Stat. 977, 27 U.S.C.A. Sec. 201.
Federal Communications Act of 1934, 48 Stat. 1064, 47 U.S.C.A. 151 ff.
Federal Trade Commission Act, 38 Stat. 717, 15 U.S.C. Sec. 41 ff. (1914), as amended by the Wheeler-Lea Act, 52 Stat. 114, 15 U.S.C.A. Supp. IV and V (1938), as amended by the Act of March 16, 1950, P.L. 459, 81st Cong.
Food, Drug and Cosmetic Act of 1938, 52 Stat. 1040, 21 U.S.C. Chap. 1.
Future Trading Act, 42 Stat. 187, Chap. 86 (1921).
Grain Futures Act, 42 Stat. 998, 7 U.S.C.A. Secs. 1–17 (1922).
Harrison, Narcotic Drug Act, 38 Stat. 785, Chap. 1 (1914).
Internal Revenue Code, Sec. 23(a).
International Communication Treaty of 1912, 37 Stat. 1565.
Interstate Commerce Act, 54 Stat. 941, 49 U.S.C. Sec. 909 (1887).
Meat Inspection Act, 34 Stat. 768, 21 U.S.C. 1 (1906).
Motor Vehicle Theft Act of 1919, 59 Stat. 536, 18 U.S.C. 2311–2313.
National Industrial Recovery Act, 48 Stat. 195, 15 U.S.C.A. Sec. 703 (1933).
Postal Law of 1789, 1 Stat. 70.
Postal Law of 1782, 1 Stat. 232.
Postal Law of 1810, 2 Stat. 592.
Postal Law of 1845, 5 Stat. 733.
Postal Law of 1872, 17 Stat. 283, 322–323, 39 U.S.C. Sec. 732.
Postal Law of 1876, 19 Stat. 90.
Postal Law of 1879, 20 Stat. 356, 359, 361, 362.
Postal Law of 1889, 25 Stat. 874, 39 U.S.C. Sec. 256 *et seq.*
Postal Law of 1890, 26 Stat. 465.
Postal Law of 1895, 28 Stat. 964, 39 U.S.C. Sec. 259.
Postal Law of 1912, 37 Stat. 553, Chap. 389.
Pure Food and Drug Act, 39 Stat. 768, 51 U.S.C. Sec. 1 ff. (1906).
Pure Food and Drug Act, 52 Stat. 1040, 21 U.S.C. Sec. 1 (1938).
Radio Act of 1910, 36 Stat. 629, 46 U.S.C.A. Sec. 484 *et seq.*
Radio Act of 1927, 48 Stat. 1064, 47 U.S.C. Sec. 151 *et seq.*
Radio Communication Act of 1912, 37 Stat. 302, 47 U.S.C.A. Sec. 51 *et seq.*
Robinson-Patman Act, 49 Stat. 1526, 15 U.S.C. Secs. 14, 18, 19.
Securities Act of 1933, 48 Stat. 74, 15 U.S.C. Sec. 77(e).
Sherman Act, 26 Stat. 209 (1890), 15 U.S.C.A. Sec. 1 (1934).

Trade Mark Act of 1948, 64 Stat. 459, 15 U.S.C. Secs. 1051–1072, 1091–1096, and 1111–1127.

United States Act Prohibiting the Use of the Flag for Advertising Purposes, 61 Stat. 641, 4 U.S.C. Sec. 3.

United States Constitution, Article XVIII.

United States Criminal Code, 64 Stat. 194, 18 U.S.C. Sec. 1464.

Webb Kenyon Act, 37 Stat. 699, Chap. 90 (1913), 49 Stat. 877, 27 U.S.C. 122 (1935).

Wool Products Labeling Act, 54 Stat. 1128, 15 U.S.C. Sec. 68.

TABLE OF CASES

INDEX OF NAMES

INDEX OF SUBJECTS